Contrapractice

BEYOND THE MODERN
Series editors: Clive Dilnot, Eduardo Staszowski and Virginia Tassinari

To contend with the scale and intractability of the multiple and interacting crises that are threatening to engulf us is to have to change how we think of both thought and acting. The separation of critical thought and technological and economic acting-in-the-world has eviscerated the ability to bring together theory and practice for anything other than merely instrumental ends.

At the same time, neither the human sciences – which historically have feared intervention – nor models of acting that eschew depth understanding can alone suffice to redirect catastrophe. One consequence of these failures is that they cause us to lose sight of other objective possibilities for the world. Envisioning the latter must be the real subject of thought and practice today.

This is the motivation for this new series of books.

Recognizing that the key challenge of our time is to invent a modernity capable of redressing the blind march toward disaster, they focus on teasing out what is immanently possible within what-now-is. Operating at the intersections of fields previously kept distinct, they explore both the conditions of such a re-invention and the articulation of configurations of thought, material practices and politics that can potentially realize transformative possibilities in the world.

In so doing their aim is to help lay groundwork for an ontological shift; for the transformations in thought, imagination, and capability necessary for engendering peaceful egalitarian rather than catastrophic modes of bringing the future into being.

Published and Forthcoming

Relationality: An Emergent Politics of Life Beyond the Human
Arturo Escobar, Michal Osterweil and Kriti Sharma

The Power of Maybes: Machines, Uncertainty and Design Futures
Betti Marenko

(Designing) Beyond the Modern
Eduardo Staszowski and Virginia Tassinari

Contrapractice: Action Against Defuturing
Tony Fry with opening and closing dialogues with Dulmini Perera

Designing Politics: Materiality, Agency, and Embodied Deliberation
Anke Gruendel

The Possibility of the Artificial/The Urgency of the Possible
Clive Dilnot

Contrapractice

Action Against Defuturing

Tony Fry

with opening and closing
dialogues with

Dulmini Perera

BLOOMSBURY VISUAL ARTS

LONDON • NEW YORK • OXFORD • NEW DELHI • SYDNEY

BLOOMSBURY VISUAL ARTS
Bloomsbury Publishing Plc, 50 Bedford Square, London, WC1B 3DP, UK
Bloomsbury Publishing Inc, 1359 Broadway, New York, NY 10018, USA
Bloomsbury Publishing Ireland, 29 Earlsfort Terrace, Dublin 2, D02 AY28, Ireland

BLOOMSBURY, BLOOMSBURY VISUAL ARTS and the Diana logo
are trademarks of Bloomsbury Publishing Plc

First published in Great Britain 2026

Cover design by Andrew LeClair

A catalogue record for this book is available from the British Library.

A catalog record for this book is available from the Library of Congress.

ISBN: HB: 978-1-3504-4850-6
PB: 978-1-3504-4849-0
ePDF: 978-1-3504-4852-0
eBook: 978-1-3504-4851-3

Series: Beyond the Modern

Typeset by Integra Software Services Pvt. Ltd.
Printed and bound in India

For product safety related questions contact productsafety@bloomsbury.com.

To find out more about our authors and books visit www.bloomsbury.com
and sign up for our newsletters.

Contents

Preface

This book is not a discrete 'stand-alone' object: it is a work among works from which much of its thinking is emulated. Depending on a reader's reading history, identifiable multiple lines of connection can be discerned. More than this, it is a product of a dialogue over the course of its creation. This is partly registered in its opening and closing, but it also has a less definable and visible presence. What has been produced reflects numerous conversations between Dulmini Perera and myself over many months, including on the political, practice, design, systems, cybernetics, plus the exchange of texts.

The book invites being viewed as an opening move created to advance Contrapractice as a project requiring ongoing advocacy, but above all, an uptake in the development of Contrapractice practices by different practitioners in specific contexts over time. The book cannot tell someone how to transform their particular practice, but it can give them a better understanding of the nature of practice, and why practices require to be transformed across a myriad of contexts and applications, plus prompts to begin this process with their own practice.

In keeping with the spirit of the series, the project contrapractice, and the form of its presentation, is transdisciplinary.

Its concept, 'contrapractice', emanates from two histories. One is a history of writing on design history and philosophy, political theory, conflict, environmental issues, and some fiction, all evidenced by publications. Less well-known is a long history of practice which predated and accompanied an academic career and not only informed what I wrote but why I did so.

Conflict and politics, in various ways, have been enduring themes, having been born in a time of war and grown up amid its physical and psychological destruction, served as a soldier and worked in post-conflict environments up until recent decades. Working professionally as a designer, including political campaigns, and in a design cooperative with cultural theorists on 'alternative' technologies and modes of organisation. Especially influential was being a founding member and director of the EcoDesign Foundation (EDF) in Sydney, from 1992 to 2002. The organization was an early leader in sustainable design theory and practice. This, included our installing on the school building we leased in 1993 what was the largest photovoltaic array in Sydney, plus an independent tanked water supply. The build fit-out we undertook was based on recycled/recyclable materials. EDF undertook sustainable design projects for the federal and state Environment Protection Authorities, and other government agencies. It worked with a major corporation, several leading architectural practices as sustainable design consultants, the Australian Institute of Engineers, as a professional development education provider to the Sydney chapter of the Australian Institute of Architects (including on design for a changing climate); ran off-campus courses for three Sydney universities; produced publications and organised exhibitions and competitions. It also managed a federally funded multi-million-dollar solar lighting R&D project, and was the environmental design manager for two Sydney 2000 Olympics projects. All of this activity cut across the mainstream, and inflected the careers of everyone who worked for EDF.

The last theme to mention is the work on climate change and cities. Most notably, membership of a forty-person design team city-move workshop in Gallivare, Northern Sweden in (2009); a climate change metrofitting risk analysis of Cincinnati, workshop leader, Green Building Council (sponsor) Cincinnati (2013); sea level rises Impacts in South Florida', Florida Atlantic University (2013); hardwood tree plantation establishment and management, Ravensbourne (Queensland) (2003–2015); master's projects, impact of sea level rises in the Pearl River Delta, HKPU (2015–2017). Two books on this issue were also published (2015, 2017). Most recently, I led a workshop and participated in a project with architects, faculty members from architecture at Canberra University, and from design and the Institute for Climate, Energy and Disaster Solutions at the Australian National University – this, to conceptualise and promote the adoption of a strategy to relocate cities at risk from climate change impacts in Australia.

The point of relating this history is to indicate that the concept of contrapractice is not an abstract creation but is underpinned by a whole range of practices where, by degree, it was present in a nascent form. As such, it was historically and existentially prefigured. From lessons learnt, a proliferation of contrapractices are viewed as having significant potential as transformative agents as they would be responsive to need in critical/crisis conditions.

As argued elsewhere, neither mainstream politics nor economics is capable of dealing with the 'complexity of the complexity' of what is unfolding at a planetary level.[1] As can be recognised, the US public voted in 2024 to make a bad situation worse and, in their structural myopia, have accelerated disasters: enviro-climatic and geopolitical. The 'stage is set' for enviro-climatic, biological and social disasters of an epic scale. At the same time, AI is on a trajectory that is/will reduce human agency, and create another kind of crisis. So, the prospect is terrifying. While a new political imagination is needed, how it could transform the political landscape is hard to contemplate, let alone answer. Meanwhile, the

---

[1]   Tony Fry and Madina Tlostanova, *A New Political Imagination, Making the Case* (London: Routledge, 2021).

development of forms of political subversion, without idealistic expectation of their ability to effect major change, is crucial in the face of the changes that will be wrought by disaster(s).

So said, for me, striving for a path to action displaces investing in hope.[2] In this respect, the politics of the coming future centres on gaining the capacity to adaptively respond to unacceptable change. For all of its no doubt limitations, I see contrapractice, as a means to engage, and eventually overcome, all those practices that, by default if not intent, negate (defuture) the very possibility of the continuity of the relational interdependence of life itself. As such, it is not a single overarching practice, with a reducible form or agency, but a specifically created operational other to every particular practice of negation. To advance, contrapractice requires to be understood, developed and deployed by all practitioners who are against the ongoing terminal trajectory of unsustainability. There is no greater political need, for without acting to sustain the evolving conditions upon which life depends there is nothing. The refusal of helplessness is the first and essential act of survival. It's not easy to pitch the proto-practice of contrapractice in a way that will capture imaginations and prompt adoption – I'm not a populist communicator – nonetheless, this communication is the task at hand.

The form of the book is slightly unusual. While it has an argument detailed over four chapters authored by myself, it opens with a dialogue between me and *Dulmini Perera*. This exchange introduces a number of the concerns that have shaped our conversation, and how they have influenced our conceptualisation of contrapractice, and its contextualisation by the concept and actuality of defuturing as a particular worldly condition reframing of practice. The book closes with a conversation with *Perera*. Our exchanges are not only revelatory but mediate projectively and retrospectively the thinking that informs the intent and tensions of the book.

The book's Introduction firmly places all that follows in the context of convergent crises that the received divisions of knowledge (that shape the ways

---

[2] The words 'action' and 'practice' appear numerous times in this text. They are not interchangeable, but practice is clearly a form of action. In general terms: **Action** is dynamic, ordered or disordered, chaotic or directed, directional, intentional and spontaneous, reactive and proactive. Etymologically action(n) is from mid-fourteenth-century *accioun*, 'cause or grounds for a lawsuit', from Anglo-French *accioun*, Old French *accion, action* (twelfth century) 'action; lawsuit, case', from Latin *actionem* (nominative *actio*) 'a putting in motion; a performing, a doing; public acts, official conduct; lawsuit, legal action' (source also of Spanish *accion*, Italian *azione*), noun of action from past-participle stem of *agere* 'to do', https://www.etymonline.com/. Theoretically, action is interestingly considered by Hannah Arendt, *The Human Condition* (Chicago: The University of Chicago Press, 1958), 175–247.

 Practice, likewise in general terms, is considered, ordered, purposeful, repeatable – both are consequential (and can be positive or negative. Etymologically, practice arrives from Ancient Greek *prāktikē* (practice, experience), *prāktikós*, (practical), and from *prássō* (I do), passing to the Latin *prāctica* (practical affairs), to modern usage *praticare* (Italian), *Practicar* (Portuguese) and practice (English). A transposition of the Italian *praticare* to the English evokes the spirit of contrapractice, https://www.etymonline.com/. Theoretically, practice is considered at length in Chapter 2.

we all understand the worlds of our existence) disaggregate. So much of this knowledge was structured and developed before the arrival of the intertwined global complexity of contemporary social, industrial, techno-scientific and geopolitical systems, and their unintended impacts on the biophysical world. The ability to create and accelerate change has totally outstripped any collective ability to understand and appropriately deal with unconsidered consequences. At present, there is a huge divide between what needs to be understood and the extent of available understanding (not least by the planet's political leadership). What the argument of this work makes clear is that not only is a greater and futural understanding of coming risks and dangers essential, but equally so is the development of transformative responsive action – contrapractice. So framed, contrapractice arrives to begin to meet an expressed need to understand and redress the defuturing agency of so many taken-for-granted practices.

The first chapter contributes to this aim by revisiting and reviewing the first published exposition of defuturing in 1999, as it presented ways of understanding the structural future-negating dynamics of industrial society. It also reflects upon how current global circumstances have added to this dynamic with increasingly disastrous consequences. To support the case for contrapractice. Chapter 2 considers how practice historically has been theorised – in doing so, it exposes a present condition of insufficient understanding in the contexts of a global enviro-climatic crisis, together with the material and immaterial impacts of digital technologies. In response to what prior chapters argued, Chapter 3 elaborates contrapractice as an organic form of action (organic understood as action that takes on a life of its own, spreads and grows, via the action of practitioners) in response to imperatives coming from the presented complexity of accelerating defuturing forces. The final chapter looks back on arguments made as markers of the passing epoch, as they portend the form the emergent one.

Acknowledgements

There are three people whose contributions have stamped themselves on this book. First is Dulmini Perera; this, for her contributions to it, constructive comments on drafts and insightful insights expressed during our numerous Zoom conversations. Next is a special thanks to the Series editor and my long-time friend Clive Dilnot; this, for his comradeship, constructive suggestions and astute observations on the text. Finally, a special thanks once again to Anne-Marie Willis, my partner and in-house critical reader.

Opening Dialogue

Tony Fry and Dulmini Perera

The concerns that have shaped our conversation, and our conceptualization of contrapractice, are contextualized by the worldly actuality of defuturing and how it demands a reframing of how practice is understood and engaged. More specifically, our overall aim is to set a path that helps to lead the development and rise of contrapractices as redirective forces against the continuing acceleration of defuturing as a structural condition and as a specific ideological objective of a radical technocentric political globally dispersed fraternity. At the same time, the intent is also to direct contrapractices toward the Sustainment of all means of futuring in what are increasingly challenging times.

So positioned, the stated principle of contrapractice is the redirection of practice toward Sustainment. While having some nascent forms, it is an ethos and an open project inviting widespread contributions across practices in general. In this respect, the politics of contrapractice is organic: it is enabled by distributed action by practitioners who perceive opportunities to intervene and act across a range of contexts and scales. In this respect, its intent metaphorically is to create sparks that create an unstoppable process of affirmative futural change. The spirit is, as put by a slogan of the anti-apartheid movement in South Africa decades ago, captured in the song 'Biko': 'You can blow out a candle, but not fire, once the blaze begins to catch, the wind will blow it higher'.

Such action is informed and prompted by an analytic that exposes the defuturing propensity of extant practices. Clearly, in many cases, their negative dispositions are not hard to discern as they are materially evident. But others will not be self-evident and may, for example, be embedded in the unquestioned values of habitual actions of a practice.

Seven topics – danger, change, time, world, technology, complexity and dialogue – are woven into our exchange. They act to register and ground the significance of the need for contrapractice and for it to be recognized, advanced and employed.

We assert that defuturing practices have to be exposed, contested, eliminated and replaced by contrapractices that sustain life in all its dimensions. Here then is the primary mission of contrapractices. Dulmini opens:

TIME, CHANGE AND DANGER

DP: *The metaphorical term 'the end times' captures the present as it connotes the end of the world as we have collectively known it. When you and I first met during Corona times, the notion of endings/beginnings and the very accelerating nature of the change of change, and (at least from my perspective) the ever-growing inability to think of agency was at the back of my head. I think this condition, or at least a version of it, is something you had already thought about, mostly because of your work on 'defuturing'. Our conversation started then. I think we both agree that the linguistic/ logical means used to evoke to explain the changing nature of the change never seems to grasp the complexity of the pertaining condition of existence. But we do need to move beyond the more simple and linear understanding[s] of cause and effect that are mobilized to frame these conditions, shouldn't we?*

TF: Often, it is an analysis of an effect, a consequence, that leads to the identification of a cause. So it is with the epochal change that is now underway as a result of convergence of the growing impacts of a changing climate, geopolitical instability, the consequences of rapid technological change and substantive political inertia that all combine to damage the fundamental conditions of life itself. While a recognition of this 'event' constituting the start of a new epoch is still inchoate, there is a widespread sense that the conditions of all life on planet Earth are once again dramatically altering. The starkest registration of this moment is characterized by the announced commencement of a sixth extinction event. As will be shortly shown, to understand what is happening requires revisiting the distant past.

DP: *Since the premise of this book is set as framed by the emergent conditions of epochal change, how would you characterize the most important characteristics of this situation?*

TF: I believe this moment can be characterized in several ways: A mass extinction event is when 50 per cent or more of all plant and animal life dies. The first of these events was 440 million years ago, the most recent 64 million years ago. For hominoids, who appeared around 7 million years ago (*Sahelanthropus tchadensis* being the first of the species), the most traumatic event was the Ice Age, which commenced 2.58 million years ago (there had been a previous Ice Age 34 million years ago). Our species, *Homo sapiens*, arrived during a period of interglacial warming approximately 300,000 years ago. As the planet warmed at the start of the current interglacial period 12,000–11,500 years ago, which ended the Ice Age (but not a cycle of warming and cooling). The commencement of this period marked the start of the current epoch. At this moment, the process of 'human settlement' and of agriculture gradually began in the Fertile Crescent of the Levant (but the claim is not exclusive – there were similar developments in Central America and in China).

Settlement was generative of conditions that accelerated the advancement of existing and newly created technologies (in areas like shelter/building fabrication, agriculture, water management, ceramics, textiles, and eventually metal (the first being copper)).[1] With this quantum increase in the capacity to employ technology to advance material condition of settled populations 'our' impacts on the natural environment imperceptibly began. Even though impacts were initially inconsequential, and populations were very small, they opened the way towards the present neo-Promethean bio-machinic age of terrestrial and atmospheric transformation.

Up until the present, there have been graduated polarities of inequity: rich/poor; developed/undeveloped; North/South. Notwithstanding the colonial violence and economic exploitation of modernity, there was also a Eurocentric humanist idealism that believed that the gaps dividing global populations could be closed and poverty eliminated by 'development'. The postdevelopment discourse has exposed its liberatory failure. But the signs emanating from the opening of the new epoch are indicating that the gap is dramatically changing structurally, and widening.

As will be discussed in detail later, three major trends are unevenly arriving: the still slow growth of the displaced and abandoned as areas of the planet become uninhabitable (due to heat, lack of water, fire and flood); the mass of the population globally being forced to adapt their material environment and ways of life and work in order to retain a semblance of their existing way of life; and, the super-rich corporate techno-elites increasingly establishing protective environments for themselves as global conditions worsen, including in terms of 'human security'. Some of these people are buying islands, and life in the artificial space of dome-structures is being explored. Likewise, others are adding luxury multi-room bunkers to their homes.

These conditions of population fragmentation suggest a breakup of any residual notion of a single world of difference and the emergence of three totally different realities, each with its own mode of being. What is new is the coming scale and extent of the break, and the degree it will render existing geopolitical structures redundant. While the schematic picture of the change is of stark difference, its realization is likely to be messy, fractious and protracted.

DP: *In other words, what you are saying is that past and present practices of world making have brought this perilous situation into existence, which in your work you have called defuturing.*

---

[1]   The first use of a stone as a tool was over 500,000 years ago. *Homo sapiens* entered a world of a vast array, albeit unevenly developed, of stone, wooden and bone tools. Chris Stringer, *The Origin of Our Species* (London: Allen Lane, 2011).

TF: Yes, and they are still being enabled in multiple ways. But, they have to be contested, eliminated and replaced by contrapractices that sustain life in all its dimensions. The task of elimination and substitution is the primary mission of contrapractices.

DP: *But if you frame it in that way, it sounds like all practices have only defuturing consequences? I think we need to be more nuanced about perhaps the degrees to which different practices are related to defuturing as well as the ability of them to be 'futural'.*

TF: You are right. We – a multitude in all our differences who oppose the forces that defuture – have to be careful not to assert that all practices defuture. By degree, from the indiscernible to the discernible, practices bring worlds at every scale in and out of being. As such, they are forces of creation and destruction. The problem is that there is often a disparity between intent, claim and actuality, with negative consequences only being retrospectively identified. Thus, in sum:

- There are practices that defuture
- There is a need to eliminate as many of these defuturing practices as possible
- There is a need to create as many practices as possible that are contra to those that defuture
- There are practices that future, and there is a need to increase as many of these as possible

DP: *There is a lot to be done in order to make present all the practices that beg to be eliminated. I can't help but think about the enormity of the scale and ambition of the mission of contrapractice. It seems like a vast collective task extending across time.*

TF: Two dynamics frame the agency of contrapractice. One goes to the time it would take for it to gain sufficient agency to have real transformative power. Notionally let's suggest this would take decades. The second acknowledges that the critical situation of 'life on Earth' is accelerating and therefore the situation is becoming ever-more serious. So situated, It follows that contrapractice has to become normative and in so doing migrate from its function being offensive to defensive. However, the immediate task at hand is to start to create contrapractices and demonstrate their efficacy as the material expression of the logic of 'Sustainment'.

DP: *Is it not the case that everything dies / ends but, in that process, things are continually born/begin.*

TF: This is true of 'the cycle of life', but defuturing has the ability to break the cycle and prevent rebirth and regeneration – hence to the emergent condition of extinction – so said, Sustainment simply names the continuity 'the cycle of life'.

DP: *For me the bigger question is how we understand 'what to sustain' or 'what to conserve'. This is always more complex than the way this question is framed in most mainstream sustainability, conservation and repair discourses at present.*

TF: Beyond the natural elements, there is no way to reductively list *'what to sustain' or 'what to conserve'*. As indicated, Sustainment is what ensures the continuity and potential of all living systems to be futural, and this can be conditional. For example, fire can be an agent of destruction or creation. It needs to be understood as both in interconnected ways. Understandings of the discourse of sustainability, conservation and repair are uneven, relative and lack fully resolved abstracted definitions and definitive practices. While Sustainment maintains the continuity of life beyond just bare life, for 'us' it overarches the biological and the cultural, the intellectual and practical. So said, if conscious of the imperative of Sustainment, 'we' act within the limits of our available knowledge, although without certainty, and thereafter act with judgement.

One essential for the Sustainment, and thus continuity of our being, and that of all our others, is the condition and complexity of 'our' relational interdependence. The recognition of this has to be, and is, at the core of how contrapractice is constituted and enacted. One cannot overemphasize that no matter who 'we' are, without Sustainment 'we' have nothing. By implication, to restate, it is essential to eliminate those things, practices and worlds that perpetuate the unsustainable. Likewise, the realization of the project of Sustainment also requires the delegitimization of the epistemological ground of knowledge that underpins practices and values that enable the continuity of the unsustainable, and this means the commencement of an enduring incremental remaking of education at every level that is, directly and indirectly, directive of practice.

Being in danger

DP: *The convergent dynamics of enviro-climatic, geopolitical and techno-social changes have created a unique critical planetary moment of danger – one in which our species are both in danger and its source. Contributing to systemic change as you mentioned is directly related to the ways in which different agents identify their relation to the planetary moment of danger.*

TF: The problem is danger, writ large as defuturing in process. For those persons with political and economic power, as well as the 'distracted masses', it has not/does not arrive. The disaggregated ways projected dangers are presented and 'recognized' not only conceal their actual temporal interconnectedness, but in so doing also undermine the very possibility of appropriate response. A significant part of the problem is the way in which problems are objectified, then presented as in need of solutions. While some might be able to be solved, many are structural conditions that demand a response, that while mitigating their impact, cannot eliminate their cause. For example, the impacted climate system, the propensity to make war, the loss of biodiversity are not 'to hand' and cannot be 'solved', but responsive action is absolutely vital

The climate of change

DP: *I am always sceptical of 'climate solutions' framed within a period of relative stability of the warming cycle that assures the planet will continue to warm until the flip into cooling commences. The ways these processes are framed in time seems quite inadequate. When we speak of climate change, I think it is important to unpack perhaps the very climate of that change, and the distinct events that help us think of the nature of climate change and its historicity.*

TF: The climate is dynamic: it does not have the possibility of a normative condition of stability. The glacial-interglacial process, known as the Milankovitch cycle, names the basis of the dynamic process, and it centres on the relation between the Earth and the Sun. The process is determined by three factors: the Earth's orbit is not a perfect circle (the variation is called eccentricity); the angle of the Earth's axis is tilted (this variation is called obliquity); and the direction of the Earth's axis is pointed and creates seasonal contrasts between hemispheres (this variation is called precession).[2] The U.S. Geological Survey indicates that the interglacial periods last about 20,000 years. The current period has several more thousand years to run. Anthropogenic induced warming, which the Intergovernmental Panel on Climate Change (IPCC) has stated is irreversible, amplifies the process of natural warming.[3] However, the data reporting the level of warming by greenhous gas (GHG) emissions is open to question. For example, the mode of emissions accounting creates an illusory picture as military emissions are not counted.[4] The key relation between climate and people is evidenced by the history of migration.[5]

[2]   NASA Science, https://science.nasa.gov/science-research/earth-science/milankovitch-orbital-cycles-and-their-role-in-earths-climate/ (accessed 8 January 2025).
[3]   IPCC, Synthesis Report of the Sixth Assessment Report, 2023, https://www.ipcc.ch/ar6-syr/ (accessed 8 January 2023).
[4]   Chelsea Harvey, 'Warfare's Climate Emissions Are Huge but Uncounted', E&E News, *Scientific American*, June 1, 2024, https://www.scientificamerican.com/article/warfares-climate-emissions-are-huge-but-uncounted/ (accessed 10 March 2023). Nations aren't required to report military pollution under the Paris Agreement. The article cites a 2022 report indicating that military emissions account for 5.5 per cent of global emissions (this is equal to Russia 4.4 per cent plus Australia 1.1 per cent). Clearly, as the current expectation is that conflict will increase rather than diminish, it can be therefore expected that this level will rise.
[5]   The historicity of migration is indivisible from climate change, the evolution of our species, and hominoid inter-species genetic changes (traceable via mitochondrial DNA). Most significantly, a key factor in prehistoric migration was seeking refuge during the Ice Age. Drought, the existence of lower sea levels, land bridges that no longer exist with current sea levels, glacial mass and geological transformation. The abundance of a source of food, or a lack of it, was another key factors driving or enabling migration. Chris Stringer, 'What Makes a Modern Human', *Nature* 485, no. 7396 (2012): 33–5; David Reich, *Who We Are And How We Got Here – Ancient DNA and the New Science of the Human Past* (New York: Pantheon Books, 2018); and Thomas Litt, Jürgen Richter and Frank Schäbitz, *The Journey of Modern Humans from Africa to Europe* (Stuttgart: Schweizerbart Science Publishers, 2021).

The more one looks at the planetary, climatic and geological past of the planet the more an oscillation between trauma, instability and stability becomes apparent. Besides extinction events, there are the impacts of gigantic volcanic eruptions, sea level rises and falls, asteroid impacts, supernova/gamma ray bursts, global cooling, global warming, and *anoxis* events (lack of oxygen in the oceans).

These distant events all have a relevance to our species and the present. The commencement of the current extinction event needs to be seen in this context – the issue is thus not total extinction but the 'nature' of the form of life that survives. Evolutionary biologists have, as mentioned, indicated that a sixth major extinction event has commenced.[6] Unlike the other five such events, collectively 'we', from the start of industrialization, started to become a major causal factor. The two key open questions are thus: what percentage of species will survive, and what will they be?

DP: *I guess this is another way of speaking about our current planetary moment, also identified by the notion of the Anthropocene. This term has already been reframed by many thinkers and practitioners from multiple geopolitical and disciplinary contexts who are equally attempting to engage the multiple existential crises by pointing toward various specificities and potentials related to this condition. Jason Moore's 'Capitalocene', Donna Haraway's 'Chthulucene', Alf Hornborg's 'Technocene', Jussi Parikka's 'Anthrobscene', Anna Tsing's 'Plantationocene' are a few named examples. But I think what is important in this book is that we relate these events to a certain 'defuturing impetus'.*

TF: Certainly, all such characterizations of the current 'state of the planet' share a common consequence: defuturing. Central to this developing defuturing impetus was the creation of an insatiable carbon economy. But, we moderns have also created an instant extinction option: a major nuclear conflagration of immediate mass destruction and a subsequent nuclear winter created by a massive fallout of radioactive dust and debris.

Life, all life, is now lived in the worsening conditions of warming within, the eleventh interglacial event, and in the shadow of a nuclear conflagration – a risk heightened by the geopolitical instability increased by the environmental and social impacts of climate change. Increased levels of instability, and therefore uncertainty, are now normative.

---

[6]   Elizabeth Kolbert, *The Sixth Extinction, An Unnatural History* (New York: Henry Holt and Company, 2014).

Time 'out of joint' – 'the now' and 'the then'

TF: Recourse to the Anthropocene, as the name of the current critical planetary moment, while conceptually understood by a few, and sensed by many, is nevertheless not something that is properly understood by the population at large. Moreover, it clearly does not adequately capture the dynamic and relational causal complexity of the formation and consequences of the now-unfolding 'heat age', which is now an existential reality for billions of people. Neither does the reduction of the current global state of criticality to a named meta-crisis register the accompanying geopolitical breakup underway, and created by, the forces of ideological polarization, or the increasing global techno-economic divisions. Such a future is already overwhelming the present. I guess what distinguishes change in these previous contexts from accelerating change in the anthropogenic context is the question of entropy and heat, layered onto geopolitical instability. These issues are clearly central to the discussions in the book. While it has parallels with the concerns of other projects, it digresses and centres on practice as it underscores a process (defuturing) like the overheating project of Thomas Hyland Erikson and more design architecture-related inquiries that are foregrounded in *Hot Cities: A Transdisciplinary Agenda*. However, the very notion of the 'heat age' and 'heat' folds back into a larger frame and greater complexity.

In early September 2023, the United Nations' weather agency announced that the planet had just experienced its hottest three months on record (Alex Blair, 2023).[7] By June to August 2024, this record was broken – clearly, this pattern has continued. The lived reality of heat is deadly. For instance, in the South American countries of Guyana and Suriname, they are experiencing over 180 days per year with temperatures over 45–50+ degrees Celsius – as a result, women are losing babies, infants are dying, and so are old people.[8] There are fourteen countries that are experiencing temperatures between 50–60 degrees Celsius – this is killer hear, especially for outdoor workers. Loss of life, water, crops, employment and places of settlement will all increase everywhere.

Likewise, in September 2023, *The Guardian* reported that 'Antarctica is likely warming at almost twice the rate of the rest of the world and faster than climate change models are predicting, with potentially far-reaching implications for global sea level rise, according to a scientific study'.[9] Then, a few days later, *The Washington Post* reported:

[7]   Alex Blair, 'UN Warns "Climate Breakdown Has Begun" After Hottest Northern Hemisphere Summer on Record', news.com.au, 7 September 2023, https://www.news.com.au/technology/environment/climate-change/un-warns-climate-breakdown-has-begun-after-hottest-northern-hemisphere-summer-on-record/news-story/bb8437677864d5c9b950b5dc5a521f4f (accessed 11 November 2023).

[8]   The seriousness of the situation in Guyana is captured in the graphics of the World Bank Knowledge Portal, 2024, https://climateknowledgeportal.worldbank.org/country/guyana/heat-risk (accessed 14 October 20 24).

[9]   Graham Readfearn, 'Antarctica Warming', *The Guardian*, 8 September 2023, https://www.theguardian.com/world/2023/sep/08/antarctica-warming-much-faster-than-models-predicted-in-deeply-concerning-sign-for-sea-levels (accessed 14 February 2024).

Pakistan is the epicentre of a new global wave of disease and death linked to climate change, according to a *Washington Post* analysis of climate data, based on leading scientific studies, interviews with experts and reporting from some of the places bearing the brunt of Earth's heating. This examination of climate-fuelled illnesses – tied to hotter temperatures, and swifter passage of pathogens and toxins – shows how countries across the globe are ill-prepared for the insidious, intensifying risks to almost every facet of human health.[10]

Another heat story, the next day, *The Washington Post* carries a report on a melting Alaskan glacier flooding the town of Juneau and destroying houses.[11] The reports of the increasingly serious impacts of climate change actually now arrive on an almost daily basis.

NASA indicates that the planet is now the warmest it has been for 125,000 years.[12] Effectively, this can be read as a futural marker of a deep coming crisis. Warming as an event needs to be seen as a continuing, growing relational pattern of effects rather than just a singular issue.

DP: *I think part of the current entropic condition and the loss of biological diversity indicates a broader problem of diversity, such as techno-diversity and most importantly reduced diversity in way of thinking and imagining. Thomas Hyland Erikson, who draws from the cybernetic work of Gregory Bateson, for example, identifies this as a loss of flexibility or the decrease of a system's ability to adapt and remain committed to continuous change. For Bernard Stiegler, this then relates to the very questions of knowledge and an inability to think otherwise that is represented by a form of what he calls 'systemic stupidity'. Perhaps you can say something more about how the question of the entropic relates to questions of knowledge.*

TF: An adequate answer to the relation between the entropic and knowledge would require a level and explanation outside the scope and intent of this exchange. So, what follows is an abridged account.

Biological science exposes the anti-entropic functions within the systems of life. The individual body or plant is intrinsically entropic – it exhausts itself and dies. Yet its reproductive capability is counter-entropic, thus life continues.

[10]   Annie Gowen, Nico Niko Kommenda and Saiyna Bashir, 'Pakistan Bears the Brunt of Global Extreme Heat Illness and Mortality', *Washington Post*, 2023, https://www.washingtonpost.com/climateenvironment/interactive/2023/pakistan-extreme-heat-health-impacts death (accessed 22 October 2023).

[11]   Joshua Partlow, 'Alaska Glacier Melting', *Washington Post*, 4 September 2023, https://www.washingtonpost.com/climate-environment/2023/09/04/juneau-flood-alaska-glacier-mendenhall/ (accessed 2 December 2023).

[12]   Then there is the larger historical frame that places the historicity of climate change as a central force of the origins of our species and its future. But the relational complexity does not have a narrative. Jeff Tollefson, 'Climate Change is Hitting the Planet Faster Than Scientists Originally Thought', *Nature* 28 February 2022, https://www.nature.com/articles/d41586-022-00585-7 (accessed 20 December 2022).

Hominoids intervened in this process and externalized and extended it exosomatically – they created technologies that denaturalized natural cycles. Made environments, and the practices that created them, gave protection against 'the ravages of nature'. The more technologies advanced, the greater the ability to exploit 'nature' and extend life. For this to be possible, knowledge was created and developed that directed worldly action. But at a certain point, the counter-entropic union of biology, knowledge and technology became destructively dynamic. Effectively, the evolution of knowledge, and its produced exosomatic capability, became increasingly powerful – the futural negentropic agency turned, became dystopic and in doing so began to defuture. The result is what has been named as the Anthropocene (an uneven totalization of difference) understood in actuality as an 'Entropocene'. This account is a very condensed summary of a complexity Bernard Stiegler detailed at length in *The Neganthropocene*.[13] In sum: entropic relates to 'questions knowledge' (that are continually productive in 'advances' of technology) that delinks it from counter-entropic functions within the 'creation/destruction of cycle of life'. The denaturalized conditions of the replication of this cycle means the rate of defuturing from the techno-natural synthesis of unSustainment ever-increases, de facto setting a path to the sixth extinction event. Futuring so positioned names an action against this propensity.

STATE OF THE WORLDS: FRACTURE ZONES

DP: *Obviously, there are many unseen, but also more visible, effects of these changing conditions. But one example that I always found useful to imagine in our arguments is the one that you often bring up in our conversations, which relates to the broad-scale strategic relocation project that you are developing for Australian communities at risk. Relocation and displacement is clearly going to be a massive planetary issue in the coming decades.*

TF: There is a certain kind of plural continuum by which 'the world' is still mostly viewed – indigenous people living in remote areas of the planet, the poor of Africa, Asia and Central and South America living in informal settlements, nations suffering in conditions of conflict and economic hardship, newly industrial nation struggling or prospering and old wealthy living the material decay of the afterlife of modernity. Climate change impacts, as indicated, will completely transform the reality of all these situations. The data arrives, the narrative does not. The scale of coming population displacement will create a redistribution of people at a scale never before known. The vast majority of these people will be abandoned to their fate. Great swathes of the planet will be rendered uninhabitable. The socio-political disruption produced will cause major economic and security problems. Nations will be unable to maintain border

---

13   Bernard Stiegler, *The Neganthropocene* (trans Daniel Ross) (London: New Humanities Press, 2018).

security, humanitarian organizations will be totally overwhelmed, economies will crash – all the while climate impacts will increase. The combination of all these factors will be primary drivers of the retreat of corporate techno-elites into the forms of protective spaces in part first envisioned by Buckminster Fuller in the 1950s and '60s, and conceptually extended by Peter Sloterdijk in his three-volume exposition of past and future modes of earthly dwelling in 'Spheres'.[14] The latter-day conditions of protection are as much bio-technical as they are spatial. As such, they are/will be about forms of being, and the consolidation of the lifeworld of corporate power, as well as being about physical modes of dwelling.

As was touched on earlier, life between the poles of displacement/abandonment and retraction/protectionism will be the condition of existence of the vast majority of the global population. As said, the reality of this picture of the change will not be 'neat'; rather the interface between the different emergent conditions of existence is likely to be messy and fractious. The unfolding of the complexity of this complexity is beyond speculation. However, what is evident is that the relation of the majority to a changing planetary environment will be pragmatically and adaptively responsive. But 'unevenly' according to circumstances: 'they/we' will make their situation as best it can be with the means available.

What the now forming three fracture zones of the displaced and abandoned, the adaptive majority and the isolated protectionism of the corporate techno-elites shows is that there cannot, and will not, be any universal address to the future now unfolding.

Many of the displaced and abandoned will socially regress into a state of bare life. Their fate largely defined by what they can find in, or take from, the environment of traverse and arrival, their lives dependent upon their skills and knowledge, resourcefulness and ingenuity. Many will survive, many won't.

A scenario of the world created by the corporate techno-elites can be envisaged, although the actuality will be more complex and nuanced than outlined. Many of the causal factors that will bring such a world into existence already exist in inchoate forms technically, organizationally and politically, as is evident in the actions and 'empires' of the extant international entrepreneurial billionaire class. The world they create will likely be exclusionary, militarized, artificial and diverse in constructed form. It will almost certainly be economically interconnected, and technologically sustained enviro-biophysically. A transhuman mode of being could well become dominant, marking a process of species evolutionary transformation. Almost certainly, it will employ the means of power it has at its disposal to command the appropriation of the material resources external to the environment it requires. Corporate governance and the rule of CEOs will likely be the political norm. The relation between the formation of corporate

---

[14]   Peter Sloterdijk, *Bubbles, Spheres Volume 1* (Cambridge, MA: MIT Press, 2011 [German edition,1998]); *Globes: Spheres Volume II* (Cambridge, MA: MIT Press, 2014 [German edition,1999]); and *Foam, Volume III* (Cambridge, MA: MIT Press 2016, [German edition, 2004]).

nations will be competitive. The condition of limitation of this world is that of scale in relation to material intensity and operational infrastructure. There would be internal issues of containment of materials and resources pro rata population. But there would also be issues of the containment of colonizing outreach into the other fracture zones.

CONTRAPRACTICES

TF: Against the backdrop of the displaced and abandoned, the world of corporate techno-elites will be technocentric and exclusive. Driven by circumstances, contrapractice will be a primary option for the adaptive majority, and be essential for their future and their ongoing viability. Specifically, the imperative to adapt would extend over the built environment they occupy, the way they produce food, the material goods they make, the services they employ and their ways of work and living. In addition, practices contra to incursions of the displaced and by colonizing extractive action by corporate techno-elites would become essential.[15]

DP: *In many ways, is not the imperative of this project to make present the scale and diversity of the project of adaptation that is needed across almost every sphere of life as a major setting into which contrapractice has to arrive? So, we try to make the scale of the danger clear, while at the same time present-ing the actual and developing options responsive to already unfolding crises.*

TF: The project of adaptation will determine if *Homo sapiens* has a future. The status quo of extant 'everyday life' cannot be, and will not be, sustained. The scale and rate of change – enviro-climatic, technological, economic and socio-cultural – will exceed the temporal condition of our being, and may occur at a speed beyond our species' natural adaptive capability, thus forcing the adoption of artificial means. What has to be grasped is that the lead into the coming epoch has started to emplace an overarching world dramatically different from, and alien to, the one currently occupied

DP: *I have a question, when you mention the notion of 'our species' and how they bring forth worlds. I think we need to make clear that although there is one planet, there are many worlds, and these worlds are also not all created by 'our species'. But I think there is more to be said about framing these 'worlds' and their consecutive ways of 'worlding' (how worlds bring forth worlds) in relation to contrapractice?*

TF: Jaoscob Von Uexküll (1864–1944) a century ago discussed the species-specific, spatio-temporal, 'self-in-world' of the *Umwelt* (understood as condition

---

[15]   Contrapractice so contextualized will be addressed in detail in Chapter 3.

of existence – and environment) that prompted a debate on *Welt as Umwelt*.[16] But as the philosopher Josef Pieper makes clear, while all forms of life live in an *Umwelt*, persons live in a *Welt*. Famously, Martin Heidegger argued in his 1929–30 *Fundamental Concepts of Metaphysics* that a stone is worldless, animals are 'poor of world' and that humans have a world – in so doing they bring Others into their world to constitute it.[17]

World is a conceptual construct that different thinkers have configured in different ways. Other species (animals, insects and plants) have environmental conditions upon which 'we' project the idea of the world. Practices brings forth environmental 'worldly' changes by intent and by default upon the 'natural world' (an anthropocentric designation) and the world of our fabrication. Because of a lack of comprehension of consequences (unrealized and realized) so many of our practices defuture the environment of our dependence, and that of all other species. Defuturing has become elemental to our collective conduct, if unevenly and in the difference, of our plural cosmo-cultural worlds.

For our species, there are many worlds within the world of our created material and cultural fabrication. But they do not exist in pluriversal harmony, or in the same temporal register. Some are under erasure, there are/will be antagonistic relations between many of them. The 'world' is constituted from competing ideological power blocs that edge toward conflict.[18] Overlapping with this conflict of fracture zone is the population of displacement and abandonment, who in the scattering will move *en mass* looking for, and taking means of survival, crossing borders uninvited and being met with violence. The division between the world's privileged, and their technologically enabled means of survival, the abandoned and the rest is an emerging fracturing destined to increase.

DP: *Well, I think this does provide a very different way to understand the geometries of the different worlds that emerge as a result of acceleration as these worlds transformatively articulate within the planetary biophysical worlds of dependence and difference that are impacted by global seismic shifts in power and force.*

TF. The world of our species occupation is not a unified whole; it is, as indicated, plural and becoming more so. For instance, the worlds of Indigenous people

---

[16] The concept of 'Umwelt' was detailed in *Staatsbiologie*, a book on biological science published by Baron Jakob von Uexküll in 1920.

[17] Martin Heidegger, *The Fundamental Concepts of Metaphysics* (trans Willian Mc Neill and Nicolas Walker) (Bloomington: Indiana University Press, 1995), 196–9. See also Tony Fry, *Becoming Human by Design* (Oxford: Berg, 2012), 66–71.

[18] *Institute for the Study of War*, the projective power of China into the South China Sea and its commitment to 'retake' Taiwan and the U.S. opposition to this aim; Israel and the tinder box of the Middle East; the rogue state danger of North Korea, and the indications the Russian is planning a war with NATO. Russian Offensive Campaign Assessment, March 20, 2024. https://understandingwar.org/backgrounder/russian-offensive-campaign-assessment-march-20-2024 (accessed 6 July 2024).

and the worlds of the poorest nations of the Global South are disproportionately affected by the reverberations of planetary material change produced by the world of rich and powerful nations. Under the impacts of climate change, geopolitical pressures and worldly structures, as said, are fracturing and differences are becoming more overt; this with the result that the possibility of mutual coexistence ('the pluriverse') is disappearing.

Tool-being now

DP: *It is also important to understand how these processes of fracturing relate to questions of technology, as well as how our 'tool-being' (as you have argued elsewhere) relates to our own ontogenesis.*

TF: To understand this movement, one has to return to a process of ontogenesis experienced by our species as inheritors of the worlds of 'tool-being' created by earlier hominoids. *Homo sapiens* came into being in environments where stone tools, and those they shaped in bone and wood, were in wide use. The estimate is that around seventy types of stone tools were in use at the time our species came into being.

The use of tools played a significant evolutionary role in hominoid physical and cognitive development over many millennia.[19] Tools put in place an indiscernible pattern of mutual transformation of worldly being and beings – the use of tools started to change the beings that used them, but also, at first indiscernibly, the environment of use. This recursive pattern has never been broken. However, the rates of change of beings and their worlds, in situated difference, continually increased over millennia, as did the enacted consequences of the dialectic of creation and destruction, futuring and defuturing (Fry, 2021).

DP: *This change (the acceleration of acceleration) was dramatically evident by the early modern age, with the contrast between indigenous and proto-industrializing population. How does tool-being, as you have defined it, factor into this process?*

TF. First, from our inception, and from our prior hominoid forebears, there was a propensity to act without concern for environmental consequences. But, in the distant past, numbers were small and the impact minor and so able to be environmentally absorbed. But once tools became more efficient, things started to change (for example, deforestation was a problem in ancient China

---

[19]   A. Muller, C. Shipton and C. Clarkson, 'Stone toolmaking difficulty and the evolution of hominin technological skills'. *Nature, Sci Rep* 12 no. 5883 (2022), https://doi.org/10.1038/s41598-022-09914-2 (accessed 9 January 2023). Fry, *Becoming Human By Design*; Stringer, *The Origin of Our Species*; and Bernard Stiegler, *Technics and Time, 1, The Fault of Epimetheus*, trans. Richard Beardsworth with George Collins (Stanford: Stanford University Press, 1998).

and Greece). Then, when modern technologies started to arrive, the situation got a lot worse. The faster technological development accelerated the greater the extent of defuturing.

What, however, remained a constant until the recent past – although unevenly – has been a failure to recognize what has been/is being destroyed, and the consequences. The defuturing implicit in and with futuring went, and still to a significant degree, goes unnoticed. Defuturing for the collective body of our species is akin to autoimmunity for the individual: it is auto-destructive. Whereas for the body it marks a failure of the immune system, for the collective body it marks a regulatory failure of a combination of the economic, social and political orders. By default, this allows a process of negation to emerge and to continue unencumbered.

DP: *I guess we can say that at its most extreme, this is most evident in extractivism and in productivism, as a logic (that underscored the structuring of labour processes and their mechanization), and in economic growth predicated upon unrestrained productivity. But I think this links to the difficulty of understanding the condition we are in, in the first place. Particularly being situated in the contexts of architecture and design, I still hear a lot of discussion around this within a 'problem-solution' framework. Current division and categories of available knowledge, in their lack of relationality, expose representational incapability of making 'the state of the world', and many of its most critical specific problems present. I think there is disjuncture between those practices that make worlds within the world, and those that comprehend the consequences of such action.*

TF: The disposition to disaggregate causality of a relational element of the unstable whole conceals the wider condition of the interwoven instability that demands responsive action. While the dangers are extensive, situated and critical, and while some of the problems are insurmountable, as said, responsive action is essential. However, the possibility of doing so is not universal. For the displaced and abandoned, all that is possible is to respond to their plight. For the accelerationist corporate techno-elite, their aim is to disarticulate from worldly conditions and to create environments independent from them. This leaves the adaptive majority as the only agent able to take responsive action for interests that include, but exceed, their own.

DP: *It follows that the claim of contrapractice(s) to intervene to redress this situation is limited, so is it still vital? Moreover, contrapractices are not 'ready-made' and present 'to hand'. So is it a second-order task with an objective still in-formation.*

TF: The complexity of this task arrives out of an evolving analytic of the flow and feedback of causal forces of fragmentation and negation in their situated relatedness – this as they are intersected by forces of change. The context of intervention is always of the 'complexity of complexity' as a confluence of 'the natural' with 'the unnatural' fabrications and systems of our species creation as they articulate a reality, by varied degrees of exposure, in which all life now dwells. This reality overrides the binary division of natural/unnatural, nature/culture and the elementalism of assemblages.

Climate change intrinsically changes 'the natural world' and always has done so. Anthropogenically induced global warming is amplifying the 'natural' warming intrinsic to the current interglacial cycle, with the distinction between natural and unnatural impacts now blurring. The significance of such change, only exists from an anthropocentric perspective. In the schema of planetary trauma, the present crises are geologically minor. So situated, there is a chronophobic failure to think in time past and future.

The primary task is to try to overcome defuturing as a means to do this. Contrapractice is, and links to, several secondary tasks in industry and education which would be expected to support this aim.

DP: *From what you have been saying ontologically, a sense of the world, and of being in it, will change for everyone according to their circumstances. Psychologically, how the past, present and future are viewed by many people will also change according to these circumstances. I guess then the political order will equally transform in different ways?*

TF: In terms of the short-term political order, some changes are predictable (authoritarianism can be expected to increase, but likewise, some form of resistant reaction against it will arrive). Economically, changes will be dramatic: economic breakdown – from the serious to the catastrophic, coming from environmental and climate change impacts – is likely, with resulting social dysfunction and conflict. But as fragmentation increases, the political will reconfigure: displacement will produce political breakdown. Corporate techno-elitism will fuse corporate capitalism with a political order and dictatorial CEO rule. The adaptive majority will likely generate forms of democratic, and postdemocratic, pluralism.

DP: *So, if I am to sum up some of the things you said about this condition, I think the most important thing in the way the heat age and breakdown are defined in the book is that they do not come with any claim to be the latest age in a series of ages. There is no telos following prior ages. Rather, what is named is an age of aberrant stages of amplified warming of unknown duration, as indicated, within the eleventh interglacial period and its possible extension, population fragmentation, possible conflict and a breakdown of the political and economic order?*

TF: Yes, however, as suggested, what will be experienced will be very different according to which fragment of life on the planet is exposed to the changed conditions. But effectively, the heat age names a milieu of constantly growing and wider unsettlement for people everywhere, displacing, as said billions over time. Living in a condition of permanent uncertainty has major impacts on mental health. It is hard to know how bad things will get, although what is clear is that the displaced will suffer the most. Of course, in several thousand years' time, the planet will also dramatically cool down. Utopian and dystopic imaginaries, especially when posed as universal, are inadequate to the imagining of coming futures.

It may be several centuries before the rate of warming stabilizes; meanwhile, the arrival of major climate impacts for huge numbers of people will continue, and they will obviously be totally devastating. It is almost certain that the vast majority of people's lives will have been disrupted by the end of this century. Along with the arrival of many new global uninhabitable wastelands. Notwithstanding current and continuing scientific research, the actual future is replete with unknowns, including the time of realization of the already started sixth extinction event.

It is also important to restate and recognize the relational complexity of the actions our species have constituted, in difference, over time. First, by implication, the number of unknowns that constitute a complexity beyond any existing ability to comprehend it ever increases (AI is a very current example – the gap between the knowledge that created it and knowledge of its eventual causal consequences is huge, meanwhile it is being uncritically embraced, not least by many governments as an economic driver). The continued advance of instrumental intelligence does not overcome ignorance; rather, it simply repositions and extends it. Second, this complexity of complexity is beyond extant political institutions to engage – this situation worsens as the fragmenting and fraught world order becomes ever more volatile. Such a political disjuncture is not just because the gap between the circumstantial conditions and intellectual reach of these institutions, and their leaders, is so wide, but also because of a large temporal gap. The time and accelerating speed of a defuturing crisis in process is just not in the same register of time as the functional operationality and collective mind of political regimes.

THE COMPOUND PROBLEM

DP: *So, we might say that the worse the situation gets, the wider the gap between the fragmentary forms of the world will get.*

TF: Yes, but it should be added that more fundamentally that the problems formed by the relational dynamic of the complexity will compound. Problems that are relationally interconnected constitute a meta-condition: a totality. It cannot be understood and engaged, as indicated, by disaggregating problems and thereafter addressing them by divisions of knowledge. What has constituted a problematic condition of existence – a reality – that cannot be fully understood and solved. This does not mean fatalistically there is no choice, but to accept this situation and just let it run its course. Rather it means acting to mitigate impacts, adapt to change, and either eliminate, redirect or transform causal practices – this is exactly what contrapractices would set out to do. There is no claim that they can instantly be created to realize this aim. Reality is plastic, its shape can be changed. The initiation of a process that can start to fulfil this aim as a realizable ambition, providing a context of thought and action *(praxis)*, is informed by establishing clearly articulated imperatives.

DP: *I do feel a bit uncomfortable with the 'totality', or trying to grasp a totality of the problem. I have seen how often attempts at dealing with the 'total' fall towards a totalitarianism as well as other rigid forms of control that this book is critical of. I guess this statement requires a qualification.*

TF: But what it does do is to communicate its scale. More fundamentally, the condition of fragmentation means totality can never be experienced in total. It also means that responses to the conditions experienced by each world fragment will always be different. There is no possibility for a totality/totalitarianism – the fragments cannot be gathered (as known and collected together). The relational complexity has no clear edge. The universal is an assumed totality, albeit without a knowledge of the total. In this sense, the total cannot be totalized.

DP: *On the one hand, it is easy to see that at present the dominance of extant divisions of knowledge is obstructing understanding of the dynamics and conditions of change, and therefore an ability to effectively respond. I think it is fair to argue that to be able to constitute modes of response, with actual transformative agency, a fundamentally new epistemological paradigm needs to be created. But do 'we' not see so many efforts at exploring and working with this relational complexity? Some in academic contexts where there seems to be some effort towards reforms. But there are also some efforts outside of it. Where could we imagine contrapractices being formed? What is their relation to institutions, if any?*

TF: Currently, 'the academy' does not provide this politico-intellectual environment of affirmative change and the ability to establish an epistemological transformation. It remains out of joint with the extent and speed of current worlding events and continues to be structured by extant divisions of knowledge, and disciplinary regimes dominantly within a universal paradigm. It has become almost totally subordinate to the instrumental needs of the current economic order, and its directive metrics. Thus, it is dominantly bonded to the academic status quo, while failing to see the condition of worldly fragmentation now underway. At the same time, within this dominant situation, there are scattered small cohorts of alienated, disenchanted and frustrated thinkers who recognize that, notwithstanding its material fabric and huge numbers of students, the university has increasingly fallen into ruins since it was first designated as having this propensity in the mid-1990s by Bill Readings (1996).[20] As he outlined, it abandoned its *raison d'etré*, folded into the commodity sphere (offering a product to customers). Subsequently, it has advanced via a business

[20]   Bill Readings, *The University in Ruins* (Cambridge, MA: Harvard University Press, 1996).

model based on being a service provider to the economy – this as a research facility and the supplier of feedstock to the extant labour market.

What the academy has failed/is failing to do is to provide the philosophical and ethical ground out of which a new epistemological foundation enabling the ability to think and responsively act in the context of the compounding complexity (of fragmentation) and crisis that is now defining the current age.

DP: *In other words, what you are saying is that contrapractice cannot claim an ability to overcome the current conditions of intellectual failure, but that it does present a means of engagement, and the potential of an interventional opening. As such, it runs against the grain of an anti-intellectual mainstream.*

TF: Yes, but within the conditions of limitation now being structured. The academy has nothing to offer the displaced. The corporate techno-elite will appropriate what it deems to be of instrumental value, and reject all other progressive views as 'woke'. In contrast, the value of the academy to the adaptive majority could be of increased and great significance if the means to create this change was formed.

So changed, it could advance paradigmatically relational knowledge and counter divisions of knowledge and disciplines that negate the very possibility of an engagement with the complexity of complexity. Likewise, it could play a key role in a new mode of politics appropriate to the conditions of reduced material consumption, increased utility and the enhancement of socio-cultural life. But this would only become possible in the context of adaptation, post-fragmentation.

DP: *So contrapractice is not a means of reforming the mainstream, or a substitute for instrumentalism, but rather a means of remaking the environments and lifeworlds of the majority of the global population who fall between the poor and disadvantaged and the wealthy and privileged?*

TF: Correct, in fact, it does imply remaking/adapting some instrumental practices, but it centrally goes to the fundamental ontological issues of 'being toward and acting in a changed world, and forming worlds of action' – this implies its involvement in adapting almost everything. Economically, institutionally, organizationally, socially and culturally. In turn, it means another way of learning and thinking about: the self, Others, the nature and agency of things, and how to affirmatively live through, and act in, deepening conditions of negation. Contrapractice so positioned is not just about change as a directed process of the Sustainment of the condition of life's dependence. It is equally an action, a capability, to create and emplace before the change of fragmentation as a means of coping with what is coming and what will arrive (mostly for the adaptive majority, and hopefully a percentage of the displaced).

It is also about a futural ontology in defuturing conditions for which no end can be seen, but has to be engaged, notwithstanding uncertainty. Coping in this setting is not so much about overcoming hardship, but more about affirmation and action to make time after the 'end times' – after the Ice Age, the foundation of the present arrived from the establishment of settlements that eventually led to the present defuturing epoch, and its opening into other contested worlds and futures. Even so, there is still a need to affirm and create futures after the unfolding of the present 'end times'. Although overwhelming, and negated by abandonment (of our others, our essential hominoid being, and for some potentially the planet all living beings inhabit), it nonetheless remains vital to affirm and embrace that imperative that bonds Sustainment to contrapractice as negating practices that defuture while advancing those that future.

DP. *I guess the point we need to highlight is not based on claiming these developments as 'solutions' but to indicate the affirmative agency of futural responsive action and how it can produce a temporal change.*

TF: Agreed.

THE DIALOGICAL: A REFLECTION ON THE NATURE OF OUR EXCHANGE

DP: *Dialogue – 'dia' means through (a passage, a path), 'logos' means speech, word, reason. Plato's 'The Symposium' (a dialogue between nine people) is taken to be the normative example of Greek dialogue. The language, rhetoric and the reasoning takes the issues discussed to the edge. The aim is not a balanced exchange, but to disrupt it: 'risk must be run if the dialogue is to be made intelligible'.[21] It requires practice, time, the ability to listen and consideration for the voice of others. This ancient mode of exchange as futural is the basis for its development as a contrapractice. As this, it is totally opposite to 'the noise' of contemporary politics and the clipped conversation and trolling of social media. Our exchanges are not presented as exemplary; rather they are aspirational.*

TF: The dialogical is an important entry to contrapractice, but it cannot be taken as given, or idealized. As such it is indivisible from creation conditions of exchange, understanding and decision.

DP: *Dialogical encounters are also ways of making time, a potential space of futuring where the existing relations between practice and structural conditions of unsustainability and defuturing may not appear as a presence. In this setting, one has to adapt to ' but as a scope, a domain which takes shape as I act upon it'.[22] At least our conversations, the ones that were generative of this book, have given me hope in this sense. Also, more importantly, I*

---

[21]   Walter Hamilton, from his introduction to *Plato The Symposium* 1951, 9.
[22]   Paulo Freire, *Pedagogy of the Oppressed* (London: Penguin Classics, 2018), 65.

think this relates to two ways one can distinguish forms of dialogue. For example, there could be projects and, in that sense, or dialogues that seek to change the content. There could be many dialogues on how to reform exist-ing practices. But then there are instances where the project is to change the very framework of the conversation. Contrapractice is about the latter. I am trying to remember something you said about the logic of contrapractice, which seemed cryptic at that time.

TF: Contrapractice can't be created by the same logic of the practice it aims to displace – this because its intent sets out to eliminate, redirect and trans-form the very ground of practice. This is to say, at its most basic, the logic of contrapractice is grounded in the overcoming of the defuturing that under-scores (mostly unknowingly) the operational agency of the many practices it will engage. Specifically:

The challenge of interlocutors is to work to understand the logic of contrapractice, to be open to learning out of the conditions of exchange, which might be fraught and grounded in difference.

The form, the claim and the reality of the conditions of worldly frag-mentation will create a situation of profound difference that requires a common interest for the possibility of the commencement of a dialogue in the service of the pragmatics of material, social, cultural and political adaptation.

The now and then of dialogue, starting at the time of the end of the epoch, presumes a certain commonality that is not futural. Fragmentation presumes a break, and a lack of goodwill. So positioned, adaptation needs a counter-narrative to material hardship centred on a realizable foundation of an affirmative culture able to provide the basis of building the ethos of future communities.

Dialogue in relation to contrapractice is predicated upon a commonality of purpose – this being the realization of the 'nature' of futural communities.

Most practices that claim to be 'dialogical' fail to arrive. Within the present milieu of this failure of conversation, the dialogic seems to be either reduced to a gesture of bringing together difference, or is completely blocked off by authoritarian monologues.

Dialogue depends on conditions of possibility, their identification and an appropriate response to them. In the knowledge of coming fragmentation (as it arrives by degree), the action required to establish these conditions needs to be prefigured. To name this task is to prompt the planning and enacting of a response within the limits of one's prevailing condition – conditions wherein practice needs to be changed, and contrapractice constituted as the means to do this.

Introduction: Defuturing, Practice, Contrapractice

Tony Fry

To begin a few scene-setting comments are presented here that prefigure examining implications of the transdisciplinary perspective of contrapractice as it challenges the efficacy of extant practices epistemologically (the knowledge embedded in them and how it is known) and functionally (what they practically do and with what consequence).

...

The specific intent of this book is to *introduce and advocate contrapractice as an appropriable redirective project of practice by practitioners to expose and negate the unsustainable and to advanced Sustainment.* By implication, this means that it directly opposes unsustainable practices coming from a lack of care, inadequate knowledge, unawareness and unthinking. These deficiencies mean that the impacts of a myriad of acquired industrial, professional, commercial, service and geopolitical practices negate the possibility of an ongoing viable future for biophysical life in general – effectively they 'defuture'. Mostly such actions are not done consciously with ill intent, but are embedded in capital logic (the naturalized and structuralized adherence to practices based upon unchecked materials extraction and economic growth), the ideological tensions of international relations, competing socio-theological orders, and in the habitus of individuals (whose actions are directed by the ways they have formally or informally learnt 'how things are done'). Thus, what the thinking that underscores contrapractice has recognized is that *nothing fundamentally changes unless practice changes.* Clearly, practices are not neutral, but in very many cases bring into being, or continue to replicate, systems, objects, processes and conduct, with material or immaterial impacts that increase structural unsustainability, and so defuture. Once acknowledged, two courses of action become clear: (i) unsustainable practices have to be eliminated, remade or replaced with ones that serve Sustainment; and (ii) organization and individuals need to be motivated, induced, instructed and in some cases compelled to change their practices. Creating such change requires strategy, argument, education/re-education, and time – it is hard and essential. In this respect, the book is an opening move. To advance its project requires ongoing advocacy, but above all, its uptake and the development of critical mass contrapractice practices – this by numerous practitioners in different fields of practices and specific contexts. Across this difference, this book cannot tell someone how to transform their particular practice, but it can give them a better understanding of the nature of practices, of transformed practice and why it's vital they be transformed across a myriad of contexts and applications.

More immediately, this book aims to affect the reader via not just an exis-tential engagement with its argument that produces a desire to embrace, explore and move to making a commitment to gaining a contrapractice capability, but to take action as a communicator of the imperative and means to transform practice. Indivisibly, this also means readers setting out to transform their own practice step by step, day by day.

...

Restating: the central proposition of contrapractice is that future-affirmative changes of practice can make substantive change to those worldly conditions wrought by defuturing by practices across diverse fields of interconnected economic, political, social and cultural life and action. Of particular concern are those practices that directly articulate with material worldly change, and have environmental consequences like: land use; extraction; material processing; design; construction/fabrication; engineering/manufacturing; servicing and main-tenance; retail food and goods production, distribution, consumption and waste disposal. So positioned, contrapractice, as a form of direct action, does not require an organization, nor funding, nor a political support and campaign to begin. It does not have a template. Rather, it has the potential to organically develop providing that examples start to accumulate and proliferate. Such examples will be discussed later. But obviously, there are particular generic practices that are of particular concern to contrapractice as direct action, and they take three forms:

- the **elimination** of unsustainable processes, practices and products and, if needed their replacement with those with sustaining ability
- the **redirection** of the agency of existing practices so they acquire sustaining ability
- and the **remaking** of a substantial part of the form and the disposition of existing practices, how they are configured to act, and to what end.

Grounded in contrapractice, all such action requires to be undertaken strategically, within specific situated conjunctural defuturing contexts of the demonstrable unsustainable practices of industrial societies, their economies and cultures. The aim is thus for contrapractice to be developed and arrive in a form determined by its engagement with, and overcoming of, those practices that it is posed against. Such action is urgent, not optional, and recognized as essential to sustain the conditions upon which 'life' depends. So situated, contrapractice is bonded to Sustainment, but not necessarily to 'sustainability' claims and practice – many of which beg interrogation. While claiming to sustain ecologies, these practices are often employed to sustain action that is unsustainable. In many cases, this is not merely as a result of ill-considered consequences by well-intentioned actors, but rather because sustainability has been unethically and widely appropriated and then employed by organizations, large and small, to cynically or in ignorance, to strategically 'green-wash' their product marketing.

Contrapractice does not fall under the rule of any particular discipline and is actually antagonistic toward the restrictive practice that defines the specificity of a discipline. Prefigured by restrictive guilds, over the late nineteenth and early twentieth centuries, there was a substantial increase in practices gaining institutional kudos by gaining professional accreditation and certification. Contrapractice directly questions the appropriateness of such action. While claimed to secure professional standards, it can also be misused to inflate and protect economic interests and derelationalize structures of knowledge and power. The unfolding enviro-climatic, security and linked governance crises of the present, that are expected to increase in the future, require greater flexibility, interconnectivity, a different ethical foundation and a basis of accountability. So challenged, while a great many practices need to change, the form of that change is clearly not uniform – this is because it needs to be responsive to the situated context in which a practice is formed, modified or employed. In particular, there is clearly a pressing imperative to respond to practices implicated in the continuation of defuturing crises, this as a directive of specific situated forms and applications fundamental to contrapractice.

Time is change, but change changes time: as such, it can negate/defuture/ unsustain or extend/future/sustain. Whatever changes, change changes everything completely, in the main imperceptibly (remember the chaos theory trope of the butterfly flapping its wings in the Amazon jungle changing the world's weather?), but sometimes it's very perceptible. We all now live at a time wherein the very conditions of life itself have to affirmatively change for it to continue as it is currently understood. Action against negative change – as it defutures by the creation of unsustainable things and conditions – is the only way that the Sustainment of life will become supreme. Change is continuous, but the continuity of life requires change to have a specific causal direction. To create this continuum, negative change, as the structural propensity toward entropy, has to be drawn out and countered.

Such action requires practices that are pitted against those that function in the service of negation. Here then is the essence of the meaning of contrapractices, in that negation is the result of practices, and what they bring into being, acting to 'defuture'. Dominantly, they have not been employed with this intent. Rather, the negative consequences of the agency of practice in the distant past were of a scale that they could be absorbed and surmounted by ecological systems. However, as such practices proliferated, and as the volume of what they produced increased, so did ecological impacts. Many centuries passed before the criticality of the situation was recognized. Even then, what started to be recognized were symptoms of the problem rather than causes. By this time, practices of negation had become embedded in industrial systems, processes, economies and everyday working, domestic and social life.

Even when the problems of damage to natural environments, their ecologies and systems became recognized and responded to, the focus has been predominantly on industrial processes and products – change being designated with the prefix 'sustainable'. Meanwhile, causality vested in occupational/professional practice had long become naturalized as the 'taking as given of how things are done' (habitus).

The time and the events of 'the world' that contrapractice addresses are not in harmony. Events are changing at a speed that renders all reflections upon them as disjunctural. The rate of change recasts the perception of both events and how they are being/have been understood. This is caused by an acceleration of the speed at which events occur and unfold, and the speed at which they are reported and mediated. This problem of temporality transposes the exercise of contrapractice. It can never *not be* a reactive action to a world 'out of joint'. The fabricated world-within-the-world, realized by intent, and from its inception, has always arrived by the same process. It begins with a conditionally responsive idea, which then moves to practice that registers the idea (if formalized, as a design) and then to one that materializes it. The immateriality of the idea is fully materially realized by the practice. The situated desire and need for change underscores the creation of the idea, as the new, as difference, that becomes realized on completion of the practice. The practice may have been especially created to technically realize the idea, but mostly it would be taken as realizable by a practice delivered by existing instrumental means: so contextualized:

Contrapractice, as it has been positioned, as effectively a practice to deploy against practices that sustain defuturing unsustainable things, environments and conditions, has no essential form as yet. It is a 'to be applied' ethos. Examples can be given, but they cannot be gathered and totalized independently from being reactive to the practice they counter.

Contrapractice: it is conjunctural, situated and dependent upon that to which it (re)acts against. It is born out of a hostility toward resistance reduced to gesture, a rejection of passivity, an alienation from the everyday reproduction of the status quo as the basis of 'a career', and as a recoil from *akrasia*.

Contrapractice wants more; it wants and desires transformative efficacy to secure viable futures.[1]

Contrapractice is not directed at a particular collection of practices or professions, but at all those practitioners who do what they do, but recoil

---

[1] Akrasia is here understood as 'acting in ways counter to what you know' – it is thus at the core of action that is wilfully unsustainable.

from taking responsibility for the unsustainable consequences of their wider actions (as practiced by themselves and/or others). So many practitioners live in a dichotomy: they love their practice, but hate the way the market employs it (and them), as well as the negative impacts their practice produces. By implication, this implies a level of knowledge and consciousness of consequences chosen to be ignored, hence *akrasia* is embedded in the dichotomy.

Contrapractice also implies a rejection of fatalism and a felt state of tension between what one knows and what one does (that is, *akrasia* as lived), and between how one views one's being in the world, and the being of one's world.

Above all, the ambition of contrapractice is to resolve a frustration that exists between wishing to act against the unsustainable beyond tokenism, but not having the means to do so. Conceptually, it is the basis of a means, realized in specific situated contrapractices as created by informed practitioners.

The frame of contrapractice is a condition of worldly fragmentation. Within the frame are worlds wrenched from the world that modernity sought to create (as unified in time, form and relation), and from the idealism of Kant's one world (as the conceptual foundation of the UN).[2] The global order is broken. Three fracture zones, as will become clear, are arriving (the zones of the abandoned, the privileged and the rest). The differences that denote them are not new, but their form and the degree of their separation is.

Fragmentation is circumscribed by the global effects of unsustainability, of which climate change is one symptom. As will be shown, not only does it denote a growing condition of geopolitical structural breakdown, a regression to spatial isolation and a major contraction in the global communications infrastructure, but also the ending of any possibility of a world order. Such a change also implies a temporal rupture, one equally as shattering of worlds that came with Western global colonial expansion and the coming of modernity. 'Now', as an asserted temporal commonality and as a communication across difference, ceases. 'Now' thereafter becomes existentially and spatially specific.

The entire period of global colonization and industrialization transformed the biophysical and enviro-climate state of the planet and the socio-cultural 'nature' of its being. The milieu of consequential causes and effects has converged, transmuted to form compounded problems and conditions of inter-woven relational complexity – a 'complexity beyond complexity' – beyond comprehension. Various concepts of 'the Anthropocene' have been evoked in the attempt to name and exposit this condition, but do so inadequately.

---

[2]   Immanuel Kant, *Perpetual Peace a Philosophical Essay*, trans. M. Campbell Smith (1795; London: George Allen & Unwin, 1917), available at https://www.gutenberg.org/ebooks/50922. See also Carlson, L. Thomas, 'Perpetual Peace: What Kant should have said", *Social Theory and Practice* 14, no. 2 (1988): 173–214.

The Holocene is the current interglacial epochal moment of warming that started 12,000 to 11,500 years ago. This moment marked the end of the Ice Age and established the conditions, most notably in the Fertile Crescent of the Levant in which settlements were to be created and agriculture commenced (there were also similar developments in Central America and China). But it equally denoted the beginning of the conditions in which the environmental impacts of *Homo sapiens* would relentlessly increase. The Holocene, as the most recent interval of the planet's interglacial cycle is named, will continue to warm for several thousand more years, but this, within a process amplified by 'Anthropogenic'-induced warming. The Anthropocene does not displace the Holocene. It is a narrative that arrived with claims of a 'geological moment' – one asserts that the Anthropocene commenced with the Industrial Revolution, which constituted a quantum leap in the impact of our species on the planet's ecosystems; another claim is that it names the commencement of the sixth extinction event. However, the transformative processes were far more graduated than any designation of specific moments of geological time suggests. Rather, they are an escalation of the process of making a world-within-the-world that commenced as a consequence of tool-being that predated *Homo sapiens* (who emerged in a world where scores of stone, bone and wooden tools were in use). What such 'tool-being' destined is an incomplete process of slow, now rapid, acceleration to biological extinction (and possible machinic continuity of a post-organic species).

Globally, causal events do not necessarily occur evenly or synchronically. Change is mostly gradual rather than a decisive moment. The division of the planet into intervals of geologic time is as much a heuristic device as it is a specific empirical moment of transition. From this perspective, the ecological impact of hominoid life on the planet looks more like an imperceptible feature of the ontological character present in the evolution of hominoids, although accelerated by the capabilities of *Homo sapiens*. From this perspective, the story starts with Homo erectus starting to use a stone as a tool in its most basic form around a million years ago.[3] By the time *Homo sapiens* arrived around 300,000 years ago, a complex range of stone, wooden and bone tools and techniques were in use. The conditions for our species to impact ecological systems were thus prefigured. Population numbers were small, impacts were low and the ability of environments to recover from them was high. But this changed and accelerated in time.

A thousand years before steel was first made in Europe in the sixteenth century, it was being made in China. The relation between fossil fuels (coal and wood), industry and greenhouse gas emissions was predetermined long before the problems shifted in scale and began to be accelerated in the late sixteenth century.

---

[3]   Fry, *Becoming Human by Design.*

The transition processes of worlds (continuous world making) centre on a recursive process of escalating ontogenic individuation.[4] Within this, the symbolic and material making of our species' world(s) of habitation was progressively, but unevenly, inter-relationally transformative of the maker and their environment. While the agency of *Homo sapiens* increased imperceptibly over millennia, it did so in geo-developmental and cosmological differences. The result over time was the rise of ancient civilizations, each with its own sense of its world as *the* world. China presents a clear example, with its cosmology founded on an understanding of a self-generating organism that was constantly changing and interacting as a correlation between the biological world and the world constituted by people. As such, it understood the nation as being at the centre of all other worlds (Zhongguo – the Middle Kingdom), deeming all these worlds as marginal. How its being was cosmologically perceived is not too distant from the concept of ontogenesis (the process of an individual organism growing organically that has been transposed to a material form, information and the social).

Anthropos, as a collective designation of our species, came out of Greek civilization, and became conflated with the Latin root of human (humus: earth). The Greek designation of *Homo sapiens* as Anthropos (translated as 'humans') started its passage to become normative with the arrival of Greek thought in Western Europe in the Middle Ages (500–1500 CE). Its process of globalization began around the end of the fifteenth and the start of the sixteenth centuries with the commencement of the West's colonial expansion. This historicity reframes the impact of the agency of Anthropos before the start in the Industrial Revolution in the mid-eighteenth century.

Western colonial conquest, enabling extractivism by forced labour and an ever-increasing technological capability, together with mercantile capitalism and Christianity (as an imposed means of civilization, and as a basis of 'humanization'), sought to universalize Anthropos (as the civilized being) while also negating indigenous modes of ungodly being. The bringing of 'Western civilization' was equally the imposition of Anthropos (the 'human') on the cosmologies of Others – who had their own understanding of the nature of being, and may not have seen themselves as a being in a binary relation to animals. For some contemporary indigenous populations, this process of imposition continues. The West's action of ontological colonization, while extensive, was never fully realized.

Clearly, the arrival and advance of the 'Capitalist mode of production' (enabled by its 'means of production', and ensuing industrial society) became the most powerful planetary force of enviro-ecological destruction. But the dialectical relation of creation and destruction is intrinsic, and relative to, levels of 'our' denaturalization, and is indivisible from the technological means and techniques that, in difference, techno-scientific corporate elites have now created and go

---

[4]   Gilbert Simondon, *Individuation in Light of Notions of Form and Information*, trans Taylor Adkins (first published in France, 1964; Minneapolis: Minnesota University Press, 2020).

on creating. A continually increasing destructive capability (from extractivism to the psycho-social) is elemental to the intent and action of advancing productivity and economic development.

In sum, the noted distinction between the Holocene and the Anthropocene is problematic, as is the universalism of the Anthropocene's designation of cause and effect. In totalizing the causal agency of 'the human', the unequal distribution of harm done between the least and the most economically and technologically developed is glossed over. Conversely, the fact is that while everyone experiences the negative impacts of such defuturing, those who caused the least harm are the most exposed to it.

Viewed futurally, the actual differences are going to become far more significant as the environmental impact of 'our species' gets even more uneven and fragmented, and thereafter the nemesis of Anthropos will become more apparent. More than this, not only will the fracturing temporal disjunction be far more overt. The temporal rupture indicated, and the related pluralization of 'now', will place a great swathe of the global population in a state of social regress, create an environment and lifeworld of transhuman existence, and leave vast numbers struggling to adapt to substantial change in all aspects of life.

The entire approach of government, the corporate sector and NGOs completely fails to recognize the emergent scale and shift in the form of unsustainability that relational disruptive impacts increasingly emanating from climate change and its geopolitical consequences will bring.

More specifically, the attempt to constitute new practices designated as sustainable and as delivering 'sustainability' has failed, on three counts. **First**, in the current moment, they have supplemented existing unsustainable practices taken as given values and methods, rather than eliminating and replacing them. **Second**, what these practices bring into being is something with the claim of being sustainable, but so often what is sustained is the unsustainable, performatively and structurally. Electric vehicles provide a clear example. They can only claim to be sustainable if they are totally produced via renewable energy, eliminate all non-renewable embodied energy in their production, do not have batteries made from lithium that has been mined by socially and materially unsustainable means, are operationally recharged by renewable energy, made by a socially sustainable workforce and have an end-of-life infrastructure so that all toxic materials are removed and safely disposed of, with all recyclable material recovered and delivered into the recycling process. The way electric vehicles are marketed and promoted is indicative of the inflated rhetoric and relativism of claims of sustainability. The attainment of sustainability, along with increased productivity and economic expansion, is unrealizable.

The fundamental claim of products deemed sustainable is that they advance 'ecologically sustainable development' (ESD), which means sustaining the existing economic paradigm of development with 'industries and products' claimed to be sustainable. Such action is in contrast to the imperative of the 'development of ecological Sustainment' (DES) – which does not aim to coexist with existing practices that defuture but rather to destroy them while creating futuring methods to eliminate *the need* for unsustainable products, or to replace them with a viable futural service. What it fundamentally recognizes is that to set out to change existing processes and products as primary agents in the delivery of 'solutions' is at best insufficient, at worst a path to failure.

Moreover, it is becoming clearer that there are no immediate solutions to hand to many deepening crises that are objectively unfolding. Some of these crises just don't have the solutions – they have created conditions of structural and irreversible change. Nonetheless, they demand a redirective and mediatory response – of which contrapractice has to become a significant example. The pursuit of de-relational 'solutions' (like geoengineering) is actually adding to the compounding problem. Thus, contrapractice is not being seen as a ready-to-hand panacea. Rather, what it recognizes is that unless habitually enacted practices (deemed as the given ways 'things' are constituted) are changed, then little fundamentally changes. Learning to comprehend the futural onto-material causal agency posited with practice, as it futures or defutures, is essential. Doing so becomes a vital attribute to acquire for all socially and environmentally aware and responsible practitioners. Effectively, this means an adoption of contrapractice *modus operandi* and therefore a transformation of the *habitas* that naturalizes the knowledge, the way it is communicated, and how a practice is enacted and overridden as given (and so uncritically adopted). In essence, the 'how' of a practice has to be directed by the 'why' of the 'what' it brings into being.

So understood, contrapractice is a task, a project, at present with only a few potentially developable examples. So said, this work is a prompt and an opening invitation aimed at contributing to the advancement of this objective. First, by working to communicate the profile and principles of contrapractice as an urgently needed praxeological mode of responsive action. Second, by working to advance and proliferate specific forms of contrapractice.

The idea of contrapractice requires it to be disseminated, engaged, contextually developed, tested, well understood and strategically deployed at scale. In this respect, this book seeks its moment, an audience and efficacy. The fundamental and broadest objective of contrapractice is thus, as indicated, to invert ESD to DES – the Development of Ecological Sustainment.

A SUMMARY OF THE CASE FOR CONTRAPRACTICE

This case is made from five viewpoints:

1   that numerous defuturing practices are going to be elemental to conditions of breakdown, as such, they will be causally implicated in the spread of crisis and dysfunction. This situation automatically creates the need for contrapractices that are contextually responsive and futural.

2   that defuturing is being *accelerated* apace by a political failure, at every level of government everywhere. To grasp and appropriately respond to the seriousness and dangers of convergence of environ-

climatic, geopolitical and techno-social crises requires the creation and realization of a new political imagination.

3   that the unsustainable political policies (of government and corporations), and their enactment by supporting practices, are a directive of defuturing by: endorsing, promoting and not adequately regulating industrial processes; manufactured products; commercial services and modes of education. Nothing changes unless this practice is made present.

4   that the discernible impacts of defuturing practices, as they are embedded in normative everyday economic and socio-cultural conduct, requires action to counter and reverse their agency. This requirement underscores the need for, and the basis of, operational forms of contrapractices that can be seen as directly confronting and displacing those practices that enable and perpetuate the continuity of the production, promotion and use of all things that defuture.

5   that the pace at which defuturing crises are accelerating cannot be overestimated. The consequences are not absolutely clear, yet even with available and inadequate knowledge, it is evident that coming changes are going to be dramatic and herald the start of a new epoch. It is fully recognized that there are no immediate solutions to overcome deepening crises that are objectively unfolding. Moreover, as said, some of these crises don't have solutions – they have created conditions of structural and irreversible change. Nonetheless, they demand a redirective and mediatory response. The pursuit of de-relational 'solutions' (like geoengineering) is actually adding to the compounding problem. Thus, while contrapractice cannot be seen as a ready-to-hand panacea it can be developed as a crucial and major response to much that threatens. Its potential rests with the organic power of the appropriation and plural application of the principle. Understanding it opens into the possibility of adopting it as a task, as a project.

Contrapractice has the ability to overcome a perception and feeling of helplessness. It does not require a structure other than that of the practice to surmount; it does not require an organization, but it does require taking action and expending effort. This work, in making the argument, unpacking the idea and providing a few potentially developable examples, aims to prompt action to advance the embedded objective of contrapractice. It invites being disseminated, engaged, contextually developed, tested, well understood *and* strategically deployed, and at scale. In this respect, this book seeks its moment, an audience, an opening move and efficacy.

1   Defuturing Now

Tony Fry

Defuturing is a fundamental characteristic of the present age. It names the ongoing consequences of unsustainability as a continuous process of the negation of planetary life. As such, it is the historical collateral product of the processes and practices of the construction of the fabricated worlds within the given world, which together constitute the condition of our existence, which we all share by degree with all our Others. As beings who have always destroyed in order to create (felling a tree to acquire timber being a simple example), prior to industrialization, the amount of damage done could *mostly* be absorbed by an environment able to ecologically recover. But with the arrival of industrial society, the situation changed. As its output continually expanded, and the size and demands of its population, the volume of extracted material correspondingly increased. The result was not only that environmental damage reached a scale that exceeded the ability for it to recover, but in doing so, the conditions of dependence on biological life continued to be diminished. Not only did a process of the reduction of biodiversity begin, but environmental conditions able to support life also started to be lost. With the recognition of atmospheric damage being done by CO_2 emissions from combustion of fossil fuels, and other activities that release methane and other gases, the situation worsened and continues to do so. Effectively, in the reduction of the condition of life's dependence, the finitude of life is equally reduced. Hence, the designation of this process as 'defuturing'. Powered by ongoing unsustainable practices of extraction, production, consumption, overt destruction (war), and the increasing impacts of climate change, defuturing becomes an ever more critical feature of the 'being of being'. So positioned, defuturing clearly constitutes an object that necessitates a concept and principle of resistance, hence the creation and sought enactment of contrapractices.

To introduce the concept of defuturing and then to consider how to make sense of it in the complexity of the rapidly changing present epoch, the chapter opens with an outline of how the concept was initially understood when it was first introduced.

BACK TO 1999: A COMMENTARY

A New Design Philosophy, An Introduction to Defuturing was published in Australia by NSW University Press in 1999.[1] The basic aim of the book's introduction was first to establish defuturing as a way of exposing and understanding historical unsustainable agency, this especially of designed things, be they objects, systems or institutions. Likewise, it was also about showing it to be a method of inquiry. The book made the case for Sustainment as an imperative, the basis of a design practice and a means toward the continuous epic project of creating material conditions for and of Sustainment. Underscoring the way that history, causality, practice and 'the natural' were understood, was relationality as it was acknowledged as the epistemological foundation of Sustainment.

PART 1

This part focussed on technology, with Chapter 1, 'Technology, Warring and the Crisis of History', opening by making clear the need to rethink technology and war. While this need was true in 1999, it is even more so now. Between the time when the chapter addressed technology being in flux, warring and the crisis of history and the present, it's evident that change has become even more rapid and that war is now even more technological. These changes make the issues raised even more relevant to engage than when they were first addressed. Technological complexity was originally addressed through a progression from the Greeks' recognition of structure as the basis of productivism – creation arriving by the manipulation of structural elements in making something systematically via the art of *techné*.

By the late twentieth century, complex systems of production had become intrinsic to industry and its management. As new technologies have continued to be developed, the means of production have become ever more directed by digital information 'feeding' robotic and automated systems, with new levels of complexity created and reached. Causally, in one direction, this complexity extended to human and technology interfaces and interactions. In another, many technological 'things' become more remote from their user; this with their complexity only reachable via the mediated interface of analytic sensors. Thus, technological 'advances' structured dependence upon a supplier, or their service agents. Besides being an economic impost, such form of product design

---

[1]   The book was based on a public lecture series presented at the University of Technology, Sydney in 1997. Entitled 'A total rewriting of the past, present and future of design' – there were ten lectures in the series delivered in the evening to students, teaching staff, members of the EcoDesign Foundation and the public.

disempowers technologically literate product owners and prompts product, or a whole composite component, replacement rather than repair.

The relation between technology, human action and negative impacts upon enviro-climate and ecological systems has been long established. But, as a technological society, the scale and use of technology and consumerism have increased these impacts substantially. Yet the recognition of the defuturing impacts of the technologies still remains insufficiently exposited. Even when knowledge of defuturing exists, the damage continues. The desire for the benefits – financial and functional – of the unsustainable overwhelms reason and recognition of environmental costs. Psychological and economic investment is one of the features of the relational complexity of complexity of 'the compound problem'. It takes causality beyond the reach of any available rational disciplinary epistemology. The convergence of unknowing and the unknowable has been constituted by the acquisition and application of instrumental knowledge that travelled with a Eurocentric propensity and a philosophical essentialism. At its most basic, Western thought became dominated by numerous forms, the (metaphysical) question of 'how', while neglecting the (ontological) question of why. Here is the foundation of the technocentric defuturing error of continually bringing things into being without considering and gaining knowledge of the consequences beyond mostly biological effects, be it the cell phone, the nuclear bomb, the Internet or a myriad of other things care and harm so often arrive by chance and in each other's company.

At the general level, the virtual now characterizes the digitally represented other of the materially real. More particularly, Deleuze claimed an aspect of reality as being ideal and real, which implies a non-materially reducible reality as elemental to the real. Whereas for Baudrillard, the contemporary world is a simulacrum wherein the real and the virtual, as imaged, are indistinguishable. Other examples of thinking the virtual exist aplenty. To mobilize the virtual is to claim the agency of the immaterial. Yes, 'it' has agency, but claims made of it are problematic and often inflated.

Rosi Braidotti's Neo-Materialist writing on the virtual makes this tendency very clear. She presents an amazing construction of abstractions, fictive theory, confusion, insight and idealism that takes the form of a narrative of entanglement (acknowledged as a vogue term of the moment spawned from quantum computing) of words, ideas, opinions, propositions and inducted theory all winding themselves around each other in knotted threads.[2] Her Neo-Materialism has ways of defining matter as embodied, embedded, relational and affective. It is claimed to be 'a more comprehensive understanding of matter itself'.[3] It is also claimed as an overarching philosophical engagement with the 'ontological core of matter'. What could be the ontological core of matter in general that slides between its being just matter and living matter? She assumes that 'matter is vital,

[2]   Rosi Braidotti, 'The Virtual as Affirmation *Praxis*: A Neo-Materialist Approach', *Humanities* 11, no. 62 (2023), http://doi.org/10.3390/h11030062 (accessed 2 February 2023).
[3]   Ibid., 1.

intelligent and self-organizing' and that 'non-humans' are geological, zoological, ecological, and technological plus 'others'. Nothing supports these unconstrained generalizations. Next, 'The vitality of matter today has been extended to the technological apparatus, which is live, smart and self-correcting'. Yes, there is a bio-technological nexus, but the 'technological apparatus' is plural, multivalent, complex, simple, and certainly not exclusively self-correcting (much of it also defutures). But then the next claim: material entities and their 'individuation, depend upon, require and co-exist with other entities they encounter'.[4] How?

Neo/New Materialism and posthumanism (as a posthuman materialism) are posed as interchangeable. Posthumanism focuses on the complexity of *the system* (my emphasis) of 'human exceptionalism within neoliberal, biogenetic and cognitive capitalism'.[5] Besides such notion of system being a prefigured projection, is not exceptionalism at odds with system? Conversely, the human as universally imposed by colonial conquest, strove to erase the exception of the designated mode of beings of other cosmologies. This ability to create projected relations evidences the virtual in action as a functioning reality. For example: 'A vital materialist philosophy of becoming stresses trans-species, inter-species and relational collaboration, not only with the material ecosystems and their non-human entities, but also with technological apparatus and artifacts'.[6] Is extractivism in fact collaboration? Are not Braidotti's statements totally ungrounded and unlocated – what is it that becomes, where does it become? It seems as if speculative realism has become speculative phenomenology.

Such an approach to matter unbounded allows it to morph into imma-teriality materialized, where 'dematerialization' becomes 'reconfigured into another kind of matter: codes, numbers, storage, algorithms, etc'.[7] How can the agency of the immaterial, although having material consequences, become matter? It reads like magical hermeneutics. Obviously, things that are material are dematerialized and things immaterial are materialized, but there is a clear difference between unmediated becoming and mediated making becoming the actualization of the virtual.

The virtual is treated as if it were an independent agency, arriving, posited with virtue, as a thing in itself without ownership having migrated from an adjective to a noun. Wherein a meaning of the virtual from the fifteenth century – 'being something in essence or effect, though not actually or in fact' now folds into a meaning appropriated from computing in the twentieth century: 'not physically existing but made to appear by software'.[8]

The crisis of the crisis of history circa 1999 still stands. Its narrative continues, its point of view is always present and mostly strives to hide itself from view. History arrives as power asserted or negated. What remains, as a constant presence, is the shadow of historicity and the realization of the end times – here

---

[4]   Ibid., 2.
[5]   Ibid., 3.
[6]   Ibid.
[7]   Ibid.
[8]   On the meaning of 'virtual', https://www.etymonline.com/word/virtual#etymonline.

is the end of the notion that history is without end, that history has a *telos*, and the realization that the present age contains forces (in which we ourselves are numbered) with terminal agency. Defuturing, so positioned, not only negates the future but also erases the past as it arrives in the present as implicit in ongoing events.

The three chapters of part two drew the connections between the history of modernity and defuturing. While colonialism was mentioned in passing, it and the complex issue of decoloniality rigorously engaged, would be a key feature of the relation now. Likewise, so would defuturing in its now higher order. Modernity (and its afterlife), coloniality (and its technological dimension as a force of domination and as a means of materials extraction), and defuturing (in its still accelerating form) now need to be seen as a triadic relation.

PART 2: HISTORY, MODERNITY AND DEFUTURING

Chapter 2, 'Made in America: A World Production' examined the rise of the United States as the industrial foundation of what was to become a globally hegemonic means of mass production, epitomized by Henry Ford in 1913 by the introduction of the in-line assembly as linked to an inventory of precision-made interchangeable parts. Although dominant for many years, the system was challenged by General Motors' 'gang system', which overtook Ford in 1930. The application of systemized productive methods (a productivism) became paradigmatic across many industries and ideologies globally. However, its momentum was seriously interrupted for a decade by the Great Depression of the 1930s in the USA. The situation was reversed by two major forces: the rise of mass consumption and the volume of war goods production for the Second World War. Crucially, mass production now can be seen equally as mass destruction. The First World War, with the machine gun, most graphically put this in place – as mass-produced weapons producing mass destruction. More generally, such a means of production created jobs, component industries and higher disposable incomes, but equally it drove increased destruction from materials extraction, the destruction of building national highway networks and, as is well known now, the creation of toxic land and air pollutants. Making begets unmaking: the ethical issue is always, 'can the former justify the latter?'

Chapter 3 directly addressed the arrival of streamlining in design as it became a force of economic and cultural transformation, especially from the 1930s onward. Born out of aerodynamic theory and wind tunnel testing, the streamline aesthetic fetishized speed and acceleration. What the F. D. Roosevelt's New Deal program combined was infrastructure development, which electrified rural America and produced jobs, the introduction of hire purchase enabling buying goods on credit, while marketing created the *desire* for streamlined products (from cars to toasters, ashtrays to fridges and washing machines). Streamlining was made to be the style of the age. The whole spectacle of streamlining was celebrated and displayed at the enormously popular New York World's Fair of 1939. It presented the modern world as a streamlined utopia. Effectively, it lit the fuse of hyper-consumption with its explosion coming after the war. In the creation of a consumption-driven economic recovery of the USA, the paradigm of global modern economic development as consumption-led was established. Here, 'progress' ushered in the supercharged motor of mass enviro-climatic destruction, now explicitly evidenced by the impacts of global warming. The full motion of the carbon economy was unleashed, with automobile-centric urban development, unchecked energy generation and its consumption from the activities of factories, the home, travel and leisure.

What is now clear is that holding consumption in check is proving to be impossible. It rules political regimes, no matter their ideology; they live or die by maintaining desired levels of consumption – almost everything is keyed to it, not least jobs, production and political stability. Consumption, as a driver of an economy, in its current unrestrained form, is one of the causal factors of unsustainability, and like war, it is a most avaricious driving force. What's new is how the platforms of electronic media have extended the reach and specific targeting of marketing, this, not least, by filtered big data and the use of 'influencers'. The psycho-technologies of social media have even further embedded consumerism, based upon techniques of installed desires, in the life of the mind.

Chapter 4 considered the idea of Total Design in Europe. Whereas the USA was the powerhouse of the industrial modern, with style firmly bonded to the market and the ideology and political economy of capitalism, Europe was more aesthetically and politically ideologically divided. At the level of design, this was registered by the German Bauhaus, and the lesser-known but influential USSR Vkhutemas (among the design avant-garde). Neither had a material articulation to mass production, but both had idealized notions of it and the power of design. The Bauhaus was led by the grand vision of the modern and the aesthetic of modernity, delivered by a new model of the designing subject. The Vkhutemas influenced the Bauhaus, not least via recruited teaching staff who migrated to it from Soviet Russia. The design ethos of the Vkhutemas was to deliver the new modern world of the USSR. As such, it idealistically saw design as part of the cultural dimension of the nation's revolution and, as a key agent in the creation of social transformation. Stalin did not share this view. His command economy determinism did not go beyond the horizon of food and factories. In both cases, the imposed total design of the political vision of the USSR and Germany displaced all other projected futures. Stalin's communist totalitarianism obliterated the institution's ambition with its imposed and repressive regime of change. The more stylized anti-modern fascist brutality of Hitler's Nazi Germany was equally hostile. Neither the Vkhutemas nor the Bauhaus delivered a mass-produced projection of the future to capture the imagination of 'the masses', thus neither gained the economic impact that streamlining had in the USA to stimulate the rise of mass globalizing consumption. More broadly and geopolitically, the current retention and stresses of extant political structures (bonded to the pacification of the 'masses' – be the Chinese, Russian, European, North American and others – by enabling globalizing consumerist ways of life) underpin a faltering political culture that defutures. In no way has the global economy weakened the cultural and political hold of nationalism, or bridged political and cultural difference.

Europe's aspiration to reassert its past global political and economic power, via an economic union, has never been realized – national interests undercut a fully achieved commonality, with Brexit marking an extreme expression of the dominance of a nationalist sensibility. What has become ever clearer since 1999, and exemplified by the very limited attainments of nations globally to reduce GHG emissions, is that curtailing defuturing and advancing Sustainment demands fundamental political and cultural change at a structural level. Rather than this being sought via more political idealism, the position that underscore contrapractice is that new transformation and redirective practices need grounding in a material pragmatics of the demands of Sustainment. That hyper-consumption cannot and will not be sustained suggests this change may become possible.

PART 3: ONE POINT: FOUR LOCATIONS

This part circled around four pivoting points of view: the body, time, the televisual and computing. Each viewpoint exposed a particular ambiguous relation to futuring and defuturing and an interwoven complexity. The body has a duration; it is situated in time; Aristotle and Einstein told us that time is that in which events occur. Thus, the existence of each body is an event in (as well as of) time. The televisual is a mode of seeing in imaged space and durational time – it constitutes the view of the world through the 'world picture' as an event. A world of bodies of difference is part of the picture.

Things change bodies. For example, as elemental to engendering a sedentary practice, a computer changes bodies. More fundamentally, computing is structurally embedded in a directional advancement of technology that marginalizes the body, and if it reaches its zenith (singularity), renders it redundant. Television, computers, and electronic devices have now merged, enabling viewers to become part of the viewed. Thus, the televisual not only brings the world close without bringing it near, but now it gives the individual the possibility of production and projection (as evidenced by TikTok). Others appear to be brought close, while remaining where they are in a different space-time.

Chapter 5 registered the body as an object of design that can, and has, been positioned as futural (the desired form), but equally has enabled it to be defutured (the defiled, disdained, aberrant and abject). The body as organism is not generally seen as such. The organism as animal (with the socio-cultural being as supplement) is negated. The symbolic form of the body overdetermines perceptions of its animal physicality. Yet performatively, it is seen and measured as such. So viewed, the body becomes an object of design transformed by specialist practitioners, such as dietitians, experts in body mechanics, sports physicians, performance coaches and so on. The chapter interrogated the body as an assemblage differentially created according to particular practices (like sport) and ideologically mobilized historically (in, for example, its service to capitalism, fascism and communism). The body is treated as malleable – the body of dance, fashion, sport, militarization, sexual pleasure, suffering, masculinity, femininity, trans-sexuality and more. In every case, each form of the body can be, and is, appropriated and classified politically (via the triad of race, class and gender).

Looking at the body through the frame of defuturing now, several changes over time are evident. The body/environment relation is changing. It is now widely recognized that global warming, higher levels of carbon dioxide in the air, are making pollen seasons longer and more intense – this, worsening allergy and asthma symptoms, especially in children. Obesity has dramatically increased, with some projections suggesting it will soon outstrip malnutrition globally. The body's relation to food is changing – heat reduces levels of nutrition. In wealthy nations, cosmetic surgery is dramatically increasing (looking old is not 'cool') – in the USA, in 2021, such surgery increased by 51 per cent. Its technology is becoming more advanced (with tools like ultrasonic saws). It is also becoming cheaper, and the number of cosmetic surgeons is increasing.[9] The pursuit of the perfect body and the concealment of age (time) become normative for significant sections of the wealthy and vain. Again, dominantly in the Global North, LGBT culture is also having some effect on recoding the body as image. The ambiguity of these actions, as expressions of difference, is equally productive and reflective of increasing social divisions.

Chapter 6 addressed disjunctural time by showing that the year 1926 was not the same time and moment in China and the USA – this being a general global situation that modernity and globalization have exploited. The action of modernity was predicated upon a destruction of the past (the termination of tradition), but equally also of the future (an induction into defuturing). Traditions examined in the chapter expose re-makeable elements generative of cosmotechnical innovation (to be shown later). The very basis of modernity has been 'development' based on the notion of the 'underdevelopment' of undeveloped nations catching up with developed nations. The obvious flaw in such an idea was that the developed nations do not stop developing and stay on hold waiting to be caught up with. This was not how development was seen in China. By 1999, it was already a very fast-growing economy, but it was paying a high price for this growth environmentally and culturally (the past was seen as a block to progress that needed to be erased).

As already acknowledged, China is now a powerful nation and the planet's second-largest economy. It exercises its economic power globally via its 'one belt and one road' policy introduced in 2013 (now active in over 150 nations). The policy is based on extending the nation's power and influence by investing in Asia, Africa and Europe. The aim of this network of projects

---

[9]   Joss Wilson, 'Cosmetic surgery is on the rise with technology and Hollywood is at the center of it', *Forbes*, January 18, 2023, https://www.forbes.com/sites/joshwilson/2023/01/18/cosmetic-surgery-is-on-the-rise-with-technology-and-hollywood-is-at-the-centre-of-it/?sh=7da9fcd51d91 (accessed 2 March 2023).

is the creation of conditions of interdependence to advance China's economy and technological capability. The purchase of agricultural land in debt-ridden Africa by China is seen as a 'land grab' to help ensure its food security (but such action is criticized by the African Development Bank and development organization). The overwhelming critique of China as a force of defuturing goes to the huge environmental impact of its unrestrained economic growth and associated environmental impacts. It has been estimated that 90 per cent of China's groundwater is contaminated, the nation is the planet's greatest source of plastics waste and plastic in the oceans, its development has had a huge impact on the loss of biodiversity, and China, in spite of recent efforts, has massive problems with air quality. Moreover, its economic expansion has now slowed, and youth unemployment is very high. However, and futurally, it is China's military modernization, expansionism and extension that is seen by many nations regionally and globally as a significant threat, with a potential invasion of Taiwan, at some future moment almost certain.[10] This situation is seen to have the ability to trigger a US intervention and the possibility of a nuclear war.

One clear absence from the book, and not just the introduction but the entire work, was a substantial engagement with colonialism (recognizing it was aided by technology and design) and thereafter decoloniality.

Colonial imposition did not just impose a Christian cosmology and the imperatives of modernity on many nations, but it also tried to erase indigenous cosmological orders whenever it could, while also imposing 'the human' (Anthropos) as a mode of being. In the act of imposing a designated identity, colonizers overtly set out to destroy the designated being of others.[11] Decoloniality so situated is required to address the habitus and the socio-cultural regime of power, of an imposed epistemology. As such, it implies a profound transformation of the colonized subject's existence in the afterlife of colonialism, its values and institutions, together with self-directed projects of restoration and new creation.[12]

Chapter 7, Televisual in-human Design, directly addressed the ontologically designing power of the televisual (the technology of television as it has gone technically and culturally beyond itself and the way of seeing it has generated). It is a highly developed example of 'things' having a designing power without intent. Rather than emanating from the material qualities of technological and culturally constituted 'things', ontologically what the televisual fundamentally designs are not predominantly behaviours but desires, imaginations and imaginaries. It brings the content of populated and unpopulated worlds into view and mind (aesthetically, technically, culturally, anthropologically, historically, geographically, environmentally). It is a major agent in the formation of an ecology of the image. This is an ecology we all inhabit – *how* we see informs and filters *what* we see, directly and from all mediated sources. Perception/

---

[10]   This moment is most likely before the 100th anniversary of the Chinese Revolution in 2049.

[11]   Walter D. Mignolo and Catherine E. Walsh, *On Decoloniality, Concepts, Analytics, Praxis* (Durham: Duke University Press, 2018), 164.

[12]   Ibid., 239.

recognition are via this ecology/memory nexus. There is a direct correlation between images and action, non-reducible to a linear cause and effect, but set in a relational context of movement and change. How 'we' act in the world is thus indivisible from how it is seen.

Considering the televisual within the concerns of the defuturing now, in the digitalization of everyday life, it has had profound transformative consequences for vast numbers of people, especially in advanced economies and in enclaves of relative wealth in the Global South. First of all, there is the omnipresence of the plurality of its technological means of delivery: laptops, tablets, phones and television. Next, there is the Internet environment and the mix of software systems, search engines, platforms, gaming apps, websites, streaming services and more. In the year 2000, only 7 per cent of the world was online; fifteen years later, between 75 and 90 per cent of people in most wealthy nations were 'connected'.

Meanwhile, in most of Africa, it was, and remains, only around 5 per cent of the population.[13] Overarching all of these details is the scale and modalities of the televisual image – from emojis to animated movies, from CAD and Sketch-up rendered images, from building walk-throughs to image-recognition automatic weapons, from 'tick-tok' to instructional simulators, from telemovies to zoom meetings, from virtual reality to the supermarket auto-checkout and ever onward – all these development have arrived in a matter of a few decades. It is perhaps impossible to contemplate in any real detail how imagination and the power of visualization is changing, or how this techno-driven trend will mutate over many coming decades. However, one consequence seems to become apparent: the power of the written word is being defutured (which is not to say it is under complete erasure). This, in part, transpires to be a class, culture and intergenerational phenomenon. It means a transformation of education, as it is generative of: (i) a higher order of visual engagement without an increase in visual literacy; and (ii) a more instrumental and literal relation to the written word. What education hereafter produces is a more transactional and functional/operative mode of worldly engagement. Such a shift removes not only a great swathe of critical knowledge but also a diminishment of a disposition toward informed critical enquiry. Without question, the cognitive changes produced by the futural ecology of the image and the continued instrumentalization of education in 'the University in Ruins' are going to be considerable.[14]

Chapter 8 marked a major extension not just in the continued increase in the power of technology, but its presence in everyday and psycho-social life, and not exclusively in affluent nations. The expanding technosphere, including a corresponding growth in techno-culture, as indicated, has been especially

---

[13]   *Our World Data*, 2023, https://ourworldindata.org/internet (accessed 22 February 2023).
[14]   The reference to the *University in Ruins* is not just to Bill Readings (1996) book and the loss of the spirit and the project of the university, in its role being subordinated to the labour market, but also in the loss if its educational normative status in setting the *telos* and content of learning. 'Learning to learn, and becoming learned' has been replaced by 'learning to function' predominantly in the economy.

evident in the extended domain of the televisual. In 1999, considerable attention was given to the characterization of the computer's power as a 'reason machine', not least in the service of productivism. With the advances in machine learning, this capability has not only considerably advanced but is taking on a techno-life of its own, and without any identifiable condition of limit. However, this does not imply uninterrupted linear progress. Four particular 'developments' make this clear. The first is the arrival of artificial intelligence in the everyday; next, is the problematic impact of algorithms; third is the coming of quantum computing; and last is the less recognized and even more controversial issue of techno-culture colonialism.

FORWARD FROM 2025: REMARKS ON CHANGE

In reviewing the 2021 message of *Defuturing, A New Design Philosophy*[15] now and in relation to the book's initial arrival in 1999, five perspectives on change will be presented as framed by the concerns of the 1999 book but viewed from the present. While significant, they do not represent the totality of global changes that have occurred during the quarter of a century that divides the first and second printing of the book. At the same time, it is equally important to acknowledge that the second book also evidenced a directional continuity of many of the historical trends established in the first book. Five areas of change will be reviewed: 1. Warring; 2. The Political, Modernity and Universalism; 3. Coloniality/Decoloniality; 4. Making, Tools and Technology; and 5. Accelerationism – all are elemental to the totality of change that has occurred, need to be seen as overlapping (and thus are not ordered hierarchically), and are situated within wider conditions of transformation and existential crises.

The context of change

Defuturing practices and their material effects are deeply embedded in the everyday economic and socio-cultural life of industrialized and industrializing nations, and associated critical global conditions. They and their impacts have gathered pace and scale This is especially evident in the geopolitical power shifts in Asia, especially in the rise of China as a major global economic and military force, the repositioning of how Russia in now seen, the ascent of North Korea and Iran as pariah nations, and the increased impacts of globalized consumer-ism (including in the production of waste, not least plastic[16]) over the last two and a half decades.

---

[15]   The original title was changed on reprint; previously, it was *A New Design Philosophy: An Introduction to Defuturing*.

[16]   Consumer-generated waste reached a new order of magnitude, with plastic waste forming a mass in the north-central Pacific Ocean the size of Ireland.

But above all, the volume of materials extraction and utilization, increased industrial production and the global extension of consumerism (notwithstanding continuing inequity) have driven the uptake of fossil fuel-generated energy and of related greenhouse gas emissions. As a result, enviro-climatic problems have escalated enormously, climate change impacts have constantly increased and loss of biodiversity has been massive – this, to the extent that a sixth extinction event has been announced.[17] Ever more people are being displaced by a changing climate, with increasing levels of heat killing especially older adults and infants.[18] Current research indicates that this situation is going to get much worse. Likewise, so will floods, droughts, wildfires and rising sea level, including from Arctic and Antarctic ice melting. All these events are arriving with increasing impacts and at a faster rate. Displaced population numbers are expected to reach a billion and rising by the middle of the century. Public health is expected to worsen, including from the growing global danger of vector-borne diseases. More broadly, so far over eight million people have died from Covid-19, with it heralded as the first of many pandemics that will occur as a result of pressures on ecologies and their interface with peri-urban environments as rapid urbanization continues unabated, especially in Africa. The city of Lagos is a dramatic example. By 2100, it is projected to have become the world's largest city with a population of more than eighty million people, by which time the global population will be over ten billion.[19] More people in cities, more construction (formal and informal), means more GHG emissions.

All these issues link to hyper-critical problems of food security and fresh water availability. As demand increases, the supply will reduce, but at the same time, higher temperatures reduce the levels of nutrition in food crops.[20] No matter how it is attempted to be represented, the seriousness, the suffering and the dangers of the collective forms and forces of defuturing are beyond imagination and challenge the ability of imagination.

Alongside the critical conditions outlined is an equally troubling manifestation of failure of thought, evident in the 'real politic' of the everyday and the machinations of the geopolitical. This observation overarches the outlining of the five changes to be considered.

[17] Elizabeth Kolbert, *The Sixth Extinction, An Unnatural History* (New York: Henry Holt, 2014).

[18] Saudi Arabia, Iran, Iraq, Kuwait, Israel, Tunisia, Libya, Mali, Ethiopia, Sudan, Pakistan, Mexico, and Guyana are just some of the nation's experiencing temperatures of over 50°C.

[19] By 2100, thirteen of the world's twenty biggest urban areas will be in Africa. *Washington Post*, Report on Urban Africa, 20 November 2021, https://www.washingtonpost.com/world/interactive/2021/africa-cities/?utm_campaign=wp_main&utm_medium=social&utm_source=facebook&fbclid=IwY2xjawHz_M1leHRuA2FlbQIxMQABHXIa6vijARTUmB9XsFAWly-4BVbPOs6pVrVREza6CT30nWhtkUvlhhAJ0w_aem_TVVAiptVGZ7EELtbiEMbVQ (accessed 9 April 2022).

[20] A. Giri, S. Heckathorn, S. Mishra and C. Krause, 'Heat Stress Decreases Levels of Nutrient-Uptake', *Plants* 6, no. 1, (2017), https://doi.org/10.3390/plants6010006 (accessed 27 October 2022).

Change one: Warring in the twenty-first century

The destruction capability of the technologies of war has significantly increased, especially in the advancement, proliferation and capabilities of missiles and the ever-increasing use of drones (as Ukraine's war against Russia has graphically illustrated). At the time of writing, there are fifty-six substantial armed conflicts in progress globally, and many smaller ones. This is the highest number of conflicts since the Second World War, and during the period July 2023 to June 2024, there was a 15 per cent increase from the previous year (which itself was up 13 per cent on the year before).[21]

In common with other industries, the uptake of artificial intelligence (AI) and robotics has been common across multiple warfighting applications, most controversially is their use in the creation of fully autonomous weapons. At the same time, the propensity to make war and the volatility of international relations bring major war ever closer.[22]

As planetary enviro-climatic conditions have become more critical, so has geopolitical instability increased. Chinese expansionism, the fear of nuclear war, heightened by Russia's invasion of Ukraine and the subsequent conflict, are omnipresent, continuous concerns. Ukraine's now insecure support from NATO is contrasted by Russia's direct assistance from North Korea, arms support from Iran and economic help from China. As a result, there is an enduring danger of the scale of the war escalating. Meanwhile, Russia is now seen by the West as a pariah state, together with its outlier supporters.

These relations prefigure a more unstable future. Geopolitically, the world's power blocs are now more sharply delineated, and as seen, the global order is now more fragmented. The Middle East is equally precarious as a result of the war in Gaza, which deepened the regional hostility toward nuclear-armed Israel. Turning to China, its territorial encroachment into, and military presence in, the South China Sea, together with its aggressive disposition toward Taiwan, and the growth of its military power, combine to make the Pacific region perilous. Certainly, this is how it is viewed by many Western and Pacific powers. Meanwhile, some non-aligned nations that feel threatened by China look towards the USA and its allies for protection, while others, especially in Africa, still veer toward support for a weakened Russia. The action of these African nations directly connects to the structural instabilities within this continent. Currently, there are over thirty armed conflicts in Africa underway, the most serious being in Sudan, Burkina Faso, Mali, Mozambique, Nigeria and Somalia. Further in the background of immediate risk is the longstanding tension between nuclear-armed India and Pakistan.

[21] Armed Conflict Location and Event Data, https://acleddata.com/conflict-index/index-july-2024/ (accessed 10 January 2025).

[22] The US Council on Foreign Relations Conflict Tracker currently (2024–2025) lists 110 medium to small wars underway, https://www.cfr.org/global-conflict-tracker (accessed 10 January 2025).

It is against the background of crises emanating from the compound problem that conditions of conflict will increase. They can be expected to take three forms: escalating contemporary territorial conflicts; insurgencies and asymmetrical conflicts within many nations as climate impacts and population movements destabilize border security, and as some nations' economies crash as the costs of climate impacts massively increase; and third, the dispossessed fighting for survival, with elites defending their spaces of privilege with private defence forces.

The level of instability from the situations outlined is going to get worse as the impacts of climate change increase, as the contest for natural resources escalates, and especially as vast numbers of displaced people move *en masse* within and between nations (crossing borders illegally).

What the conflict in Ukraine has exposed is the ever-increasing power of the technologies of war. Advanced electronic communication and surveillance technology, sophisticated supply chains and the certain arrival of autonomous weapons systems are a continuum of extending the capability of conventional means of war fighting. The arms industry is clearly no longer discrete: an 'off the shelf' affordable drone can be a sophisticated toy, a crop inspection device for farmers, or modified to provide location data to direct artillery fire, or a means to drop a grenade into an open turret hatch of a tank, or be an auto-destructive explosive weapon. At the other extreme, large ocean-going drones can sink a warship, or an airborne drone can travel a long distance and strike and destroy an oil refinery, a large aerial command and control centre or a hangar full of aircraft. At the highest end of weapons development are LAWS (Lethal Autonomous Weapons Systems). They have the ability to identify a target and destroy it without any human intervention at any point.[23] Currently, they are unregulated, and because the major 'rogue nations' will not introduce regulation, it is unlikely that any nation will.

What this situation reiterates is the fact that there is now no longer any clear distinction between military and non-military technologies, the industrial military complex and the industrial production in general of computer chips, algorithms, sensors, image-recognition devices, guidance systems and so on – all articulate the one technological domain to the other.

These technologies, and an expansion of the means of warfighting, are transforming the very nature of war itself. What remains unclear is what will actually be the consequences of such change. The psycho-technological and the ontological designing impacts of the multiple domains of unrestricted modes of warfighting now unfolding have also dissolved, and clear distinction between war and peace.[24] In this respect, the war in Ukraine is a hybrid between the old and the new, but within a dynamic wherein the agency of the new is to make

---

[23]   ZamZam Chenna, 'Lethal Autonomous Weapon Systems', *Geopolitical Monitor*, March 26 (2004): 1–4, https://www.geopoliticalmonitor.com/lethal-autonomous-weapon-systems-a-gamechanger-demanding-regulation/ (accessed 2 April 2024).

[24]   Tony Fry, *Unstaging War, Confronting Conflict and Peace* (London: Palgrave Macmillan, 2019).

the old redundant – this tendency will continually increase. By implication, what this defines is that permanent warfare is now a normalized condition of variable intensity. De facto, the Third World War has started as a protracted process of provocations and posturing, together with pockets of conflict (large and small) existing as a general milieu in which proxy interests are always present and active. Such a situation is unlikely to remain so as already existing crises become more serious.

Unrestricted Warfare, a permanent mode of waging war, was an idea initially developed in China by two People's Liberation Army air force officers, Liang Qipao and Wang Xia Gsu, as detailed in a book by the same name in 1999.[25] It was conceived as a way of waging war on, and defeating, the United States. While it never became formally adopted as policy in China, many of the ideas it presented became influential, especially in China and Russia. Much of the book's thinking echoed and modernized the strategy of Sun Tzu's ancient and enduring 'grey war' classic, 'The Art of War' – strategically it advocated waging and winning war by devious means. The ultimate aim was to win without fighting. Translated into a contemporary context, it is war waged economically, industrially, culturally, informationally, psychologically, electronically and militarily in variable combinations. Thus, nations can be, and are, at war with nations with whom they appear to be at peace.

Change two: The political, modernity and universalism

The disjuncture between institutionalized politics and its capabilities, and the scale and depth of the compound problem that is determining the ability of the planet to sustain life, is of a scale beyond measure. The pragmatics of transformation in this situation is seemingly beyond comprehension, let alone engagement. By implication, there are only two options: fatalism or attempting the seemingly impossible, which in turn requires a conceptual repositioning of the mind in order to contemplate such a challenge.

The problem of the political and thought converge: both require a shift in focus on what are deemed to be matters of concern. A frame of reference has to be constituted that is able to overcome a gravitational pull toward the particular, the now manageable and the familiar. Just to get into a position to contemplate what *has* to be contemplated requires a discipline of exclusion directed at invested and familiar preoccupations. This goes directly to the entire project of contrapractice, for it is not merely an action against the form and agency of defuturing practices but is equally a process against many practices of the self. As such, it is a 'discipline of exclusion'. What is being recognized

---

[25] Unrestricted Warfare employs all means – military, political, industrial, economic, informational, psychological – in waging war. It was, as stated, conceived by two Chinese Air Force colonels as a strategy to defeat the USA. While not officially adopted, the idea has been influential, including in Russia. Qiao Liang and Wang Xiangsui, *Unrestricted Warfare* [FBIS Translated Text], (Beijing: PLA Literature and Arts Publishing House, 1999).

and embraced is an ability of 'overcoming' that does not rest with a voluntarist act of cognition, but with a reconfiguration of one's habitus by the *praxis* that is contrapractice. As such, this implies working towards the seemingly impossible, as it is taken to constitute conditions of possibility, exploration and action without certainty (but as experimentation).

Over the past two decades, the character of the politics of many Western democratic nations has altered. Democracy has been placed under stress with the arrival of neo-populist authoritarian governments and the rise of far-right parties and sensibilities. These trends have been evident, by degree, in many nations, not least in France, Britain, the United States, Hungary, Italy and Argentina. Over the coming decades, as suggested, climate change will become far more politically destabilizing as impacts become more severe. As indicated, vast numbers of people will be displaced and huge numbers of communities will need to be relocated. There will also be a proliferation of associated health problems. Again, restating the economic impacts will become huge as severe problems converge. Not only could any of these impacts trigger civil unrest and conflict within and between nations, but they could also cause a total breakdown of the ability of a nation to be governed.

Viewing the worldly situations is always from a particular position within a world geospatially and geo-culturally, but where you're situated also defines an epistemological location. The very view of the world, as represented in an atlas, is dominantly from the Global North. Likewise, how the world is theorized and discussed is massively influenced by Eurocentric thought. Such thinking cannot be divorced from modernity, coloniality and hegemonic universalism. To understand this, the two dimensions of Eurocentrism need to be understood.

The first is that the extension of European power began in the early fifteenth century and continued to the early twentieth century. The founding symbol of this moment was the 'discovery' of the New World in 1492, and the commencement of its colonization. Subsequently, colonialization was globalized by thirteen of the forty-four European nations.[26] During this period, they possessed or controlled two hundred and eighty-seven colonies across the Middle East, the Asia Pacific, Africa and the Americas. Of these colonies, almost half were British. The extraction of wealth from them was dominated by the means provided by almost one hundred Austrian, British, Dutch, French, German, Polish-Lithuanian, Portuguese, Russian, Scandinavian, Spanish and Italian chartered trading companies.[27] These companies, together with colonized labour and the use of military forces of colonial powers, extracted the natural material wealth of the colonies. To enable this, a colonial governmental regime, and the legal and administrative system it created, imposed control over the indigenous population and facilitated the logistics of materials extraction.

---

[26]   The United Kingdom, France, Germany, Spain, Portugal, Italy, Belgium, Holland, Hungary, Sweden, Denmark, Norway and Russia.

[27]   William Bartleet Duffield, 'Chartered Companies', in *Encyclopaedia Britannica* (Vol. 5, 11th ed.), ed. Hugh Chisholm (Cambridge University Press, 1911), 950–2, https://en.wikisource.org/wiki/1911_ Encyclop%C3%A6dia_Britannica/Chartered_Companies (accessed 10 June 2025).

Second, the socio-cultural and epistemological colonial order, in the name of religious enlightenment and the bringing of civilisation and modernity, created what have been viewed as fully colonized subjects, constituted as such by 'imperial knowledge' (the fusion of Eurocentrism with epistemology). But as Walter Mignolo has pointed out, citing the example of Bolivia, Eurocentrism was not fully established everywhere, although no colonized people were without its trace.[28] In part, resistance to it is linked with the scale and vitality of indigenous culture and its traditions within a nation. Where subjection was extreme, the degree of erasure of indigenous identity was major. In the Afro-Caribbean, where the colonized population was ripped from its indigenous culture by slavery, attachments to an African cultural heritage were weakened, while colonizer imposition upon colonized subjects was forceful. To illustrate the point, there are accounts from the half a million immigrants recruited from Afro-Caribbean islands in the late 1940s and early 1950s by Britain – because of a post-war labour shortage – many of them described their boat journey as 'going home'.[29]

On writing on Eurocentrism and the origins of the European global order in 1950, Carl Schmitt, who is recognized as a heterodox legal and political thinker, stated that:

> European international law considered Christian nations to be the creators and representatives of an order applicable to the whole earth. The term 'European' meant the normal status that set the standard for the non-European part of the earth. *Civilization* was synonymous with *European* civilization.[30]

Currently, the geospatially represented world represents the notion of a world order and 'global development and modernization' is gathered under the universalizing banner of the United Nations, but as the world fractures, so does it. The economic fabric of globalization still functions, although it is increasingly fragile. But, again restating, the global powers are increasingly divided and are likely to become more so, with 'the rest' even more marginalized. There is no viable discourse of unity; the neo-Kantian spirit of one world and universal peace is all but spent. Nothing looms to replace it. All signs indicate that divisions will grow. Moreover, the last vestiges of the idealistic project of modernity – as a universal condition of emancipation from what was deemed to be limitation intrinsic to past traditions, civilisations and cultures – have now been dissipated.

---

[28]   Walter Mignolo, *The Darker Side of Western Modernity* (Durham: Duke University Press, 2011), 19–20.

[29]   B. M. Nobrega, 'We came because we were coming to the mother country', in Jack Webb et al. (eds), *Memory, Migration and (De)Colonisation in the Caribbean and Beyond* (Longman, London: Mark Wilson, 2020), https://read.uolpress.co.uk/read/memory-migration-and-de-colonisation-in-the-caribbean-and-beyond/section/03eec1b2-0296-48b4-8651-e69a1795ef86 (accessed 12 June 2025).

[30]   Carl Schmitt, *The Nomos of the Earth*, trans. G. L. Ulman (New York: Telos Press, 2006), 86.

Yet its underside, colonialism, lives on with less visibility, but with remaining technical, psycho-social and epistemological vigour.

Whereas in the past technology was mobilized by colonial powers in the service of their local population suppressive and extractive objectives, now technology, via its enabling agents, has become (from the hegemony of instrumental knowledge ruling the academy, to psycho-technologies and the bio-techno synthesis of transhumanism), an independent colonizing force in itself. It is doing this clearly not with conscious intent but rather with the inherent logic implicit in not just in its creation but as a consequence of the interpolative capability of it as an operative ontological designing agent. Technology's 'smart' enabling agents know how to instrumentally do what they do, in an enacted regime of endless technical innovations. But 'they' have no idea of the futural consequences of their actions beyond operative performance, and nothing holds them accountable – the futural impacts of the Internet, psycho-technologies and AI are unknown. What drives the process of innovation is a flow from the structuring logic of productivism toward a totalizing techno-colonialism directed at singularity, wherein technology becomes ontology that is dominant, irreversible and transcendent of biological life. Growing conditions of inequity will not halt this progression, but they will stop it from becoming universal.

Implicit in the embrace, submission and advancement of technology and a machinic mode of being is the extreme proposition and project of reactionary accelerationism. It asserts that biological ecologies of the planet are doomed, and that the future of cognate being is technological. The aim, therefore, should be to accelerate toward this objective. To move the argument forward, there is a need to look at how this extreme position has been formed, developed and promoted.

A contradiction appears: capital logic is predicated upon the production of particular commodities at the lowest cost, the capturing and command of markets, meeting its constructed needs and thereafter selling at the highest level of profit – all to enable capital accumulation. In this context, monopoly equates to another mode of colonization. The arrival of mass consumption in the early twentieth century, and its advancement by the fusion of style with desire, was predated and prefigured by this colonizing dynamic.[31] There is no contradiction between the colonization of the market, the consuming subject and the product that gains a monopoly. As Virilio showed, the relation between intent and accident is recursive. But there is a problem with techno-colonialism – less overtly characterized as a seduction, addiction, obsession or romance – but nonetheless all denoting a conjoining of our species being and the technological object as viewed by accelerationists as enhancing a subject's physical and/or cognitive performance and means of environmental survival. This bio-technical synthesis, named as the transhuman, is embraced by the techno-avant-garde as pathfinding and futural. For the extreme among them, it's seen as an induced de-naturalized evolution step toward singularity and *Homo-technicus*. Here

---

[31]   Paul Virilio, *The Original Accident* (Oxford: Polity Press, 2007).

is a switch moment that turns a faction of 'our biological species' tool-being (our being with technology from our inception as world making and self-transformative) to becoming an embodied proto-bio-technical hybrid being. As indicated, in the coming of greater global inequity, such a constructed being cannot be conceived to be, and realized as, universal. Although that may be its ambition, and projected as being attained by being the only being able to withstand the ravages of defuturing to come. Yet the majority's future being would be circumstantially determined by uneven environmental conditions and differential adaptive capabilities, which would suggest significant numbers surviving. The displaced and abandoned rest would have a more precarious future – mostly, they would have nothing other than what they can discover in the circumstances in which they find themselves.

Change three: Coloniality/decoloniality:
Against the colonization of everything

Over the past decade, the concept of decoloniality has been popularized and critically diminished. In doing so, its rigour and critical edge have been weakened, if not totally lost. A ten-minute web search produced over fifty examples of it becoming a politically correct gesture and trope. The listing included: the decolonization of literature, the workplace, national culture, transnational institutions, research methods, journalism, animals, banking, the university, art, the economy, digital rights, museum practice, Africa, knowledge, peace building, the skies, climate change, development, governance, human rights, chemistry, poetry, psychology and more. Leaving aside the questions of methods, capability and attainment, where do the results of such activity arrive and with what agency? And what of the question of ongoing, and new modes of, colonization? What this listing reminded me of was the oft-cited opening of the Preface of Foucault's *Order of Things*.[32] In it, he wrote, drawing from a passage from Borges, of 'a certain encyclopaedia' where animals are listed as (a) belonging to the emperor, (b) embalmed, (c) tame, (d) suckling pigs, (e) sirens, (f) fabulous, (g) stray dogs, etcetera. Thus, the unifying agent in both cases simply gathered an arbitrary listing that has nothing in common other than the claim of belonging to the seemingly unlimited ability of an agency of classification, and the agent to classify.

Because the individuation of everyone's habitus is unique, there is no format for its creation. In the context of decolonization, one can understate the habitus as to consequence of how the self was colonized in and by the world from which their being and practice(s) were drawn (imitation, repetition, instruction, formal and informal education, reading, writing, dialogue, and so on, and over time). Effectively, the acquisition of one's habitus is a process of individuation/colonization (that can be connected to colonialism, but not necessarily so). The

---

[32]   Michel Foucault, *The Order of Things* (1966, New York: Vintage, 1973), xv.

process can be positive or negative, enabling or disabling. All education, in all forms, is, by degree, epistemologically colonization, but this does to equate to epistemological colonialism (but it can be). The very process of bringing one's habitus to presence and subjecting it to critical review is a process of clearing: a removal of redundancy, a making of space, a revaluing and of creating openings. Obviously, the more established the habitus, the longer to task. The process can be seen as just subjectively self-reflective, or circumstantially responsive. In relation to practice, the tracking of its material consequences begs rigour, bringing embedded values into conscious consideration requires help (read instruction or directly sought from an informed other). This involves confronting fundamentals, like gaining a realization that universals are not universal, that Western thinkers dominantly naturalize an ownership of critical discourses. Eurocentric thought was made a universalizing prism of seeing and thinking 'the world'. Similarly, thinking of technology as a tool that is just directed by use, rather than always having ontological consequences on bodies and minds, is another misplaced 'given' notion. Thus, once the habitus is moved out of the unthought and into the domain of critical enquiry, things change, but again, these changes cannot be generalized.

So, decoloniality viewed at the level of the habitus comes with no grand claims and does not dismantle the colonial conceptual matrix of power.[33] Its actual interface with colonialism will depend on the particular and cultural history of the individual, which may fall on the side of the colonized or the colonizer historically. In a contemporary sense, it will depend on an individual's ontological proximity to particular regimes of power, social order, economic conditions and technologies in relation to how they see and are seen, understood and function within the complexity of the forms and forces of their lifeworld.

The pluriverse, the mutual coexistence of multiple worlds, linked to the decoloniality discourse, is being seriously disrupted as an expression of a pluralistic sensibility – this in worldly conditions of fragmentation, exclusion and an accompanying certainty of increased levels of conflict. The emergent reality is of *incompossible worlds*.

Change four: Making, tools and technology

Genetic engineering and nanotechnology are examples of the artificial, where the distinction between benefits, risks and dangers blurs. Likewise, the technologies of social media display ambiguity. Whatever their contribution to enhancing the ability of people to communicate, they also have profound ontological, psycho-social and cultural impacts that remain inadequately understood, yet socio-culturally problematic. The impact of technology has grown dramatically over recent decades. While there have been positive developments in areas like renewable energy technology and electronics, many development limitations

---

[33]   Mignolo, *The Darker Side.*

become ever more ambiguous, not least in the relation between the natural and the artificial. Overarching all technologies is constantly growing computational power – soon to be accelerated further by the commercialization of quantum computing, as it converges with the ambiguous power of AI.

Many of the people who have contributed to AI's creation have acknowledged that it has the ability to self-develop (via the power of machine learning) and go beyond any ability to be controlled.[34] Placed in the frame of the compound problem, and reduced to the most chilling dilemma, our species faces a stark double-bind: we are positioned between and defuturing condition of biological and technological extinction, with both options being of 'our' own making.[35] Here is a situation that requires to be confronted and surmounted if 'we' all are to have a future. The crisis of this crisis is that this confrontation is not being recognized, let alone engaged. This unknowing reflects a fundamental characteristic, ever-amplifying, of our specified condition of 'being with technology'. Namely, bringing it into being without understanding the consequences of what has been created, or how. Functional capability and economic return ever override thinking ethically, futurally and of securing Sustainment.

Tools prefigured our species becoming and its continuum to our technological being now.[36] It took about three-quarters of a million years from our distant hominoid ancestors using a rock to smash bone to get to its marrow, or nuts to get their kernels, to the creation and use of around seventy stone tools, and ones of wood and bone. It then took just over two hundred thousand years for *Homo sapiens* to get from this array of the most basic tools to robots, algorithms, AI, quantum computers and nano-machines. The fabricated worlds now inhabited were created by technologies created by tools. At one extreme, tools have now become immaterial and abstract, while also physically becoming a more sophisticated version of a rock smashing a nut. Tools are embedded in practice, populate our species environment and transform it; they are objects of dependence that alter our bodies, pattern our brain, are treasured and abused, are microscopic and gigantic. They are, and have always been, prosthetic extensions of our bodies and minds as they exercise our will. 'We' are tool-beings.

Graham Harman entitled his 2002 book *Tool-Being*.[37] In it he defines 'tool' as 'readiness-to-hand' and equipment.[38] For him, 'the tool *is* the mode of executing itself. *Equipment itself is existential.* It is not merely spatially located in some presence-to-hand way, but is actually *in* the world; it does not merely have some neutral presence that could be viewed from the outside, but actually

34   Josh Taylor and Alex Hern, '"Godfather of AI" Geoffrey Hinton quits Google and warns over dangers of misinformation', *Guardian*, May 2, 2023, https://www.theguardian.com/technology/2023/may/02/geoffrey-hinton-godfather-of-ai-quits-google-warns-dangers-of-machine-learning (accessed 14 August 2022).

35   Here 'our' equals a specific technological class.

36   Fry, *Becoming Human.*

37   Graham Harman, *Tool-Being, Heidegger and the Metaphysics of Objects* (Chicago: Open Court, 2002).

38   Ibid., 18.

exists in a network of forces and meanings that determine its reality'.[39] Thus, his understanding, echoing Bruno Latour's understanding of 'things',[40] is that the tool has being, hence 'tool-being'. However, I have chosen to read them in another way. Tools move our species across its mode of being. As such, tools are seen cybernetically as a 'steering'.[41] Viewed as implicated in worldly engagement (making in and of (a) world), and of the individuated self (the feedback from use as an ontologically contributing fact, in the making of the self – originally in some way bio-mechanically in use, but always cognitively), affirms that the agency of tools is always ontological. They have an ontological consequence for the user, and the world of use, even if imperceptible. Conversely, writ large over time, tools have changed the planet as is overtly evidenced by global warming as produced by the sum of the tool-created environment of industrial production, extending over centuries, creating GHG-driving global warming, and altering the climate system. Likewise, tools also have, as said, changed us bio-mechanically and cognitively (sitting at a desk in front of a computer keyboarding every day, year in, year out, does both).

Ontological design does not directly change behaviour from an exposure to the 'thing in itself', rather change comes from the practice associated with the use of 'the thing' over time – be it a cell phone or a tennis racket, a sewing machine or a chainsaw, a violin or a car. Change is the consequence of things in use. Such action over time develops skills, increases muscular memory, dexterity, levels of concentration and produces minor to significant cognitive change, does or does not do physical harm (to bodies and worlds) and more. But a person's behaviour, their worldly conduct, is constituted relationally in different situated contexts in which practice functions among variations within a complex material, psycho-social, cultural and economic environment. One that positions a subject with or without agency. This complexity undoes all reductive accounts of the efficacy of ontological design as directly transformative of behaviour.

The being of tools is always imminent. They exist, awaiting animation in use. Use is mostly predicated on intention (but obviously, reactive impulse can be circumstantially prompted). The realization of intention depends on the posited form and capability of the tool (what it is designed to do, and can do). Tool-being, so understood, requires the convergence of being with the tool and the being of the tool, which only comes to be by being made to be in its practical life.

Equipment (a complex tool, or tools articulated together in a system) has an existence in two senses: as finite matter, with a life subject to its environmental exposure; and as it is animated by the force and power that brings it

---

[39]   Ibid., 39.
[40]   Bruno Latour, 'How Better to Register the Agency of Things', The Tanner Lecture on Human Values Delivered at Yale University, 26 March 2014.
[41]   Martin Heidegger and Eugen Fink, *Heraclitus Seminars*, trans. Charles H. Seibert (Evanston: Northwestern University Press, 1979), 5–14.

into deployed use. In the current age, in its most advanced form, equipment has reached a state of autonomy (robot as tool).

The crucial distinction here is not the difference between being and non-being but animate and inanimate being. In evoking a tool, an enormous difference is called up: nano-machine (a 'nanite', in size, a millionths of a millimetre) has nothing in common with a gigantic 15,000 tonne bucket-wheel excavator other than they both have been in some way, and are, classified as tools. They are not connected by a transformative capacity, material properties, function, effect or the force that animates them. Yet they do manifest their essence by the production of an applied intentional effect. The ontological essence of a tool is not within the thing itself, but is defined by what it does. That which is ready-to-hand may use a readymade tool as a tool, but equally may take an object-to-hand and make it a tool by its use: a brick is used to hammer a wooden stake into the ground, a branch with leaves is used to sweep a shed floor, a stick is used to stir a pot of paint.

Things have a supplement. For Jacques Derrida, written language was seen as the supplement of speech. As a relational principle, the made is a supplement to the tool. Evoking Derrida, Yuk Hui remarks that his notion of the supplement and his development of pharmacology are fundamental to study today.[42] What this means for technology is that it has the ability to create or destroy, or, in the hands of a surgeon, cure or kill. Such capabilities are supplementary features of it. Likewise, tools are not just prosthetic extensions of the body, as artificial organs. They are also a means of enabling the extension of the will in acts of creation or destruction.[43] They can provide the means to materialize the imagined or to exercise violent force.

Tertiary retention is elemental to the ontic in the nature of things.[44] Considered as an object, the violin again provides a good example – the instrument of today is the sum of the cumulative memory of making violins from their inception: it embodies memory. This includes the tools and practices that make the object as well as the thing itself – in its temporality, it retains and expresses the trace of memory.[45] Technique likewise is a product of traces of incremental memory carried in an evolving practice and passed to the practitioner over time and again registered in the very nature of the created object. So while tertiary memory is ontically an element of the object, while present, it is not directly reachable. Tertiary retention is not understandable just in terms of special objects that have evolved by makers over time. It equally inhabits humble and modest objects. It is integral to all materially made things of the world, in which we are all immersed as users and makers.

---

[42] Yuk Hui, 'Writing and Cosmotechnics', *Derrida Today*, 13 January 2020, 17–32. The pharmakon was centrally addressed in Plato's *Pharmacy*, part one of Jacques Derrida, *Dissemination*, trans. Barbara Johnson (Chicago: The University of Chicago Press, 1981), 95–119.

[43] Elaine Scarry, *The Body in Pain* (Oxford: Oxford University Press, 1985), 58–9.

[44] Bernard Stiegler, *States of Shock*, trans. Daniel Ross (Oxford: Polity, 2015), 158.

[45] Stiegler, *Technics and Time*, 245–59.

Everything recedes back into, and comes forward from made things. The unreachable memory that enabled its coming into being as agency in material and cultural action is predicated on changing the nature of practice itself. This means remaking the relation between thought and action by exposing the links of practice to defuturing (via what things service) and forward to what they are made to sustain (a futural imperative of an 'overdetermination' of practice). Such remaking is constitutive of a contrapractice. But it cannot happen as an idealized model, a programmatic plan or a ready-to-hand method. It can only emerge out of the incrementally evolving specificity from critical reflective practices. Our aim here is to contribute to bringing such practices into being. This does not imply an uninterrupted passage of unbridled attainment and improvement – misdirection and mistakes are also of the ontic nature of things. The environment in which we exist, as a populated plural depository of artefactual things with differentially posited tertiary memory, co-existing with all else that inhabits the space in which they are. As such, they form part of the temporal condition in which our primary memories are formed. Things so situated, as natural, as products of technologies and as technologies themselves, are mediated and mobilized by practice, all functioning in conditions of the remembered and the forgotten.

It is against this background of making that instrumental practices will be considered, including design, as they support, replicate and extend the materiality of the status quo, as, by degree, it sustains the conditions upon which life depend, while also enfolding defuturing agents that negate it. For affirmative change to be possible, these structural conditions have to be better understood and inform the development of contrapractices, at an organic and created systemic level. This action is other than, and beyond, fragmented attempts to reform extant practices. By implication, this means building a foundation of transformative redirective action upon which contrapractices can stand.

Technology

The ability to continually increase by the power of technology has been continuous over time, with the greater the power gained, the faster the rate of technological development. The defuturing disaster has been the underside of this process. The unmaking that accompanied the world making by technology did not become recognized until the last few decades of the twentieth century. Even then, the scale of what was occurring was not grasped for several more decades. A metaphysical catastrophe had actually been at the core of this situation.

It centred on the rise of Western instrumental thought, bonded to productivism, delivering technical objects and processes of creation – to meet immediate ends – without any understanding of the associated consequences of negation that were also being produced and accumulating over time. The toxicity and emissions of mass productive industry became exposed as being destructive of biophysical ecologies and damaging to the climatic atmospheric system. Even after the arrival of this knowledge, the damage continues. Maintaining the economic benefits continues to outweigh the environmental costs. In this situation, the retained relation to instrumentalism strives to find ways to sustain high-volume material modes of production and consumption while sustaining ecological conditions of dependence. But it fails to overcome what is a structural condition of unsustainability and unchecked increasing material demands. As a result, defuturing remains directionally dominant. Yet the myopic pragmatism of economic development remains dominant and inscribes *akrasia* as the dominant and ruling condition of mind.

As already signalled, as a consequence, displaced populations that will increase in number will be abandoned to their fate by the corporate techno-elites who dominate the economic status quo. They will act to protect their interests and well-being by becoming fully post-natural bio-technical beings. Meanwhile, the vast majority of the global population will be left to adapt to changing circumstances as best they can. Between the present moment and this future, there is a whole series of events that unfold that centre on processes of acceleration that will bring them into being.

What frames the dynamic of each of these futures is the process of defuturing now being commanded by accelerationism as it is forming an incompossible world, and in so doing displacing the current way the world is differentially viewed.

Change five: Accelerationism (outlined)[46]

Accelerationism is a defining characteristic of the present epoch; as such, it needs to be understood as a plural agency and idea.

As agency, accelerationism is a structural feature of the post-industrial domain of advanced industrial capitalism and elemental to the afterlife of economic modernity (a retained attachment to continual economic growth, in contrast to political modernity – the enactment of the ideology of global development). Its central precept is that innovation to continuously accelerate productivity is normative. In turn, this means an unchecked relation to extractivism and resource utilization; this, making environmental destruction, and thus defuturing, intrinsic to accelerationism. At the same time, sections of post-industrial capitalism have established an ideological and political-economic relation to acceleration. Its aim is to disrupt the political and economic status quo to cause a shift of power from the political order of the state to the rule of advanced techno-corporations under the direction of CEOs who have cultural-political and techno-economic agendas. In the USA, the Elon Musk, Peter Thiel, Jeff Bezos, Mark Zuckerberg et al. nexus (evidenced during the 2024 election) is a messy but prefigurative indicator of this development in process. The history of the idea of accelerationism needs to be taken seriously as it informs and

---

[46]   This section is based on a summary of Accelerationism in Tony Fry, *Political Breakout* (Wilmington: Vernon Press, 2025).

underpins the trajectory of this moment, as corporate-political power expands and takes control of discursive practices.[47]

Accelerationism: an outline history of the idea

The four ways that define how accelerationism can be understood are not homogenous: one is sociological, the second is environmental and the remaining two are political. Together, they contribute to how the fracturing and unstable geopolitical and economic state of the world can be understood. As such, they expose the redundancy of the current characterization of the dysfunctional world order, as divided between the Global North and South, and the ideological division between the East and the West. Dysfunction is being advanced by conflict (and the danger of the use of nuclear weapons), democracies being under stress (with the rise of many reactionary authoritarian populist regimes), and by an inability to manage deep crises (of which global warming is the most serious). All these divisions and conditions have shared a trajectory toward geopolitical fragmentation, enviro-climatic breakdown, economic chaos and proliferating conflict. Against this backdrop, nations are showing themselves to be demonstrably politically unable to grasp and engage the scale and 'complexity of complexity' of emergent converging, and thus compounding, problems in formation. They remain preoccupied with retaining and extending their power, while myopically claiming to act in their national interests. Transnational political institutions equally show themselves to be disarticulated from the scale, dangers and depth of the crises now underway. Like governments, they continue to deploy disjunctural idealist rhetoric that calls for action based on moral imperatives (while displaying double standards) and without any means of enforcement. Meanwhile, events are underway that will accelerate conflict, the arrival of mass population displacement, increase the power of corporate techno-elites and force the majority of the global population to dramatically adaptively modify their lifeworld and material conditions in order to cope with coming enviro-climatic conditions of substantial change. Framed by this backdrop, the four modalities of acceleration already signalled will be summarized.

The first is historical and encompasses how acceleration has been understood as elemental to the dynamic of modernity. The second is an environmental condition that has been called the 'Great Acceleration'. The third accelerationist narrative is an ideological reactionary project, and the fourth, also political, but idealist, 'left' and utopian (in common with the third it also embraces accelerationism as political disruption, and as having a Promethean spirit, but it travels with the hope that its response to crisis will lead to a revitalized contemporary and enlightened socialism delivering a global future).

---

[47]   Here, disruptive corporate-political accelerationist destabilization meets discursive practices of chaos as seen in the example of Elon Musk as a high-level disrupter of the US State and as the associated reactionary enabler of alt-right language on his X platform. The aim, the restoration of order by national corporate postdemocratic governance.

Acceleration and modernity

This view of acceleration is epitomized by the German sociologist Hartmut Rosa, who in 2013 published *Social Acceleration: A New Theory of Modernity*. He argued in this book that acceleration was 'a constituent part of modernity', that societies are unable to fully manage.[48] Within the orbit of modernity, he viewed everything as accelerating, including change, the unknown and time.[49] By implication, this also meant a speeding up of processes of erasure.

Rosa makes a distinction between three types of acceleration: (i) technical acceleration of transport, production, information; (ii) social transformation, including social structures and social practices, knowledge, fashion and (iii) an acceleration of the pace of life. These dynamics are not new, but receded back to the late eighteenth century. However, they most dramatically arrived in the nineteenth and early twentieth centuries, as Karl Marx made clear when addressing production, the labour process and commodification. Likewise, so did Charles Baudelaire, in common with many writers and artists, who observed rapid change when viewing everyday life. In all cases, the disruptive force of modernity shattered traditions and established orders of life with the intent of opening a space for the arrival of the new (an intent now shared with contemporary accelerationism). Notwithstanding his insights, Rosa fails to recognize and address the inseparable darker side of modernity – not least its indivisible relation to colonialism and the enduring afterlife of its physical, cosmological and environmental violence. From his disciplinary placement in sociology,[50] the philosophical, political, ecological and economic, techno-cultural dimensions of accelerationism never really come into view.

The Great Acceleration

The Great Acceleration was first named by Paul Crutzen and Eugene Stoermerin in 2000. It is a registration of the dramatic and constantly increasing impact of human activity on the planet's geology and its ecosystems that is now overwhelming natural biogeochemical cycles.[51] Data on this process was first recorded in the mid-twentieth century. The convergence of impacts of technology, the constant growth of industrialization and industrialized society (especially in economically developed nations) and the growth in the human population plus consumerism, have all dramatically increased the scale of destruction and increased the defuturing consequences of unsustainability.

By the mid-twentieth century, there was clear evidence of fundamental shifts in, and damage to, the functioning of Earth systems. These impacts became more evident once the effects of global warming became apparent and understood. Knowledge of the seriousness of change continues to increase. It is now

---

[48]   Hartmut Rosa, *Social Acceleration: A New Theory of Modernity*, trans. Jonathan Trejo-Mathys (New York: Columbia University Press, 2015).

[49]   Ibid., 108–17.

[50]   Ibid.

[51]   Will Steffen, Paul J. Crutzen and John R. McNeill, 'The Anthropocene: Are Humans Now Overwhelming the Great Forces of Nature?'*Ambio*36, no. 8 (2007): 614–21.

recognized that global warming is irreversible, that vast areas of the planet will become unlivable, and a very significant percentage of the global population (maybe 30 per cent) will be displaced by the end of the twenty-first century.

Heretical accelerationism[52]

Extreme and reactionary political accelerationism aims to position itself to fill a coming political void after existing systems of governance fail under the pressure of breakdowns from multiple crises – crises that it itself acts it promotes and exacerbates. Such a position needs to be seen not just in the context of the 'compound problem' but as a contributing factor aggravating it. Viewing the destruction of the status quo as an act of clearing as a means to open the space for the arrival of the new, it is nihilistic – this is not a new perspective, for example, it echoes that of the Italian Futurists who saw the First World War as the destruction of a history which they deemed as preventing a new age from arriving. Rather than war as a means of clearing, politically accelerationism posits contemporary capitalism unchained as having destructive and liberatory power of clearing the past and present away.[53] Such enablement breakdown and dysfunction are now starting to be caused by the combined impacts of enviro-climatic, geopolitical and economic crises, with geopolitical insecurity and conflicts. The 'logic' of political accelerationism is that the wasteland of devastation provides the space and conditions to build conditions of techno-logical transcendence (singularity). These are not merely dangerous ideas of delusional thinkers but a project supported by named billionaire corporate leaders and silent power-broking supporters.

To understand the philosophical and political foundation of accelerationism, it is necessary to acknowledge the agency, theory and presence of its key figure, Nick Land. He taught philosophy at the University of Warwick between 1987 and 1998, and headed the Cybernetic Culture Research Unit. Land's heterodoxical thought project was expressed in his writing on the occult, cybernetics, fiction and poststructuralist philosophy.[54] He also embraced the notion of the Dark Enlightenment. His development of a political philosophy of unrestrained excess was articulated in his writing and during a drug-induced period of his life. His influence was created as much by the milieu of followers he attracted as by his writing, as it fused fact and fiction. Eventually, his relentless quest to transgress philosophical confinement took him to a point of mental breakdown and resignation from his position. However, his notion of techno-capitalist

---

[52] In this context, the term 'accelerationism' was first coined as a neologism by Benjamin Noys, *The Persistence of the Negative* (Edinburgh: Edinburgh University Press, 2010).

[53] Robin Mackay and Armen Avanessian, *Accelerate: The Accelerationist Reader* (Falmouth: Urbanomic, 2014), 4.

[54] From an antagonistic position toward philosophy and the academy, Land become more estranged and transgressive, as Robin Mackay, 'Nick Land: An Experiment in Inhumanism" (2012), (unpaginated), http://readthis.wtf/writing/nick-land-an-experiment-in-inhumanism/ outlined; he set out to establish a way of thinking and writing beyond the norms of humanist thought and to unlock 'the forces of dehumanization' and to establish a post-political position of cybernetics at the end of philosophy.

acceleration took on a life of its own in the company of rapid technological development in the early 2000s.

Land believes that China has become the economic, cultural and political embodiment of accelerationism, and he decided to live there, earning a living as a journalist. He also wrote prolifically as a blogger. His view of China was confirmed in an article on accelerationism published in *China Digital Space* in 2022.[55] It said that 'Xi Jinping is hastening the demise of the Chinese Communist Party by doubling down on his authoritarian rule, Xi often being referenced by the mock-title Accelerator-in-Chief. The article qualifies acceleration as being in 'its original sense, accelerationism'.

For Land, 'Capital is not overdeveloped nature, but underdeveloped schizophrenia', it provides the force of acceleration driving the future.[56] Land celebrates capital, as money, consumption, addictive desires and excess. So cast, in the inherent organizing ability of its materiality, he saw a force continuing beyond 'our' species extinction and a descent into chaos. Land's accelerationism, as ultra-rationalism, was predicated on the agency of machine-logic, and as positing the fate of 'our' species becoming transhuman. His thinking was viewed by hardcore accelerationist thinkers as more sophisticated and far more philosophically grounded than the left version, which was deemed to have a shallow version of technology.

While Land occupied the position as the lead philosophical thinker, Curtis Yarvin became accelerationism's principal political and economic salesperson.[57] Yarvin was a Silicon Valley computer scientist, start-up entrepreneur and far-right blogger (as aka Mencius Moldbug). He was also a pioneer 'deep state' conspiracy theorist, which was connected to and underscored by what he calls the 'Cathedral' (a power cabal of elite academics and the media). Land, who was immediately drawn to Yarvin, embraced his politics, his view of democracy as malignant, and the merit of the rule of monarch CEOs. Yarvin was also the founder of the 'Dark Enlightenment', also called the neo-reactionary movement – which Land supported. The danger of Yarvin and Land was not them gaining political power, but influencing alt-right people who do. There is a line of influence connecting Yarvin's friend billionaire Peter Thiel[58] to mentoring and support for US Vice President J.D. Vance that marks a continuum *from* neo-reactionary supremacist, quasi-fascism, Christian nationalist, to technocentric authoritarianism post-democracy mainstream accelerationists that intersects with Elon Musk and his once Trump-serving cohort. So situated, acceleration, at its end point, is technologically nihilistic and effectively the abandonment

---

[55] *China Digital Space* (June 26, 2022), https://chinadigitaltimes.net/ archive.

[56] Nick Land, *Fanged Noumena, Collected Writings 1987–2007*, Robin Mackay and Ray Brassier (eds.) (Falmouth: URBANOMIC, 2011), 313.

[57] Andre Prokop, 'Curtis Yarvin wants American democracy toppled. He has some prominent Republican fans', *Vox*, 24 October 2022, https://www.vox.com/policy-and-politics/23373795/ curtis-yarvin-neoreaction-redpill-moldbug (accessed 10 January 2023).

[58] Peter Thiel is a venture capitalist, founder of PayPal, an early investor in Facebook and creator of the Founders Fund.

of the value of organic life (and for Musk, planet Earth) – is defuturing in the driving seat. History awaits the result.

The question of the future it poses to us all is not 'will we all survive' but in the difference of a fragmented world, 'Who will survive?' and 'As what?' The facts and the fictions veil plural and uncertain futures. Uncertainty arrives in condition now the present, being clearly recognized, and structural (not only as a political, economic and environmental condition, but as globalizing psychology of being unsettled).

Accelerationist idealism

The Accelerant Reader (Mackay and Avanessian, 2014) and Alex Williams and Nick Srnicek's '*Manifesto for an Accelerationist Politics*' (2013) present themselves as the 'progressive' left voice of accelerationism. As such, they cast themselves as a provocation to the contemporary left's often endemic and ingrained technological illiteracy. Their position is triangulated between Land's embrace of the Dark Enlightenment as it tips toward violence, the alt-right corporate capital nexus and a post-Marxist left techno-utopianism.

A collection of diverse thinkers are called up to claim that accelerationist thought is historical. A lineage is drawn from Karl Marx, Samuel Butler and Thorstein Veblen to Gilles Deleuze and Félix Guattari, Jean-François Lyotard, Gilles Lipovetsky and J.G. Ballard, and then to Nick Land, Sadie Plant, Iain Hamilton Grant, and thereafter to Mark Fisher, Antoni Negri, Tiziana Terranova, Luciana Parisi, Reza Negarestani et al. Progress and regress, utopia and dystopia, futuring and defuturing all churn in the mix. *Telos* begets blindness. Any alignment of accelerationism with emancipatory forces, positing modernity as one of them, fails to grasp the darkness of the dialectic. So said, modernity cannot be delinked from the excesses of European colonialism, including the genocide of numerous indigenous peoples and the inequity that arises when undevelopment became redesignated as underdevelopment.[59]

From this Eurocentric lack of understanding of the colonizing violence of modernity and its global aftermath, Mackay and Avanessian go on to chide the left for its insufficient understanding of technology and economics, a view 'it shares with its more radical but equally technologically illiterate academic counterparts', whose view they believe lacks any grasp of concrete reality.[60] They then embrace a renewal of 'Prometheanism and rationalism', and a regression to extol a 'command of nature'.[61] Not only is their retrospective reading of an accelerationist past in error, but the social, technological, capital nexus that underscores the present fails to grasp the complexity of the dangers of the current conjuncture (named here as the compound problem). Contrary to their argument, there is no revisionary process underway. or promise of 'emancipation'.[62] While

---

[59]   J. D. Cockcroft, A. G. Frank and D. Johnson, *Dependence and Development* (New York: Doubleday, 1972).
[60]   Mackay and Avanessian, *Accelerate*, 5–6.
[61]   Ibid., 7.
[62]   Ibid., 11.

their aim is at total odds with neo-reactionary accelerationism, they equally posit technology as liberation from the extant conditions of limitation, and in doing so, they expose their lack of understanding of it. Their position is in fact retreatist and replete with extreme idealism. As such, left accelerationism aspires to be a reshaping and repurposing of socialism responsive to the contemporary contexts.

In contrast, Srnicek and Williams insist on the necessity of precise cognitive mapping, which implies epistemic acceleration, for any progressive political theory and action today.[63] But whose thinking processes are on the map? Our species is not 'one'. We are many. There is no, no foreseeable future, no technological convergence that resolves global difference, no 'Prometheanism' delivered salvation. All problems now and to come will not fall before the power of technologies present and future – all their rhetoric is just more of the same thinking in error.[64]

Neither left nor right accelerationism offer desirable or viable politico-philosophical positions. The 'left' is idealistic and naive in its analysis and view, including of the potential of its agency. The 'right' is nihilistic, reactionary and inherently authoritarian. Both embrace technology and a significant future of our species as a (promoted or implied) becoming transformed techno-mutated hybrids. The 'right' views the 'left' with contempt, while the 'left' views the 'right' with some indebtedness but also degrees of disdain.

Accelerationism and resistance

The dominant counter position against accelerationism is that it is unsustainable and can be halted by the imposition of degrowth/limits to growth (outlined in Appendix 5). But the politico-corporate power, volume of available capital and dynamic of accelerationism completely overwhelms the marginality of such de facto gestural actions. At the same time, in its destruction of the status quo and its alignment with a techno-corporate class, constituting protective environments for themselves, in a more fragmented world, protection could be expected to include a military dimension with a defensive and projective capability.

Such action would likely prompt contrapractice action within the plurality of geographic, cultural and practico-material lifeworlds of adaptive communities, who, to survive and flourish, would have become capable and resilient. Integral to the construction of the material environments of these communities – who in sum constitute the global majority – would be the regrowth of another kind of economy with its own mode of exchange, businesses, material practices and lifeworld. It could be expected that means would be created to resist aggression from the smaller but more technologically sophisticated communities of protection-seeking, for example, to command and control the management

---

[63] Alex Williams and Nick Srnicek, *#ACCELERATEMANIFESTO for an Accelerationist Politics* (2013), https://criticallegalthinking.com/2013/05/14/accelerate-manifesto-for-an-accelerationist-politics/ (accessed 12 August 2022).

[64] Ibid., 432–43.

of natural resources. In their difference, and lacking any situated knowledge, it is not possible to speculate how adaptive communities would resist control, but having the ability to do so is taken as a given.

FOUR ECOLOGIES OF TRANSITION

The vectoral force of accelerationism bisects a number of ecologies that are generative of practices that invite being seen and engaged as sites of contrapractice contestation. Such engagement would recognize the recursive dynamic of the ecological system as it cycles through processes of creation and destruction. They also can be viewed as pragmatics of new utility. Besides these pragmatics being articulated to adaptive practices, they may also provide situated opportunities to create obstructions on the pathway and resistance to singularity.

The first: An ecology of technology

The attempt to command nature by technology has been a disaster, has damaged and transformed natural systems, and created synthetic conditions that have denaturalized the natural.

Francis Bacon, in his *Novum Organum* of 1620, stated his ambition was to completely reconstruct human knowledge and establish productive sciences that not only more adequately provided a better understanding of the natural world but also facilitated a more advanced mode of applied scientific enquiry. In doing so, he created a bridge between science and technology that was to underscore notions of the domination of nature by technology. Such thought contributed to the epistemological foundation of modernity and its universalization by colonialism. The domination of the natural environment and of native peoples were brought into convergence. In the modern era, this mode of thought, moderated by humanism, arrived globally and is characterized as 'development'.

Gilbert Simondon, writing in 1958, stated that 'the world of technical objects' is 'the mediator between man and nature' and that 'man is the permanent organizer of a society of technical objects which needs him as much as musicians in an orchestra need a conductor'.[65] With the escalation of the power and presence of technology in people's lives, and in the world in general, Simondon's views have gained greater resonance, but more importantly it's become much clearer that 'the world of technical objects' has not merely mediated the relation between 'man and nature' but has transformed both – and continues to do so, to the extent that the distinction between technology and nature (via biotechnology) no longer exists.

---

[65]   Gilbert Simondon *On the Mode of Existence of Technical Objects,* trans. Cecile Malaspina and John Rogove (University of Minnesota Press, 2017), 2–3.

It is no mere coincidence that at the same time that Simondon was extoling the 'significance' of technology, the United Nations (UN) was promoting global modernization and modernity. It designated and launched the period 1960 to 1970 as the 'Development Decade'. In doing so, it projected freedom arriving in this historico-political moment of burgeoning post-colonial emancipation. All the while, freedom was being negated and control reinstated by the extension of techno-epistemological colonialization. In significant part, in the name of development, this action by the UN enabled the continuity of the Promethean force of the violence of extractivism. It should be noted that coincidentally, this moment also marked the birth of modern environmentalism – this registered by the publication of *Silent Spring* by Rachel Carson in 1962.[66]

While Simondon recognized the ontological transformative power of technology, its agency has far exceeded his projection. While this judgement can be applied to the period in which he was writing, it is even more evident now in the array of contemporary technologies, from nanotechnology to robotics and from AI to quantum computing. Ideologically, these technologies are all political potential/actual instruments of corporate accelerationism. Projected as futural, such technologies are ambiguous. They straddle the line of futuring and defuturing. They are effectively bonded to practices that not only instrumentally act in the service of defuturing but also support ways of thinking that legitimize such action.

Questioning technology and substantialism

Technology is fluid, not fixed. It directionally changes in its multiplicity rather than evolving as a totality. Much of its past travels with its present, and at times arrives from the future revitalized. This view poses a problem for those who hold to an essentialist position which wishes to firmly define technology. So framed, and after making a number of introductory comments, a number of issues are prompted by reading Andrés Vaccari, director of the Institute for Studies in Science, Technology, Culture and Development, Rio Negro University in Argentina. Vaccari's views are usefully provocative, and represent in various ways the other similar voices which merit a response from a contrapractice perspective. Doing so will contribute to clarifying the significance of substantialism for understanding technology.

The substantialist's claim is that there are stable and plural realities, formed by substances, and that all phenomena and all matter have real substance (and thus are not just a collection of forces). This opens into two problems: differentiating substance and form, and the accommodation of change. Such problems fold back into metaphysics, and the notion of the origins of thought upon which the very thinking of substance itself stands. The issue brought to technology has prompted the claim that it has real substance, rather than just being the product of a collection of forces. Martin Heidegger provides a relevant counter view in his *The Question Concerning Technology* when he confounds this binary

---

[66] Rachael Carson, *Silent Spring* (1962; Boston: Houghton Mifflin, 2003)

when he says that technology is nothing technological (which implies it is not reducible to form and/or substance), but rather it is a way of revealing. What it reveals is the actuality (truth) of (a/the) world.[67] Its essence is thus the consequence of what it does elementally in disclosing a world in being – world itself is not a phenomenon: it is an enigma that does not announce itself directly.[68] It is not just that we are all immersed in a technologically constituted worlds, but what it unites and 'makes sense of' is what is seen as being technologically disclosed by technologies of making worlds present as constructed and altered environment, as object and image (consider the iconic image of planet Earth taken from the Voyager spacecraft in 1994 as not simply a product of advanced photographic technology but also as the result the historicity of the sum of technologies that *took* the camera into space and thus made taking the image as disclosed view of 'the world' as an object in space, possible). It follows that making present is not merely disclosure but the totality of bringing to presence.

A position that argues for or against substantialism now seems like a redundant issue of metaphysics. The contemporary complexity of technology has gone beyond such polarization. It is substance and form, matter and the immaterial, object and image, energy and forces, light and sound, equipment and *techne*, the cosmological and the anthropological, time and motion. This is to say, technology is a continuous becoming, to which we are articulated, while also being trapped in an oscillating judgement of its value (be it good or bad). As such, it is equally a milieu, one that our species occupies and continuously recreates. If there is an outside of technology, it is unreachable by us – technology has become elemental to the ontic.

What has become apparent is that in its constant becoming, in its making and unmaking, technology has had profound temporal consequences: it can be futural and extend specific ontological conditions in time ('life-support'), but likewise it can, and does, defuture and so reverse and negate the conditions of life. In doing so, technology has overridden the fundamental cycling of creation and destruction upon which the continuity of life has been predicated. It constituted a bias toward destruction that over millennia has progressed from the imperceptible condition to a state of rapid, assisted, accelerated destruction (defuturing). Obviously, unchecked, defuturing is terminal.

Re-generational objects
The technological object as a focal figure in Simondon's philosophy is not seen as singular, static or inert, but evolving. As such, the object prefigures itself as transformed in an environment of individuation. Its ontological qualities engage its conditions of existence, and equally are engaged by them – this includes the ontology of the person who engages technological objects (individuation and ontological design resonate with each other). However, the plurality of

---

[67] Martin Heidegger, *The Question Concerning Technology and Other Essays*, trans. William Lovett (New York: Harper and Row, 1977).

[68] William McNeill, *The Fate of Phenomenology* (London: Rowman and Littlefield, 2020), 56.

the technical object (as distinct from *a* technical object) is not universal or fixed. They are geo-culturally situated, and the temporality of the object is not uniform. Everything just said unfolds in the context of this ecology and the other three yet to be detailed.

The time between the nature of advanced technology now and the time Simondon was writing, which was over thirty-five years ago, has to be considered when considering what he had to say. The leading edge of technology is now clearly significantly different – not least from the rise of immaterial objects and ones that transcend conditions of physical and biological limitation that he would have taken as given. Likewise, Simondon's view of technological objects and technological progress did not differentiate defuturing from futuring – a position begging to be contested with the coming of greater complexity and deeper crises. 'Progress' is now an undersubscribed myth to all but 'technocentrics'. The autonomy of the user is reduced by a technically imposed dependence on 'black box sealed' technical objects, and thereafter on 'service providers'. Certainly, Simondon recognized that transformations of the technical object had technical, environmental and 'psycho-social' consequences, but the contemporary scale of these has gone beyond his insights. Perceptual constriction is normative; thus, even now, amid the unfolding environmental impacts of climate change, there is a general failure to grasp the degree to which defuturing is an immersive condition.

It's common to present technology from a totalized view, as a continuum following an evolutionary path. But the history of technology is plural, not of one moment, and not as universally uniform. Its present retains some of its past, and its future is not singular or of one form. Technological practices are situated in space and time. For example, one part of a factory may be fully operating with an automated robotic plant, but in another part, iron is being cast into a sand mould – using a method invented in China over 3,000 years ago. Notwithstanding the efforts of modernity to create a single temporal condition, technologies still exist in different times and cosmologies. This means they exist in the company of plural ontologies, each with its own habitus. There is now no 'naturalized' condition of technology: culturally, intergenerationally, across genders and between and within the global difference, which is moving toward a quantum leap unlike any other past moment of uneven development predicated upon a *telos* of modernization and technological transfer. The emergent situation is one of disarticulated technological futures. The rhetoric and narrative of a technological *telos* continues, but it is now unanchored from the empirical reality of incommensurate technological futures.

While productivism remains global, the experiential encounter with it is incommensurate. So said: a woman attending an Computer Numerical Control (CNC)–driven knitting machine in Bangladesh, a man at the wheel of a rotary excavator in Western Australia, a woman in Canada 3D-printing disposable cameras, a woman in Poland assembling AK47 assault rifles, a man in Korea grinding lenses for telescopes are all unified by the capitalist mode of production as an abstract unifier, while divided by the concreteness of the capitalist means of production, which is concrete and plural. However, this economy will not survive as it is in the coming enviro-climatic and related economic crises.

Technogenesis and the human

Andrés Vaccari argues against a position that humans are born from techno-genesis.[69] He claims the positions adopted by Bernard Stiegler and Simondon are flawed. However, he shows little understanding of the basis of their position, which was based on paleo-anthropology research and the bio-mechanical and cognitive consequences of the interaction between early hominoids and the progression of stone, and then, bone and wooden tools. These tools were instruments of micro-environmental transformations (and precursors of tools of macro-environmental transformations), and agents of cognitive and bio-mechanical ontological change of their users (that is: technogenesis). Vaccari reduces the process of incremental change as a direct from animality to the emergence of *Homo sapiens*. But change occurred over a period of over six million years, during which time there were more than twenty hominoid species (with the use of a stone as a tool is thought to have begun around two million years ago). Vaccari caricatured a reductive moment of coevolution when there was already a whole ontological process of worlding underway.

There was no simple linear evolutionary progression. During the uneven sub-species evolutionary process, there is evidence that brain size increased by a significant percentage through the use of stone tools and the associated cognitive demands of making. There is disagreement over the degree of this increase, but a significant amount of the literature reviewed suggests it was substantial.[70] The more complex a lived environment and lives therein became, including more complex forms and uses of tools (and resulting objects of artifice), the more cognitive demands were made and the more the brain developed. By the time of the arrival of *Homo sapiens* some 300,000 years ago, it is estimated that approximately seventy types of stone tools were in use by the most advanced and established groups, as well as these were tools created from wood and bone. It follows that a substantial range of different practices were being created and employed in the making of domestic artefacts, weapons and clothing. Variations in environment (like available materials, food sources and climate) would all have had different evolutionary consequences.

Against this contentious background, and prior to discussing cosmotechnics, Vaccari states: 'Technology is a complex phenomenon that can be viewed from many perspectives'. He then welcomes pluralism, which reduces everything to equivalence and addresses cosmotechnics as problematic. 'My main concern is that notions of cosmotechnics runs the risk of reproducing what it seeks to

---

[69]   André Vaccari, 'Cosmotechnical Thought Between Substantivism and the Empirical Turn', *Foundations of Science* 27, no.394 (2022): 1280, https://philpapers.org/rec/VACCTB (accessed 19 September 2023).

[70]   Hyun K. Ko, 'Origins of Human Intelligence: The Chain of Tool-making and Brain Evolution', *Anthropological Notebooks* 22, no. 1 (2016): 5–22, http://www.drustvoantropologov.si/AN/PDF/2016_1/Anthropological_Notebooks_XXII_1_Ko.pdf (accessed 2 March 2023).

counteract – this presumes it to be a position, which it is not. He asserts, the cosmotechnical scheme needs to identify a universal "technical" component'.[71] But there is no independent agency and intent; there is no technology that is without a cosmology. The designation is applied to a cultural Other and fails to recognize that the position he occupies is itself within a cosmology (one that is Western and hegemonic). As for the 'cosmotechnical scheme', what it names is the specificity of a cosmotechnics and not an agency with an imperative determined by an intent. The very notion of 'need' for a 'universal technical component' folds into the problematic of the universal, which itself negates cosmological difference of people and their cosmology.[72]

Vaccari evokes Oswald Spengler's view of cultures as self-contained, suggesting that cosmotechnical thought reproduces this position. Besides conflating culture and cosmotechnics, and employing an outmoded Eurocentric reductionist view of culture (contrary to a contemporary well-established anthropological understanding of cultures existing in varied conditions of dynamic change).[73] The position adopted by Vaccari is disingenuous. He appears to think his remarks are helping towards 'fine-tuning the concept', but they are not. No awareness is shown of the relation of cosmology, as expressed by, and enacted in, the cosmotechnics of practices of everyday life.[74] Cosmotechnics so situated in indigenous cultures makes no distinction between how 'a world' is understood and how it is made and maintained. It constitutes a complex history and a diverse futural projection of a way of being. Rather than being seen as a figure of romanticized indigeneity, it (as recovered and reconstituted) is actually of growing significance and practice, especially for emergent displaced and adaptive populations in making a meaningful and functional life in the wake of disaster – one that awaits a narrative.

The agency of technology is obviously unevenly situated globally, and as indicated, will increasingly become so. Notwithstanding, there is a generalized totalization of technology constituted by the discursive practice of the kind of philosophy Vaccari represents. No matter the position adopted, it is overwhelmingly Eurocentric, projecting a *telos* of technology as a totalizing all-encompassing cosmic force, autonomous and expanding according to its internal logic. Notwithstanding a universal impetus and presence, technology is situationally embraced and conditionally employed. Yet appearances mislead – immaterial and virtual technology rest upon the material, be it the energy infrastructure or technology sweatshop workers in the Global South.

Labour is expendable, jobs are at risk. The annotated data of work practice is now being harvested by machine learning to train artificial intelligence

71   Vaccari, 'Cosmotechnical Thought', 1283.
72   François Jullien, *On the Universal*, trans. Michael Richardson and Krzysztof Fijalkowski (Oxford: Polity, 2014).
73   James Clifford, *The Predicament of Culture* (Cambridge, MA: Harvard University Press, 1988).
74   Eduardo Viveiros De Castro, *The Relative Native, Essays on Indigenous Conceptual Worlds* (Chicago: Hau Books, 2015).

models to replace live labour to further reduce the cost of production. For example, transitional labour (that creates its own redundancy) is employed to label images of different objects in the built environment (drawn from drive-by videos) as part of the development of algorithms needed for automated driving. Meanwhile, others edit chunks of 'feeder text' to ensure language models like ChatGPT don't churn out gibberish.[75]

In rejecting the non-neutrality of 'artefacts, machines, and techniques', technogenesis is by inference acknowledging 'artefacts, machines, and techniques' as always ontologically transformative of/for the person who attends to and uses them. Heidegger's famous hammer is a good example. The hammering (as technique), of the hammer (artefacts) changes the condition of what it hits, and the hammering affects the hammerer – its continual use produces ontological changes: the hammering arm becomes more developed, and hand/eye coordination improves. As for the status of a hammer as a 'morally innocent object of use', it can crack nuts, and so assist in the delivery of nourishment, or kill a shopkeeper in the course of a robbery.

Vaccari claimed that technology became dislocated from history.[76] At the simplest, this statement presumes both technology and history exist as totalized and independent from each other, which is clearly incorrect. It also reveals a lack of comprehension of the agency of technology in the historical advance of modernity, and the even more fundamental fact of the historicity of our species as a technological being. Technological objects functioned in conditions of historical causality. Examples are myriad: the clock in the history of navigation; its transformation of the conduct of war; and the car in the history of human mobility and the transformation of the city. These are just two examples of technology placed in a larger global frame that was central to the capitalist labour process and the history of work. Then there is the history of technology of colonialism, agriculture, war, shipping, building construction and so on. Vaccari's claims make no sense. More importantly, they reflect a wider societal condition of not making sense (including of technology and its relation to history).

The second: Psycho-technology ecologies: Delinking the switch

At a fundamental level, psycho-technologies have had profound psychological consequences. From their inception, they have amplified problems of the spatial dynamic of social interaction by creating a breakdown in a sense of proximity. What is taken to be close has been dislodged from what is near. Famously, Marshall

[75]   Rebecca Tan and Ragine Cabato, 'Behind the AI Boom, an Army of Overseas Workers in "Digital Sweatshops,"' *Washington Post*, 28 August 2023, https://www.washingtonpost.com/world/2023/08/28/scale-ai-remotasks-philippines-artificial-intelligence/ (accessed 12 September 24.

[76]   André Vaccari, 'Neosubstantivism and Cosmotechnics, Gilbert Simondon Versus the Transhumanist Synthesis', *Angelaki* 28, no. 4 (2020): 41, https://rid.unrn.edu.ar/bitstream/20.500.12049/8365/3/10.1080%400969725X.2020.1790834.pdf (accessed 8 January 2023).

McLuhan defined television as a 'cool medium' – which meant there was an unreachable divide between 'you' and it. Whatever appeared to be near was not close. No matter the image, it was cold. Social media has inverted this relation. It is hot. While not near, it is taken to be close. It seemed to engage 'you', 'touch you'. It gathered information about 'you', it 'knows you'. The reality it constructs could be/is felt to be closer than the spatial reality 'you' occupy. In some cases, it even makes those people held captivated by it delink from their reality and adopt the 'truth' of the alt-reality it presents. Consequently, with the extensive uptake of digital technology in the twenty-first century, something has changed for many, often young people, especially those in advanced economies. The relation between these people and technology has altered. It became seemingly more intimate, the proximity of technology to body and mind changed, and the time spent with 'devices' of this electronic technological domain significantly increased. Laptops, tablets and especially smartphones across the populations of industrialized and industrializing nations become omnipresent. They were a feature of everyday life as tools of work, sources delivering entertainment, and of social connectivity. Not only did these mediatory technologies have a physical and mental presence, but they also altered their 'users' proximity to the world – not least via a range of audio and visual communications and social media platforms that ideo-informationally mediated a particular view of the world. The psychological presence and consequences of technology became of a different order than other communication technologies of the past (the telegraph, telephone, the radio and TV). Most significantly, the nature of social ecology changed (and with it the 'power' of communication).

Past ways of disseminating information, ideas, knowledge (education, books, newspapers, radio, television) have, for many, again especially young people, been displaced by social media platforms, websites, blogs, and by various common interest/worldview networks and lists. Effectively, the nature of experience and the means and conditions of influence have changed. Whereas in the past, and its afterlife in the present, the representation of reality rested upon an unstated structurally embodied epistemology – often linked contextually to particular communities of knowledge (eg, science mostly mediated reality via empiricism and positivism), now this is no longer exclusively the case. There has been a reversion to mythology as the foundational basis of social ecology, especially among a substantial sector of the social media generation. One of the main markers of this situation is the widespread declaration of 'the end of truth'. Huge numbers of people in and beyond the USA view the mainstream news media as fake, and of politics being underpinned by the conspiratorial actors and actions of the 'deep state'. The issue with these claims is not their lack of veracity but that they have agency. Belief has replaced truth for a very significant percentage of 'the masses', and stupidity cohabits with intelligence.[77]

There is one other crucial factor to note, which is the correlation between social media/psychologies and mental health. In and beyond the Global North,

---

[77]   Stiegler, *States of Shock*.

there is a mental health crisis among the younger generation, as evidenced by data.[78] A graphic anecdotal indicator of this problem was told to me recently by a Chinese postgraduate student who said that 'to be young in China is to be mentally ill'.

Psycho-technological states of mind are taken to be serious conditions mostly beyond the conventional range of psychological illness – like a dependence upon a smartphone, the anxiety suffered if they could not access it, or the reduced attention span of many who have grown up in an age of digital culture. Then there is the cognitive implication of a drift away from texts that require focus and many hours to read, and toward AI summaries, memes and the image as primary sources of 'knowledge'. These trends, although not universal (but becoming so), are epistemologically serious.

While 'the market', in an era of mass media, has always battled for attention and sought to create desire for its commodities, with the coming of the digital domain and psycho-technologies, a more profound change has occurred. It comes from the speed, volume and character of content, and rate of change arriving in conditions of rapid technological, social, economic and environmental transformation. The fallout ontologically, epistemologically, bio-physically, and the psycho-social effects are becoming significant and serious. Accelerated redundancy, transitory attachments, the retention of attention requiring constant stimulation and alienation from 'the serious' being some of the features of the lifeworld of the population of digital culture. The proximity to movement (speed) and distance (between the near and the close) have transformed 'our' being (an emergent majority) in time. Effectively, this suggests defuturing can be seen here as a condition not just of materially impacting environments, ecologies, and 'our' bodies, but also of our minds. The crises of the end times are not just worldly, they are also existential, and so within 'us' and disabling.

'We' all live in what Walter Benjamin called the 'everlasting now' – neither past nor future exist as a point of reference. Memory and anticipation are overruled by the moment of instant passing gratification and instant communication. This situation of unthinking time (as change) can be empirically verified. For example, covering large areas of the body with tattoos is seeing the body as an 'everlasting now' that is not cognisant of the perception of the self and body changes with time. They are a 'sign' of an unthinking self in time – one common to people of seemingly different ages, classes, ethnicities and intellects.

Above all, the impact of the technological transformation of temporality and perceptions of the real, together with the shadow of defuturing (fear of a dark future) is disabling a crucial agency essential for constituting a more viable future: the agency of imagination.

For millions of people, especially in the geographic and post-geographic Global North, the immaterial environment of messaging (visual stimulation,

---

[78]   The World Health Organization reports that one in ten adolescents has a social media-related mental health problem, https://www.who.int/europe/news-room/25-09-2024-teens–screens-and-mental-health (accessed 2 January 2024).

distanciated social interaction and the rejection of time-invested modes of communication – like reading and writing), is unstopping.

The psycho-technology environment poses many challenges for contrapractice: how to create the means to switch over to a mediated otherness. How to make the extent of the disabling reach of psycho-technology more fully present (a problematic ontologically designing apparatus). How to rethink determinism. And above all, how to make futuring integral to being now, when defuturing is arriving as a diminishing sense of finitudinal time.

Defuturing action – as extinction in process – is destructive of the ecological totality that is life; Bateson assigns this negation to 'conscious purpose'.[79] While it is true that, for instance, the destruction enacted by extractivism is executed with such a purpose, this does not mean it was done so without a consciousness of consequence. The actuality of such action is really 'unconscious instrumentalism'. What Bateson is actually addressing is conscious intent. For instance, conscious intent directs the felling of a tree, whereas the conscious purpose of doing so is, say, to acquire timber to make a table. Defuturing is dominantly the result of a conscious intent lacking a consciousness of consequence. So understood, it requires to be viewed not just as a worldly effect, but also as the effect of a mind lacking a consciousness of the consequences of enacted intent.

Defuturing is clearly not exclusively produced by technology, nor from a failure to recognize its negative ecological consequences in general. It is also a failure to comprehend, as said, to know and understand the consequences of an enacted intent. As such, it is a failure of mind, knowledge and the ability to exercise responsibility emanating from a lack of concern, *akrasia*, the unthinking of an unquestioned habitus or the effect of an agent of critical disablement as exemplified by psycho-technologies.

The philosophy of technology is presented as the discourse with the most developed understanding of its object of concern, yet by not giving attention to defuturing, it is deficient. The correction to this deficiency implies the need for an understanding and the potential contrapractice brought to its practice – a substantial project in its own right and one that would also need to engage with the ecologies of technology and psycho-technology as well as those of mind and the geo-epistemological.

The third: A pluri-ecology of mind

Gregory Bateson retrospectively employed the concept of an 'ecology mind' in two ways: pragmatically as a gathering of performativity of interdisciplinary

---

[79]   Gregory Bateson, *Steps to an Ecology of Mind* (New York: Paladin, 1973), 117–19.

thought in a collection of writing spanning over thirty years, and conceptually.[80] He defined the concept as an 'ecology of ideas in systems or minds' beyond the containment of the individual. But then, second, he said it was also 'epistemology' – that is, 'another word for what that concept names'.[81] Bringing these views together, what is described is an environment in which ideas and thoughts come into relation with each other, circulate and constitute ways of knowing. This all occurs ontologically, but Bateson claimed it can be brought to consciousness by constituting an interdisciplinary approach created to explore this ontology. He equated such study with that of biological ecology. What emerges in his work as a general un-gathered theory of relational behaviour (of mind, psychology, ecology, cybernetics, information, conscious purpose, learning, culture) as an ordering of change.

Bateson's thought was of, and traversed, his moment. Aldous Huxley, of *The Doors of Perception* fame, appears as an implied trace. Often, his views can be placed in the shadow of the rise of late modern counter culture. But his moment was also one of being cognizant of the arrival of the reality of an 'ecological crisis' (specifically in 1973 linking back to Rachel Carson[82]), yet in contradiction, he also resonates with an idealism that appeals to, and embraces, a desired, rather than actual, collective 'we'. His thinking was prior to the intervention of psycho-technology as a mediation between mind and body, so from a contemporary perspective, his views read as dated and somewhat naive. Thus, writing on 'high civilization', he affirms 'on the technological side, whatever gadgets are necessary to promote, maintain (and even increase) wisdom of the general sort. This may well include computers and complex communications devices'.[83] Certainly, Bateson can be regarded as a pioneer of interdisciplinary thought. As such, he invites being read as a source of insightful questions and openings (not least in association with the concept of a 'double-bind') rather than of final conclusions. However, his recognition of 'of mind' remains important, notwithstanding a wider under-recognized acknowledgement of its growing salience in the problematics of the present (as indicated by references made to psycho-technologies).

---

[80]   The notion of gathering begs qualification – Heidegger's reading of Aristotle's account of the making of a sacred vessel in his *Physics* provides a useful characterization of the concept of gathering. It has its philosophical roots *in aition* as 'the being responsible for the cause' of something, and as *legein/logos* – here seen as a means of bringing forth as together into appearance, and thereafter to deliberate and comprehend (William McNeill, *The Glance of the Eye* (New York: State University of New York Press, 1999), 196). Gathering also directly links to bringing our being into being as the event of our becoming – as such, we become to be as we gather language, knowledge, skills, and all else that constitutes our embodiment and habitus via our being as an appropriative event (ibid., 316–17).

[81]   Bateson, *Steps to an Ecology of Mind*, 310.

[82]   Ibid., 465.

[83]   Ibid., 471.

In part, the current significance of 'ecology of mind' was elevated by Félix Guattari's publication of his *Three Ecologies* in 1989 (English translation 2000).[84] The ecologies Guattari explicated were: social ecology, mental ecology and environmental ecology. Besides his view that these ecologies were all well comprehended, he also considered them as treated by individuals and government with 'fatalistic passivity'.[85] What Guattari hoped for was that these ecologies would lead to a 'recomposition of the goals of the emancipatory struggle'.[86] While his ideas resonate with an 'ecology of mind', Guattari also concurs with Bateson that ideas 'cannot be contained within the psychology of the individual', but rather are organized into 'systems of minds'.[87] While Bateson places them in ecological sub-systems he calls 'context', Guattari disagrees; he sees context politically constituted by '*praxis*', as it ruptures 'the systemic pretext'.[88] He also sees the 'mental ecology' as more fluid than Bateson.[89]

Viewing an 'ecology of ideas in systems or minds' from the present, and specifically from the perspective of the form and traffic of ideas in the digital domain, and its psycho-technologies, two things are immediately clear: the agency of this ecology has dramatically increased; and the consequences of this 'development' are massive and ambiguous.

Certainly, there is now a great deal more information and ideas in circulation, but correspondingly, there is equally a great deal more misinformation and bad ideas in the mix. Overall, there is a huge amount of informational 'noise' within a vast electronic information environment operatively 'jamming' the ecology of mind as it has become a domain of contestation of perceptions, knowledge and of the psycho-cultural attachments to individuated and collective identities. The ideological spread of competing colonizing forces spans taste and style, brand and political allegiance, product choice, sexual orientation and more. At the same time, the technology and means associated with social media especially, has fostered a culture of attachment within an ecology of mind that has produced, and is producing, subjects with psychologies of dependence, reduced attention spans, and deep attachments to 'alt-realities'.[90] A review of seven studies of the psychological and emotional impact of digital technology on boys and girls between 14 and 18 conclusively reported negative outcomes, especially among girls.[91] Just as earlier technologies were created without any sense of their

[84] Félix Guattari, *The Three Ecologies*, trans. Ian Pindar and Paul Sutton (1989; London: Athlone, 2000). Deleuze and Guattari, had already briefly engaged Bateson on the double-bind and schizophrenia in their *Anti-Oedipus* ([1972] 1983) and *A Thousand Plateaus* ([1980] 1987) – the concept of plateaus being drawn from Bateson.

[85] Ibid., 41.

[86] Ibid., 49.

[87] Ibid., 54.

[88] Ibid.

[89] Ibid., 79, n.103.

[90] Johann Hari, *Stolen Focus* (New York: Crown Publishing, 2022).

[91] P. Limone and G. A. Toto, 'Psychological and Emotional Effects of Digital Technology on Digitods (14–18 Years): A Systematic Review', *Health Psychology*, 13 (2022), https://doi.org/10.3389/fpsyg.2022.938965P.

material environmental impacts, now an entire very sophisticated electronic technological domain has arrived with no more understanding of its immaterial impacts than the technologies of earlier ages. The most extreme example is AI, which is starting to be viewed by some of its creators as a possible instrument of our species' extinction.[92]

A fourth ecology: The geo-epistemological

The three ecologies that have been rehearsed are actually overarched by a fourth – a dissolving geo-epistemological ecology still situated between the Global North and South (as a geographic binary existing between and within nations). Historically, an epistemological divide has existed that devalued the Other's knowledge. Effectively, the exercise of the power of the North designated the value given to knowledge itself. Predictably, the North thus amplifies the significance and value of its own knowledge, as structurally distributed across numerous discourses, while simultaneously devaluing and marginalizing the knowledge of its Other. Such epistemological injustice is described in detail by Bonaventura de Sousa Santos.[93] Obviously, this inequity is mirrored in the reduction of the status of 'local knowledge' and its practices. However, in the coming condition of overt global fragmentation, the entire epistemological geography of power will change (and with it an ecology of mind). Part of the abandonment of the displaced will be epistemological, and elemental to the loss of value of their being that comes with such a designation. The counter-consequence of this situation is that the knowledge integral to their cosmotechnic capabilities will likely become of greatly enhanced and increased significance to them, and developed (as a matter of survival). The hyper-instrumental knowledge of corporate techno-elites will be contained within its protected condition of exclusion. As for the majority culture of adaptation, there is a huge epistemological challenge that contrapractice has to meet head-on.

Driven by the extent of enviro-climatic, social and economic change that will unfold over the remainder of the twenty-first century and beyond, the very nature of knowledge and education will transform in the face of the agenda of adaptation and associated contrapractices. Not only will the changed material conditions of life demand new knowledge, but so will the making of life that is futural and affirmative in circumstances with a high degree of loss of the extant world. Knowledge in this setting will require recovering across cultures and over time, and creating it in response to the changing circumstances. It would be presumptive to try to detail what this agenda would look like. There would obviously be a lot of instrumental content responding to changed circumstances and needs. But what is certain, in conditions of material constraint

---

[92]   As noted earlier this is very much the voice of Geoffrey Hintion – Taylor and Hern, 'Godfather of AI'.

[93]   Bonaventura de Sousa Santos, *Epistemologies of the South* (Boulder (CO): Paradigm Publishers, 2014).

and the stresses across the scale of worldly fragmentation, is that the demand for major social, cultural, political and practical transformative change will be enormous. Contrapractice here became an essential and generative means for diverse communities to find ways to cope and continue to be.

The formative ontologically directive force of technology in the coming fragmented world will play an equally significant role in the conditions of radical difference. It will fragment as 'we' and 'our' world fragments. It is actually already clear that technological futures will pluralize as fragmentation occurs. This has already been registered in acknowledging three ways: the potential relations of displacement, abandonment to recovered/recreated cosmotechnics; redirective technologies of adaptation; and the accelerationist trajectory of corporate techno-elites toward singularity. In briefly evoking such change, an enormous complexity is glossed over, not least the consequences of the fragmentation of our species by being prefigured and realized by transhumanism. These remarks firmly place technology in a relational frame wherein contrapractice, and the ontological form of the majority of 'the adaptive all will acquire their futural form'. To this end, technology begs to again be revisited and reviewed.

Epochal Change: Living in plural time

Now the modernized segment of humanity lives in global time. No matter the local time, the time of electronic communication is the 'present'. The same Internet-enabled moment can be occupied by a group of people distributed anywhere on the planet. By innovation, the epoch of the accident has been created – as Paul Virilio (2007)[94] recognized. Technology and design are at the centre of this accident through innovation.

Nuclear energy generation has had two major accidents (Chernobyl and Fukushima) and there have been an order of one hundred other small ones in which loss of life and significant damage have occurred. Then, as the war in Ukraine has shown, any nuclear power plant in a war zone is an accident waiting to happen (or a dirty bomb waiting to be activated). The potential for accidents proliferates across technology. As Yuk Hui has also argued, accidents 'come to the fore in the digital age and beyond'[95] – because they are indivisible from, and generative of, contingency (a condition of the unknown wherein whatever is, could exist otherwise if circumstances were different).[96]

Technological innovation and an increase in risks are indivisible. As, for instance, Bill Gates and Stephen Hawking warned in 2015, AI is arriving with great benefits to humanity, but equally with great destructive power.[97] More

---

[94] Virilio, *The Original Accident*.
[95] Yuk Hui, 'Algorithmic Catastrophe – the Revenge of Contingency', *Parrhesia* 23 (2015): 139.
[96] Ibid., 137.
[97] Michael Sainato, 'Stephen Hawking, Elon Musk and Bill Gates Warn About Artificial Intelligence', *Observer*, 19 August, 2015, https://observer.com/2015/08/stephen-hawking-elon-musk-and-bill-gates-warn-about-artificial-intelligence/ (accessed 10 February 2023).

recently, Geoffrey Hinton, a pioneer of neural networks, quit Google because of the dangers of AI.[98] That the technology carries risk is clear, but the forms it will take are not. Emanating from digital technologies, more generally, Bernard Stiegler made clear that psycho-technologies have the power to both capture and destroy attention, with profound consequences for the retention of knowledge and an increasing dependence on such technologies.[99] Then there are the under-considered risks of neuro-technologies – like Elon Musk's chip implant brain-computer interface technology, Neuralink. Approval to undertake human trials was gained in early 2023, and they are now underway.[100] Other prosthetic technological devices that form part of the means of developing the technological enhancement of the human body and mind are also being created. Such developments are enthusiastically embraced by technophiles; they see them as a means to fully realize a transhumanism condition. Like so many technological innovations, the ability to create and introduce them does not correspond with understanding the causal consequences of their introduction. Their introduction widens the technological divide on a planet heading toward fragmented lifeworlds.

Another technology of concern is nanotechnology. It has now reached a level of development where it is going to have a big impact on many industries, including chemistry, medicine, materials science and engineering. But the disruptive changes that may occur as a result of the most advanced form of nanotechnology (molecular production) are still largely unknown. Investigations of the physicochemical properties of nanomaterials suggest they may pose more potential toxic hazard risk to ecosystems, and thus to the human body, than previously recognized.[101]

As the rate of the acceleration of global climate and related eco-disaster increases, the duration of biological time diminishes. This moment of prospective finitude slowly, if unclearly, exposes itself in the present as an unfolding defuturing event – named by evolutionary biology as the sixth extinction event. The finitude of life does not correspond to the solar disaster five billion years away. A total extinction event would have occurred way longer before it arrived, and while the process is gradual and still distant, it is already discernible. NASA confirmed in January 2025 that 2024 was the first year the Earth's temperature exceeded 1.5°C above pre-industrial levels. The expectation now is that 2.0°C will be reached in the next ten to twenty-five years.

[98]   Taylor and Hern, 'Godfather of AI'.
[99]   Bernard Stiegler, *Taking Care of Youth and the Generations*, trans. S. Barker (Stanford: Stanford University Press, 2010).
[100] Daniel Gilbert and Faiz Siddiqui, 'Elon Musk's Neuralink Says it Has FDA Approval for Human Trials: What to Know', *Washington Post*, 26 May, 2023, https://www.washingtonpost.com/business/2023/05/25/elon-musk-neuralink-fda-approval/ (accessed 17 November 2023).
[101] Nasrollahzadeh Mmoudah and Mohammad Sajadi, 'Risks of Nanotechnology to Human Life', *Interface Science and Technology* 28 (2019), https://www.sciencedirect.com/science/article/abs/pii/B978012813586000007 (accessed 20 January 2023).

As chronophobic beings, we collectively display a reluctance to think in time, while recoiling from the reality of impermanence. The unavoidable existential arrival of the condition of defuturing places this disposition as a condition of negation at the core of our current species being. While defuturing is a condition of 'our existence' it is accompanied by refusal to recognize the criticality of this state being. Defuturing so positioned exceeds what is known, yet it demands our collective (time-making) attention.

The rhetoric of crises already carries the weariness of constant return. It does not want to be heard and uttered again – its language ever exhausts itself – and produces an automatic turning away. The essence of contrapractice does not deliver a transcendence of this reflex. But its potentiality arrives as a means of individuation whereby the position between helplessness and being help-full can become the locus of a felt and actual possibility: as action, it begets action.

The current 'complexity of the complexity' of the crises that define the present, and determine so much of the future, exposes the history of a fundamental contradiction that became the essence of industrial society. Namely, the creation of material future conditions by the means of production by every agency that negates future: here is life in the grip of a double-bind.

From one then to a plural now

The humanist objective of creating a unified world has failed. The attempt of global control by 'development' post–Second World War (by Euromodernity, and then later by a neoconservative-led project of globalization) also failed. Rather, what arrived was a terminal world order and deepening conditions of eco-political crisis and fragmentation. So framed, *Homo sapiens* face two convergent dangers that will decide the fate of our species over the next few decades.

Danger one comes from the diverse impacts of enviro-climatic crises as agricultural systems fail, as parts of the planet become un-liveable, as a result of heat, sea-level rises and extreme weather impacts, as biodiversity is increasingly reduced, as populations are displaced and as conflict increases. As evolutionary biologists and others have recognized, these (and more) impacts could result in our (and many other species) becoming extinct. Danger two comes from technology, in particular from the advancement of Artificial General Intelligence (AGI super-intelligence), fusing with neurotechnics (embraced by transhumans) and establishing proto-forms of singularity to eventually produce conscious machines. The danger here is that these machines deem 'us' as useless (there is already the expectation of a coming techno-produced 'useless class'). From the perspective of 'machinic reason', useless beings are simply eliminated. Such seeming science fiction fear fantasies are now voiced by some of the scientists who created AI.

The Industrial Revolution started in England just over 250 years ago – it was driven by the thermal energy of coal, the ability to make iron and the power of the steam engine. AI, quantum computing, neurotechnics, nanotechnology, and the prospect of the move from nuclear fission to fusion now mark the current moment and developmental stage of the technology project that began two centuries plus years ago.

The key point here on this developmental process is one of continual acceleration, generating an ever-increasing complexity and innovation accompanied by a diminishing comprehension of the futural consequences of what is being brought into being, beyond evident instrumental and discernible trends.

The speed of the arrival of artificial intelligence is extraordinary. It is now continually being inducted into operational systems across industry and services. It has a growing public presence via the introduction of ChatGPT – a 'Bot' allowing an everyday speech dialogue, and with continuing machine-learning programming, to have the ability to answer diverse questions, write, including in simulated literary styles, and generate code. Within six days of its introduction in late November 2022, ChatGPT gained 100 million users (especially in education). From this point on, its uptake has increased. At the time of writing, it is free – early use equals advancing system-driven research and development (use 'feeds' machine learning and thus its added value: the technology is not a free gift): it is also a mechanism of market development and capture. AI has no critical or moral sensibility, although acting on the information it delivers can have critical or moral consequences. It is open to abuse by scammers and phishing, and while able to write software, it can also write malware and cause problems for programmers and software developers.

The development of this type of technology has the ability to replace live labour in, for example, routine administrative occupations, further automated supply chains, and be disruptive in numerous contexts – answers given sound authoritative, and are taken to be so, even when incorrect.[102] Epistemological disruption and the production of a growing 'useless class' are two already obvious consequences. Reiterating the sentiment of Stephen Hawkins, Bill Gates, Geoffrey Hinton and others who assert that artificial intelligence could well be the best or worst idea in history. It could be a grave danger to our species. Its reception was prefigured by a prepped, uncritical culture, and its future is assured by its ability to grow this culture. The scale and defuturing implication of the autonomic (functionalized as machine learning) warrant this technology being given additional consideration as a danger, one generating an algorithmic-led catastrophe.

As philosopher of technology Yuk Hui identifies, algorithms mark a general exteriorization of reason wherein 'we find more and more that human reason is becoming less and less capable of understanding the system that it has succeeded in constructing'.[103] Besides this being elemental to the dynamic of an ever-expanding complexity of complexity, it also points to a process that is even more concerning, as this algorithm-enabled technology becomes ever more autonomous (not least in the domain of war). He goes on to say that 'The

---

[102]   These comments are drawn from sampling the 230 articles critical of ChatGPT listed by Google at the time of writing.
[103]   Hui, 'Algorithmic Catastrophe', 137.

catastrophe that arrives with algorithms must be distinguished from industrial or military accidents. These can be avoided, but the algorithmic catastrophe is increasingly beyond the capacity of human beings'.[104] By implication, this means that technology moves/has moved completely out of 'our' control (which is also to say, algorithms function in the service of singularity). A perverse inversion of metaphysics has thus occurred whereby an increase in the production of knowledge is exponentially increasing the unknown, wherein 'the black box becomes the keeper of the sole explanation'.[105]

It is against the background of these remarks that quantum computing begs to be viewed. It is on the verge of arriving: prototype machines already exist. By the time these words are read, such machines will likely have become commercially available. Thus, with this huge advance in computing power, there will also be an equally large increase of the known and unknown. *Quantum Insider Intelligence Platform* provides a brief summary that headlines the nature of this increased capability of the technology[106] – quantum computer AI systems would have a natural advantage over classical computing in many tasks because of their unique ability to apply the principles of quantum mechanics to calculations.[107] Primarily, these principles include superposition and entanglement. Superposition is the ability for quantum bits, or qubits, to seemingly be in multiple positions at once, rather than just holding the binary 1 or 0 positions of a standard bit. 'Entanglement' refers to the potential for correlations between qubits, which would exponentially increase the computational ability with each entangled qubit.

A fault-tolerant quantum computer that taps into superposition and entanglement could speed up artificial intelligence tasks, perform more of those tasks and tackle more complex tasks. Compared to classical supercomputers, which must process complex problems over long periods, fault-tolerant quantum computers can process those same challenging problems in less time and use less power. That makes implementing quantum computers more sustainable and more environmentally friendly (and marketable). They will also expand the power of corporations like Google, which are to build quantum processors and develop novel quantum algorithms. Notwithstanding the more 'environmentally friendly' computer, once linked to AI and its energy-hungry data centre, environmentally friendliness fades.

The rationalized merits of these computers are also accompanied by the latest and the most terrifying example of the unthinking of the defuturing consequences – a condition of limitation that has been historically intrinsic to the hegemonic instrumentalism of technoscience. Quantum computing will massively increase technological autonomy. It will also advance the pursuit of super-intelligence

[104] Ibid., 139.
[105] Ibid., 140.
[106] James Dargan, 'Quantum Computing Companies: A Full 2024 List', *Quantum Insider*, 29 December, 2023, https://thequantuminsider.com/2023/12/29/quantum-computing-companies/ (accessed 8 June 2024).
[107] Ibid.

and the effort of transhumanism to advance toward the sub-set of our species becoming a bio-technological hybrid (a fully realized transhuman).

Such projects, and the thinking they engender, expose an absolute colonization by technology: one that will arrive by a graduated process. The mechanism of this process is already firmly in play: the seductive agency of psycho-technologies as they take the 'deseverance' of the televisual to a higher order (the technological separation of the near and the seemingly close delivered by the image). What is produced is a condition of de-worlding: the shrinkage of one's world. What is being colonized is *time and attention*, as commanded by a created addictive relation, to a techno-functional mediated environment of flows, attractions and distractions enfolded by image compression (neo-televisual high-intensity short-lived optics). There will be no resistance to such development within the spatial conditions of techno-corporate privilege in a proto-fragmenting, or eventual fragmented, global order. Resistance from others outside this zone could be expected if their well-being is compromised or directly attacked. The form and consequence of this resistance is impossible to contemplate in the abstract. However, the interface between the techno-culture of the world corporate techno-elites and the displaced and abandoned, or the lifeworld of the adapting majority, is certain to be fraught.

***

What has just been outlined would challenge an agenda of contrapractice at the highest level. It would be a specific situated convergence of specific elements of the 'complexity of complexity', of the defuturing compound problem beyond any extant means and ability to be adequately grasped and represented. Yet it is a real possibility, and the prospect demands a response, and as such, a contrapractice. What makes this statement cogent and of substance is the empirical fact that the reactive nature of institutionalized politics across all ideologies and nations is demonstrably failing to comprehend the seriousness of the planetary compounding crises. That prefigurative and preventative action is an absolute imperative goes unrecognized. Effectively, all existing modes of political control are out of control in the context of what demands effort to attempt to create appropriate means of control. Fundamental to this situation is a crisis in imagination resulting in a failure to grasp and make present the complexity of the complexity of what threatens. There is a social and political sense of complexity, uncertainty and danger. But rather than this being confronted and engaged politically, it is recoiled against – complexity is not a marketable political commodity – the politician, especially the populist politician, poses simple solutions to reductively framed complex problems that 'the masses' can understand and connect to what they believe to be their self-interest. Not only do these 'solutions' not work, but they also contribute to masking the complexity of the actual problems to be addressed.

Contrapractice is not posed as the bringer of 'the solution', and a means to overcome the defuturing currently destined by the intertwined complexity compounding problem that threatens. But it is a means to respond to what is being ignored by failing political leadership, the politics upon which it is predicated, as well as the other claimants to delivering 'the future' – techno-corporate accelerationists bros and their hangers on.

So positioned contrapractice can take three forms: mitigation of the impacts of some defuturing practices; adaptively responding to conditions created by defuturing practices that cannot be solved or mitigated; and direct contestation with defuturing practices in the arena of the four ecologies that have been outlined.

Contrapractice: A responsive demand of the times

There is clearly a major temporal disjuncture between the compound problem as it unfolds and the perceptions and agency of political institutions. The former is moving quickly; the latter signs are almost indetectable. This implies a contrapractice has to act in time, which means in the medium of time and with a sense of urgency.

Contrapractice recognizes 'we' (in our difference), and our worlds, cannot continue to be as they are. It also recognizes that neither will change as a result of a mass voluntarist acts of transformation based upon populations gaining consciousness of the need to do so. Change will actually only happen if sufficient numbers of people 'remake otherwise' many of the practices that form 'our worlds of habitation' – so that in turn, they remake us. What this proposition rests on is that 'we' are the product of two formative agents: our genetic inheritance and the ontological designing of the materiality of our becoming (our ontogenesis). Everything from our environmental conditions, diet, parenting, physical activities, education, social customs and activities, occupation, tactile skills and more *are all constituted by practices*. Effectively, 'we' change if the practices that bring the ontological form of our being into being change. Clearly, this will not happen via a grand scheme of planned action, but as argued, it can happen if an organic contrapractice process is initiated, nurtured and generalized. The ambition is not a total transformation of everyone everywhere, but to create a sufficient critical mass to produce a milieu able to generate the momentum toward becoming futural (in difference) as a dominant condition for the adaptive majority – as they exist in engagement with the displaced and in tension with techno-elites. The trigger to effect change is conjunctural: it is that *between* the moment when confronting the criticality of the condition of 'our' being/being becomes unavoidable, *and* the moment when it becomes catastrophic.

What has been outlined will not stop population fragmentation, mass displacement and abandonment or the onto-technologically overdetermined techno-corporate elites as they retreat into protective environments, but it would posit decisive transformative agency within a diverse adaptive majority.

The magnitude of this task exceeds all others across all time and is multi-generational. Notwithstanding its magnitude (in the way outlined or variants), it is unavoidable if life, as currently understood, continues to be given value.

Contrapractice is not predicated upon a revolutionary idea, belief in a salvational force or an idealist vision – it does not promise a utopia. Rather, it simply asserts pragmatic action in the form of the labour of taking existing practices and remaking them to become means of Sustainment in conditions wherein defuturing is gaining momentum. Its potential is to make the seemingly impossible possible. In practical terms, it is within the capability of motivated practitioners, can be realized economically, but not painlessly, can span political differences, and with effort can be managed logistically (with the logic totally grounded in the foundation of reason, grasped, embraced and acted upon as an expression of collective interests). Such action requires generative political momentum to take it to a start line, and thereafter an ever-growing number of people finding their own way to turn their own practice to a futural contrapractice, with momentum and directionality overcoming an inevitable unevenness. While contrapractice can be conceptually elaborated and illustrated, its realization depends on it being recognized and acted in response by large numbers of practitioners (the critical mass) who see no other choice.

The agency of contrapractice exposes the poverty of the academy. It can be seen in a large array of theoretically sophisticated and insightful academics, with a high level of understanding of pressing contemporary issues, but whose work is completely devoid of *praxis*. Thus, they stay inside their academic bubble, forsaking the attempt to acquire political agency in worlds beyond tenured or contracted security. But then there is also that large number who function within the academy as 'casual educators' who have less to lose.

While the academy is the very place where one would have expected an informed and critical leadership to be educated, and a nation's culture to be advanced. But any potential for this has gone. In its place is the corporatization of the institution, ruled by its business model, delivering feedstock to the labour market and evaluated by the metric of graduate employment. Instrumentalized pedagogy has become hegemonic; clearly, there are exceptions, but they are few. Meanwhile, the political domain of public life is populated by politicians, leaders of industry and commerce, NGOs and institutions who increasingly display contempt for theory, contemporary critical thought and speculative ideas.

Another credible kind of education appropriate to the current planetary condition of criticality is needed. It cannot come from the attempt to create an alternative academy able to displace the academic status quo. The attempt to do this has been tried numerous times and has failed, as have attempts to radically reform existing curricula. Change from imperatives coming to the fore, in the face of the systemic defuturing breakdown, could, if there were numbers, posit contrapractice as a potential and credible action, able to trigger transformations exposing the necessity of Sustainment and action toward it. Education itself needs to become a contrapractice, which in turn brings contrapractice into a direct relation with the entire curriculum in terms of its ethos, content and purpose. It implies and requires a total revision of the very epistemological foundation and relational geometry of knowledge, historically and futurally, in response to the fundamental changes in planetary conditions, environmentally, geopolitically and politically, in the context of governance and the socio-cultural.

In a condition of deep planetary crisis, the politicization of knowledge would be essential, as would defining the futural role of the institution on the basis of a developed comprehension of the critical context of the 'complexity of the complexity' in which it was situated. Central to this task, and against this backdrop, would be an identification of possibilities and dangers.

Such a process of remaking would have to overcome the ruling instrumental paradigm, reconstitute the very project of the academy in ruins, and at least equal the scale and temporal reach of the Enlightenment's constitution of the modern university, plus recreate the practice of learning. How the institution would articulate with the displaced and their means of coping (or not), and the world making. As would the unavoidable issue of the world of the techno-corporate elites. Establishing a foundation of futural relational knowledge (not based on divisions, but relations of knowledge) would be a condition of operational functionality, and the means of setting institutional directions that deal with the question of knowledge and a world of fragmentation.

2   On Practice

Tony Fry

Existentially, practice is intrinsic to our species being and is enacted in purposely directed action. As such, it has been the means by which the fabricated worlds that we all occupy and engage in have been created over eons. Ontologically, practices are recursively transformative of ourselves and our world(s). As processes over time, they have been constantly expanded, disciplined, organized into specialisms, increased in complexity and changed as circumstances demanded. They span the formal and informal, the everyday and the totality of our species' productive endeavours. So contextualized, practices are constituted from acts of appropriation, instruction, innovation, development, self and organizational management and controlled application. Extending across culture and economy, the material and the immaterial, they gather (as in collecting together and comprehending) and mobilize a historical and futural transformative ability of processes, objects, environment, subjects – including practitioners themselves. Practices are exclusive, but this has not acted as a condition of limitation, as they are able to function in conditions of cooperation. At the same time, practices extending across defence, the spiritual, the pedagogic, economy, governance, law, physical and mental health, the social, agriculture, nutrition, transport and industry, the arts and more, have a long history of self, organizational, economic and governmental control: this, by imposed restrictions by practitioners themselves, guilds, educational, training, and professional organization accrediting bodies and by government laws and regulations.

Control over the independent agency of practitioners started to be systemically diminished by the management of labour in and by advance of modern capitalist industries. The auto industry was paradigmatic in pioneering such change.

Two forces of transformation converged. The first was the introduction of in-line production by Henry Ford in 1913, and then the five-dollar day in

1914. His actions were strategic: it meant industrial craft workers abandoning their skill and independence for a higher income. As a result, Ford was able to control the labour process and gain higher industry output via a designed production system. The second overlapping force started to emerge around the same time, with the publication of Frederick Winslow Taylor's *Principles of Scientific Management* in 1911. What it put in place was convergence between a technical and a managerial system of control, which established an enduring norm of industrial production. Both these developments were advanced by the introduction of operational management during the Second World War, which aimed to further increase the rate of production to meet the insatiable material demands of the war machine (and thereafter post-war industrial and civil reconstruction). Operational management brought to the equation a higher order of science, computation and logic of control. Stafford Beer was one of the leading thinkers of this 'innovation', and his work made connections that have prefigured current systems. He linked operational management with cybernetic means of managerial control, which in turn linked to developments in mathematical modelling and linear programming.[1] In turn, this prompted 'a flood of new algorithms and theoretical developments' in the 1950s.[2] What resulted was an ever-increasing level of automation, and with it a greater convergence between management, systems and supply chain logistics. This developmental trajectory has continued unabated and globally within the North and the South, including with the production management system of the South being managed by corporate headquarters in the North (Tesla, VW and Apple being prime examples).

By the mid-1970s, the relation between capital, labour practices and automation had become a critical concern. A swathe of publications made the history and consequences of these developments clear. Four of the most notable texts that evidence this history are: Harry Braverman, *Labour and Monopoly Capitalism* (which knits together the relations between labour and management, science and technology, monopoly capital, and the transformation of work and class); Pat Walker (ed.), *Between Labour and Capital* (which marked the rise of the 'professional managerial class', resulting in an expansion of the field of management and the diminishment of the power of organized labour); David Noble, *Forces of Production* (which registered the history of the rise of the means of systems of command and control enabled by automated technology); and Doreen Massey, *Spatial Division of Labour* (which put the changes of production, technology and labour into the global context of inequity).[3] These accounts of change took place alongside the rise of a powerful Japanese economy driven by automation, managerial systems and a highly disciplined

---

[1]   Maurice W. Kirby, *Operational Research in War and Peace* (London: Imperial College Press, 2003), 9–11.
[2]   Ibid., 14.
[3]   Harry Braverman, *Labour and Monopoly Capitalism* (New York: Monthly Review Press, 1974); Pat Walker (ed.), *Between Labour and Capital* (Brighton: Harvester Press, 1979); David F. Noble, *Forces of Production* (Oxford: Oxford University Press, 1986); and Doreen Massey, *Spatial Division of Labour* (London: Macmillan, 1984).

control of labour that influenced the West (not least by 'just-in-time mode' inventory management). This period of change also included the rise of China as an industrial power. Overall, this history, besides denoting major transformations of especially industrial and management practice, also produced, as will be shown, a considerable amount of new practice theory.

The march of the union between technology and management systems has not stopped. The proliferation of AI will further deplete independent practitioner practices. At the same time, on a planet of deeply fragmenting futures, circumstances will demand new, recovered practices, as well as contrapractices. This will certainly be so with populations who will have been displaced and abandoned, and in common with the majority of people globally, striving to adapt to a changed and changing biophysical environment and lifeworld. Their need recasts, elevates and extends the significance of practices of survival. It is against this backdrop that issues of how practice has been thought and how this thinking poses questions for contrapractice now need consideration.

PRACTICE REFRAMED

Initiative action comes before practice as it is objectified consciously.[4] The ordering of action to realize a specific end constitutes practice – a bird builds a nest, a squirrel hoards nuts, a beaver builds a dam, bees construct honeycombs, a farmer farms – these are practices. Once practice becomes conscious, learning to apply rule-governed action with intent becomes possible. Thereafter, practice becomes directional and evolves. Its evolution is a variable mixture of recurrent action, reflective change, refinement and modification.

Historically established practices acquire a given status. Technique, materials and context may change, but the territorial domain as a practice among practices mostly says the same, as does the perception of the practitioner, and what they do: a carpenter, accountant, architect, surgeon and so on connotes an occupational identity and a commonly understood functionality. In this respect, practice dominantly acts performatively and collectively to sustain the operation of the extant world. It follows that if worldly conditions need to change then practice has to be delinked from a replication of 'the same'. Fundamental re-directional change thus requires the transformation of practice and what it brings into being. Without this, in the current context of industrial societies, there is a continuity of the unsustainable being sustained. At present, at its most basic, practices currently fail to take responsibility for what they bring into situated worlds, consequently in time. Which is not the same as meeting

---

[4] Etymologically practice arrives from Ancient Greek *prāktikḗ* (practice, experience), *prāktikós* (practical), and from *prássō* (I do), passing to the Latin *prāctica* (practical affairs), to modern usage *praticare* (Italian), Practicar (Portuguese) and practice (English). A transposition of the Italian *praticare* to the English evokes the spirit of contrapractice, https://www.etymonline.com/.

performance and safety standards. Extreme examples, like nuclear weapons, giant open-cast mining bucket excavators and neurological chip implants may all meet object-based operational standards, but this does not mean *what they do* is safe, consequently, and thus futurally. Practice reifies intent, but so often what results is unintended. So many practices posit an endpoint, a product. But every product is a pro (forward) duct (connection). They are posited with a positive or negative destiny, open to being deflected by will or accident. So, while a practice in its conception may seek to determine a specific use and consequence, it can never fully do so. The oft reported use of a hammer, a car and a kitchen knife as a weapon in a crime are three examples that make the point. Likewise, laws, medication and financial instruments all equally have a history of intended and unintended misuse.

Theory arrives before practice as a means of foundational direction. For example, penal theory is predicated on punishment based on a moral principle of the duration of the punishment of incarceration being proportional to the severity of the crime committed. The theoretical proposition of incarceration is that it is an act of retribution that functions as a deterrence, and affords the possibility of rehabilitation. The efficacy of such theory remains open to question. Here, theory itself becomes an object of critical interrogation, as the history of criminology affirms and as seminal works like Michel Foucault's *Discipline and Punish* illustrate.[5]

Wayfinding a sense of practice

Practice theory (which is also called praxeology) is an area of social theory within anthropology and sociology that examines society and culture as it is operationally structured and exercises agency. Its conceptual roots are grounded in: structuralism – the fundamental concept of structure, within structural linguistics and anthropology,[6] and in the structure of literature within literary theory and culture.

Practice theory should not be confused with professional, academic and creative practices, theorizing their particular practice (with or without the influence of practice theory). Although this does illuminate a certain understanding of practice, it mostly fails to position practice in the world beyond an effect upon the practitioner (as agency and knowledge), and practice in the world as 'world formative'. So while practice theory needs to be acknowledged and engaged, contrapractice requires to be understood as not just challenging what

[5]   Michel Foucault, *Discipline and Punish*, trans. Alan Sheridan (Harmondsworth: Penguin Books, 1979).
[6]   Key thinkers in structural linguistics and anthropology are Ferdinand de Saussure (1857–1913), Jean Piaget (1896–1980) and Claude Lévi-Strauss (1908–2009); and in the structure of literature and literary culture, Roman Jakobson (1896–1982), Roland Barthes (1915–1980), Jacques Derrida (1930–2004) and Terry Eagleton (1943–).

many existing practices do (often by default sustaining the unsustainable) but also how they have been made sense of.

To engage in practice in general, a clear distinction needs to be made between social and material practice and what articulates them. This is not done by many theorists of practice who totalize claims of practice while actually addressing it as a specificity. Thus, for example, social practice is presented as *the* domain of practice, whereas it is itself a 'discursive practice' among others that equally have material consequences. For Foucault discursive practices are understood as expressive acts with material consequences that are operational and function within specific historical and contingent circumstances. It is in this context that they produce knowledge and posit meaning – specifically knowledge which is linked to (the exercise of) power. Discursive practice also 'systematically form the objects of which they speak'.[7]

So framed, practice as it will be presented here is seen to be material and the social, the everyday and specialized, the inculcated and the instructed, the active and the passive, the individual and institutional, voluntary and imposed. They extend across industries and professions, the tutored and the habitual, the discursive and the concealed, the experiential and the doctrinal, the performative and the contemplative – the extension and sub-division of such listing is suggestive of, but does not elucidate the complexity of the diversity of practice.

While such complexity is being recognized here, as said, there is no intention to engage in a microscopic exposition of specific practices. But rather to register a theoretical understanding of practice, as an agent in the formation of the materiality of the worlding (agency) of worlds as they future or defuture in their industrialized (rather than purely natural) hybridized materiality.

This ecology of this materiality, in varying degrees, enfolds design processes that contributed to understanding design beyond the circumscription [of] overtly designated design practices. Practice so broadly configured recognizes that social, political and economic practices are not independent from world-making/ unmaking, or material practices of fabrication in its widest sense. The relation between the one and the others is mediated by a variable mix of directive forces: habitus, desire, design, pragmatic conditions (from environmental circumstances), as well as political influences and economic imperatives, all of which, to a degree, inform the action and the situatedness of material practice. Yet in the growing condition of criticality of the 'complexity of complexity' of current planetary conditions, as has been indicated, there is insufficient grasp of consequences. Again, this underscores contrapractice coming from a critique and thereafter going to another kind of formulating and exercising of practice. It should be added that in the conditions of extreme complexity the demands upon contrapractice are not, and clearly cannot be, universally even, either within or between nations. Moreover, in conditions of global fragmentation and structural inequity, the demand for contrapractice would exponentially increase as the challenges to be faced become more serious.

---

[7]   Michel Foucault, *The Archaeology of Knowledge*, trans. A.M. Sheridan Smith (London: Tavistock Publications, 1985), 49.

The implication of what had just been outlined is that a temporal shift in the nature of defuturing is underway. Historically, the unconsidered consequences of the extractive power, productive output and environmental impacts of modernized and modernizing nations, with growing populations, have accelerated entropy (hence have initiated the planet's sixth extinction event). As a result, the driver of defuturing has shifted from the ongoing causality of the actions of industrialized societies to the actions of autonomous denaturalized systems that have gained a momentum of their own. Thus, the loss of biodiversity begets an ongoing loss; climate change impacts beget new impacts. Systemic ecological breakdowns and dysfunction likewise create a recursive dynamic. A feature of emergent conditions is an increase in unsolvable biological and climatic problems. As the horizon of finitude nears, the time for responsive action becomes ever more urgent. The form of this action has to be less concerned with the pursuit of solutions to intractable problems and more concerned with adapting to changing enviro-climatic, geopolitical, and socio-cultural conditions (environmental impacts will increase, as will geopolitical insecurity, global population growth and displacement). Instability will become normative. Existing practices are not conceived to respond to such situations; rather, they were formed by and for a 'world' predicated upon a productivist paradigm (growth in its widest and most specific sense). Whereas to become futural is, for instance, to have a futurally determined direction. But this will not arrive as a massive coordinated project of political transformation. Rather, it will come from an organic proliferation of projects and contrapractices.

In 'world making and unmaking', the adopted framing of practice is dominantly productivist, instrumental and defuturing. In contrast, the intent and outcome of contrapractice is to redirect and reconfigure such framing.[8] As François Jullien points out, action is unstable and unsustainable practices register this instability. They carry risk, and with it the possibility of creating unforeseen circumstances.[9]

Jullien also proceeds to critique the West's preoccupation with a particular form of action. In particular, the creation of efficiency: as it has the ability to impose, be mono-directional and negate complexity and difference – all in the service of productivism as it constitutes the core of capital accumulation. In doing so, as assigned 'productive' time, the distance between now and finitude is negated. The forces of defuturing have travelled under the banner of advancing the need for efficiency; this, not just as a means to speed the passage of progress, but as a value in itself.[10] As such, efficiency is embedded in a reductive

---

[8]   Immanuel Kant asked the question 'what is a frame' and answered 'the Parergon'. It is 'detached' and is outside the work it frames, and divides it from the milieu in which it is located. It is a hybrid of inside and outside and thus an object of betweenness (61–3), Jacques Derrida, *The Truth in Painting*, trans. Geoff Bennington and Ian McLeod (Chicago, The University of Chicago Press, 1987), 15–148.

[9]   François Jullien, *A Treatise on Efficacy*, trans. Janet Lloyd (Honolulu: University of Hawai'i Press, 2004), 9.

[10] Ibid., 120–36.

sensibility that eliminates all that is deemed not functional, especially within the creation and advancement of practices in the service of the capitalist mode of production. Efficiency is central, extolled and elemental to the productivist economy of acceleration.

Reiteration: reframed and redirected, practices have to have the ability to install transformative action that anticipates and acts against defuturing – an action that has been named as 'contrapractice'.

The mantra of contrapractices, in support of futuring, is not saving time, but making it. Contrapractice, so situated in the global context of the impetus of defuturing, is a particular *praxis* informed, as stated, by the negation of finitude (that *is* defuturing), and by the formation of new situated discursive practices.

What this means is that a specific contrapractice is conjuncturally constituted in a particular worldly setting against a practice/agency that is actively defuturing. In this respect, it is not brought to a context but a product of it, while being informed by knowledge and experience of the practice it is acting against. In doing so, its primary objective is to destroy, delegitimize and replace the practice it opposes, which means in operational terms: its logic; its epistemological basis; the deconstruction of its foundation; and, in theoretical and communicative terms, the authority of its discourse. At the same time, a contrapractice, as will be shown, fills the created void with its futural agency. Such actions may be social, economic or cultural; material or immaterial; new, adaptive or redirective. Such action is not the norm, and as Jullien has stated, the history of knowledge is vast; the history of action is slight.[11] The implication of what is being argued is that practice, at present and notwithstanding practice theory, has not been adequately thought out. However, such a claim has to be substantiated.

To gain a critically reflexive view of this constitutive environment of self and world becoming, a phenomenology of practice is needed, within which what underscores the plurality of the agency of forms of practice is made visible – this to inform contrapractice in a mobilization against practices that defuture. To progress this, six fields of interrogation of how practice has been thought and positioned will be considered, but prefigured with a brief historical and cultural overview. This, followed by a comment on four Western thinkers on practice: Pierre Bourdieu, Michel de Certeau, Peter Sloterdijk, Michel Foucault, and then four closing reframing notes – the first undercutting a Eurocentric perspective of practice as linked to the next three: *praxis*, praxeology and *metis*. In doing so, the case will be made for why the problematic of the Eurocentricity of practice theory needs to be displaced, and enabled to engage practice within the differences of worlds; this, opening other ways of thinking contrapractice.

A historical cultural overview

Writ large, the emergence and advancement of practices are indivisible from historicity and ethno-pluralization of the coming into being of our species. The

---

[11]   Ibid., 185.

prehistoric use of tools, well before the arrival of *Homo sapiens*, played a major ontological and cognitive role in hominoid development – including in brain size.[12] The history of practice, as a category (*practisen*), is deeply embedded in Eurocentric thought from the late fourteenth century onward. Phenomenologically, practice is obviously present in all cultures, but differentially enacted within their cosmologies and their cosmotechnics.

For example, the Chinese understanding of practice was not theoretically formative of values and conduct, but resulted from adapting to the propensity of circumstances. As such, it was not predicated on making judgement or taking action (exercising a practice). Rather, it focussed on the efficacy of behaviour and was determined by the extent to which a person refrains from trying to manage things.[13] In this respect, conforming to how things have been produced (including practices themselves) is how things are managed. Tradition is recursive, yet accommodates graduated change. Likewise, the ontological repetition of a practice adjusts to circumstantial change. 'It is enough to go along with change, change that is forever regulation, change that helps create harmony'.[14]

Historically, the development of practices follows winding paths. Numerous examples illustrate this; for instance, the study of Alchemy has a history spanning more than four thousand years and is indivisible from the history of chemistry. It was practiced globally, including in Egypt, Greece, Byzantium, India and across many Islamic nations, as well as in East Asia. Another example is the *Yinz Zao Fa Shi*, a major work detailing building construction practices in China in 1103 CE. Diverse examples are presented in Joseph Needham's twenty-seven volume *The History of Science and Civilisation in China* that records vast numbers of practices across the sciences, arts, crafts and industries. There is equally a large literature of the history of practice in the West, including Vannoccio Biringuccio's *Pirotechnica*, a study of the emergence of metallurgy produced in 1540 CE. It was followed a few years later by Georgus Agricola's influential *DeMetallica* (1566 CE) a major study of mining, iron making, associated technical appliances and practices and chemistry.

In every case, 'progress' was the result of the expected and unexpected, intent and accident, deviation and return to the winding path.

The oriental and occidental partly converged on the founding moment of the theorizing of practice in the fourth-century BCE. Aristotle stated practice to be 'the moral foundation of the good', while Confucian philosophy defined the good as the materiality of efficacy reality as a given.[15] Such thinking has not been assigned to the arcane, but survives in the present. Neo-Aristotelian moral philosopher Alister McIntyre in *After Virtue* argues that the 'good' needs to be seen

---

12 Fry, *Becoming Human*; Stringer, *The Origin of Our Species*.
13 François Jullien, *The Propensity of Things, Towards a History of Efficacy in China*, trans. Janet Lloyd (New York: Zone Books, 1995).
14 Ibid., 265.
15 Ibid., 264.

as the result of action goal-oriented practices.[16] While François Jullien explains the materialism of efficiency as a condition that is good, emanates from efficacy as a quality and result of practice.[17] Insofar as practice, to be, requires rules, derived from theory (prefigured action, from simple to complex), the nature of the theory is central to the intended consequences of the practice. In considering the relation between theory and practice, Kant, in an argument presented in 1793, forcefully pointed out that practice, as one form of action, once studied on the basis of having been informed by theory, transmutes to *praxis*. Moreover, if practice is informed by bad theory, it 'can aid the corruption of human life and human society'.[18] Defuturing arrives by and as bad practices, and links to particularly bad practices that have a direct relation to knowledge models and organizational processes set in motion within the industrial revolution.[19]

In 1675, at the dawn of the industrial revolution, the French Academy of Science undertook a systematic study of more than two hundred work practices and techniques, from mechanics to baking. Then, with the arrival of the Industrial Revolution, vast numbers of existing practices were modernized and extended while new ones were developed. Many of them were documented in Andrew Ure's massive two volume *Dictionary of Arts, Manufacture and Mines*, of 1853. This work reflected an interest in labour practice and process that were to become especially associated with Karl Marx (who was already influenced by Ure's book *The Philosophy of Manufacture* of 1835).

By the mid-nineteenth century, the study of work practices became a practice in its own right – this, made famous by, as already registered, Frederick Winslow Taylor, who in 1890, while chief engineer of the Midvale Steel Works in Philadelphia, studied the labour process of skilled and unskilled workers, his aim was to gain knowledge to increase their efficiency. The influence of his research, published as *The Principles of Scientific Management* massively accelerated productivity in the USA and the industrial world globally – especially when it was linked to *in-line production* introduced by Henry Ford in 1913, then later when linked to the *gang system* introduced by Alfred Sloan at General Motors in the early 1920s. The contemporary system of fully automated industrial production and its propensity for accelerated defuturing was prefigured by this moment.[20]

The transformation of industrial work practices in the first quarter of the twentieth century not only changed the means of production but the nature of work itself. Not only did a huge number of workers with craft skills abandon them

[16] Alister McIntyre, *After Virtue* (South Bend: University of Notre Dame Press, 1981), 191.
[17] Jullien, *A Treatise on Efficacy*, 120–1.
[18] Jeffrey, G. Murphy, 'Kant on Theory and Practice', *Theory and Practice* 37 (1995): 47–78, https://www.jstor.org/stable/24219524 (accessed 12 March 2023).
[19] Resilient ecologies can absorb damage and recover. Likewise, Sustainment does not imply the total elimination of defuturing action, but rather a continuous ability to recover from, and contain, it.
[20] This history is addressed in detail by Fry Tony, *Defuturing: A New Design Philosophy* (London: Bloomsbury, 2021).

for the higher wages paid to semi-skilled workers on production lines (which became the manufacturing paradigm for scores of industries) but the culture and view of the function of work changed – including changing notions of skill sensibility, and the nature of practice (in sum, the worker's habitus). In turn, this generated a huge increase of industrial production, while accelerating an expansion of mass marketing and consumption, and consequently transformed the culture of everyday life. These developments expanded a whole range of service sector *job practices* in areas like advertising, marketing, office work, sales, as well as in finance and law.

The more one considers practice, the more apparent it becomes that it not only fundamentally is a means of making an intended material or immaterial object present – via a disciplined and ordered recursive act – but it also registers worldly transformation by a continuous process of mostly imperceptible change. To grasp this is to comprehend the rationale and potentiality of contrapractice. Practice extends across all cultures, notwithstanding how it is understood, named and employed. All of us are a product of the practices to which we have been exposed and have employed. We, ontologically, are among those things it brings into being. Practice constitutes our capabilities and shapes much of our individuation and identity as 'we' create and adopt it.

The historical presence of practice touches everyone. The material and social, economic materiality of practice is part of the fabric of all of our lives, as 'we' are implicated as producers and recipients of its defuturing and futuring agency. While modernity's appropriation and creation of practices transformed work rather than reaching a hiatus, automated transformations of labour processes, advanced technologies and the rise of new service industries have all further accelerated increasingly sophisticated and complex worldly change. Combined with speeded extractionism, increased productivity and hyper-consumption, this material plethora of affordances has added to an entropic propensity intrinsic to defuturing. This means that a response to this situation, one that advances Sustainment, becomes increasingly pressing. Contrapractice has the potential to be a significant response to this need, but it requires an expansive uptake and enormous momentum. Such demand, no matter how challenging, must be placed in the realm of the tangible and possible.

(WAYS OF) FRAMING PRACTICE

As indicated, the fundamental aim and agency of contrapractice is to eliminate all practices that defuture. In order to do this, the nature of practice needs to be better understood. To do this, the limitations of how practice has been theorized requires to be exposed. With this intent, consideration will be given to the four theorists already mentioned: Bourdieu, De Certeau, Sloterdijk and Foucault.

Bourdieu: Recognition and misrecognition

Pierre Bourdieu is seen as one of the most significant theorists of practice. Importantly, he recognized that everyday practices are not purely consciously directed and mediated by language, but are social, tacit and embodied.[21] However, there are significant issues arising from his understanding of practice that are especially evident in his *Outline of Theory of Practice* and *Logic of Practice*. From the perspective of an [imminent] contrapractice, his exposition and influential address to the concept of habitus present problems.

Essentially, habitus animates practice as it is situationally employed. The conditions that form a contrapractice (the situated, epistemological, political, cultural and pragmatic) are similar to those that constitute a habitus, except that habitus is not politically directed. What is at stake here is not the significance and existence of habitus, but the relation between how it is formed, understood and functions in the underpinning of defuturing practices.

Bourdieu viewed practice with a certain ambivalence. For example, he opened chapter five of his *Logic of Practice* by saying, 'It is not easy to speak of practices other than negatively – especially those practices that are seemingly most mechanical, most opposed to the logic of thought and discourse'.[22] For Bourdieu 'has a logic which is not the logic of the logician' – a statement rests upon a totalizing position that is essentially abstract and Eurocentric.[23] The notion that it is possible to speak universally for all practice is erroneous. However, the most influential aspect of his engagement with practice is what he had to say about habitus.[24]

The key to understanding the way Bourdieu explains habitus is detailed in his *Outline of Theory of Practice* and thereafter reiterated in the *Logic of Practice*.

He presents habitus as a result of a formal and an informal induction into rules, conventions and actions of conformity; as such, it has a determinist bias and while able to deal with contradiction, it cannot accommodate resistance. As indicated, the tendency of habitus is to reproduce 'the same'. Notwithstanding his anthropological history, Bourdieu's work, as said, is Eurocentric and registers a lack of recognition of difference, with the exception of an overarching concern with class, across his entire oeuvre. Effectively, what Bourdieu constructed with habitus was a model that could not be easily accommodated during the time of its introduction. It produced a recoil before becoming influential,[25] but now

---

[21] For more detail here see point 1, Appendix 1.
[22] Pierre Bourdieu, *The Logic of Practice*, trans. Richard Nice (Stanford: Stanford University Press, 1992), 80.
[23] Ibid., 86. For more detail here see point 2, Appendix 1.
[24] Bourdieu goes on to further qualify practice see point 3, Appendix 1.
[25] It was deemed to be very deterministic, functionalist and lacking the ability to accommodate and respond to social change.

is problematic in this age of digital culture and social media as supplementary inculcation, along with contested notions of gender and identity, and pluriversal cultures in growing conditions of involuntary migration. Habitus so resituated is not redundant but begs being retheorized, as cultural difference, fluidity and tensions are increasing in many urban centres globally in conditions of discontinuity that diminish its explanatory agency in its current dominant form. As societies and populations become increasingly fragmented, and with climate change-driven migration destined to dramatically increase, conditions of sociocultural discontinuity will arrive and diminish the explanatory ability of habitus as it is currently understood – this as a mode of transmission of knowledge/practice in a milieu of relative stability.

Such a situation of change places many practices in conditions of growing insecurity and contestation, as well as of unrestrained appropriation and pragmatic adaptive innovation. The ensuing milieu undercuts Bourdieu's understanding of the dynamics of power via his notion of 'doxa', as it combines orthodox and heterodox norms and beliefs and common understandings as they are contested in 'competing discourses'.[26]

Fundamentally, Bourdieu's thinking acknowledges that the gaining of habitus is indivisible from inter-social engagement and individuation.[27] However, the associative milieu of past encounter (environments, products (material and cultural), practices, skills and knowledge and social formations) is now overlayed with another order of complexity. This does not make habitus redundant, but it does require revision. Futures (from workplaces to biophysical environments) are now more unstable and unpredictable; the techno-social, the communication domain and media have changed (thus, so has how 'the world', social interaction and knowledge are mediated and engaged). Indivisible from these changes are the impacts of rapid technological developments and transformations of the conditions and 'nature' of being. Gilbert Simondon understood such change as 'continuous genesis' whereby being is disrupted in its becoming – ontologically, individuation and habitus overlap in/as the ongoing becoming of being.[28] However, as is already evident, unstable conditions of being are creating problematic psycho-social conditions of individuation (from almost a now innate tension of life lived in a state of heightened uncertainty to the impact of psychotechnologies). Effectively, practice produces a replicable effect of some kind (change of movement, function of system, object, image, sound) in the world, together with an ongoing incremental, accumulative transformation of the practitioner (be it physical, cognitive, tactile or psycho-social and dispositional, all producing an ontological condition of perceptible, but mostly imperceptible, continuous change[29]). Difference exists here as a matter

26   Bourdieu, *Outline of A Theory of Practice*, 168.
27   For a further critique of habitus see point 4, Appendix 1.
28   Gilbert Simondon, 'The Genesis of the Individual', in *Incorporations*, edited by Jonathan Crary and Sanford Kwinter (New York: Zone Books, 1992), 297–319.
29   See point 5, Appendix 1 on the restrictive way Bourdieu viewed 'things' and change.

of degree and emphasis between what is intended to be brought into being and the actuality and effect of what is created.

Contrapractice, practice, habitus

In conditions of viability, habitus constituted in the establishment and operation of contrapractices is a means by which contrapractice becomes naturalized, and thus organic. But neither habitus nor contrapractice can arrive naturally. To exist, any future union of their agency requires an overall political project from a critical mass of the global population striving to become futural in a geopolitically fragmenting world. Thus positioned, habitus needs to be rethought, revised and liberated from Bourdieu. In particular:

1   Bourdieu's binary relational/mechanical distinctions are too crude and do not accommodate *the complexity and diversity of contemporary immaterial practices*

2   *Historically, forms of* habitus cannot deal with the arrival of the breakdown of clear distinctions, of those between nature/culture, artificial/natural, biology/technology.[30]

3   Bourdieu qualifies the habitus as 'the durability installed generative principle of regulated improvisations produces practices which tend to reproduce the regularities immanent in the objective conditions of their production'. He states this indicating a situation 'defined by the cognitive and motivating structures making up the habitus'.[31] *In this context, habitus emanating from contrapractice would establish and replicate the adaptive conditions of another and futural ground of 'the regularities immanent in the objective conditions of their production'.*[32]

4   Bourdieu continually subverted his empirical bias with a subjective inference. But also, as a 'product of history' that produces 'individual and collective practices'.[33] *In this context, habitus emanating from contrapractice formed in the present would essentially act against habitus extending the practices of the defuturing element of the status quo.*

5   Habitus functions as 'the product of a work of inculcation and appropriation as necessary in order for those products of collective history … objective structures … to succeed in reproducing themselves more or less completely, in the form of dispositions'.[34]

[30]   For more critique here see point 4, Appendix 1.
[31]   Bourdieu, *Outline of A Theory of Practice*, 78.
[32]   Bourdieu's understanding of the relation of habitus to production is present, but not perceived, see point 6, Appendix 1.
[33]   Bourdieu, *Outline of A Theory of Practice*, 82.
[34]   Ibid., 85.

In this context, habitus emanating from contrapractice would be an overcoming, not a reproducing.

6   Bourdieu provides examples of both objective structures and dispositions. It is through habitus that 'the structure which has produced it governs practice, not by the processes of mechanical determinism, but through the mediation of the orientations and limits it assigns to the habitus' operation of invention'.[35] *By implication, and futurally, habitus is not fixed, but fluid – it changes with circumstances.*

7   Habitus is gained from information transfer, formal and informal instruction, dialogue and a great deal of observation informing an imitation of observed action. There is never a pure transmission, for all communication is transformed in its circumstantial and experiential process of mediation – *this holds true.*

8   Habitus results from lived experience grounded in 'trial and error'.[36] *But it is now equally, and will increasingly be, a product of the experience of a response to 'crisis and disaster'.*

9   As a process, habitus acts to install 'generative principles' of 'regulated improvisation'. The resulting practices 'relating to the objective structure defining the social conditions of the production of habitus', and its conditions of operation.[37] *Such a process would futurally install circumstantially reactive pragmatic adaptation.*

10 None of this is a product of conscious acquisition; it comes from what Bourdieu called 'learned ignorance' in which knowledge of principles arrives via the gaining of practical knowledge[38] and by pedagogic action[39] – education is seen as an inductive and appropriative event. *In this context, habitus emanating from contrapractice requires exposure to an inculcated/existential learning, and gaining deployable knowledge, of defuturing.*

Other perspectives

Three other theorists of practice will be considered: Michel de Certeau, Peter Sloterdijk and Michel Foucault.

The focus of de Certeau is upon: change and the everyday; who considers the environment of change, and the transformation of the self. Sloterdijk gives special attention to change of the self. Both thinkers are addressed respectively in Appendices 2 and 3, while Michel Foucault is considered briefly below. They, and

---

35   Ibid., 95.
36   Ibid., 88.
37   Ibid., 78.
38   Ibid.
39   Ibid., 63.

Bourdieu, all need to be read and viewed against the unfolding crisis of climate change, population displacement and associated geopolitical fragmentation.

The arriving conditions of change are going to reconfigure the ground of everyday life everywhere by degree (the propensity to retain an attachment to 'normality' notwithstanding). The very ground of emancipatory politics will be/is being shattered. One of noticeable example will be that discourse of decoloniality, which will be overwhelmed by the scale and consequence of the displacement and abandonment of dominantly 'postcolonial' populations

Michel Foucault and discursive practices

For Foucault, discursive practices are understood as expressive acts with a material consequence, that are operational and function within specific historical, specific and contingent circumstances. Like habitus, they have particular salience for contrapractice. As such, and in this context, they produce knowledge and posit meaning – specifically knowledge which is linked to power. Discursive practices, for example, 'systematically form the objects of which they speak'.[40] A lecture is a discursive practice (one now being rendered unfashionable in education). So characterized, it is not merely signs, language and utterances but a practice with an 'enunciative function presented in a statement' (the environment in which signs exist).[41] It is not understood linguistically but operationally – as with 'laws of possibility, rules of existence' for that which the discourse names.[42]

David Beer provides an illuminating digression and states: in considering Foucault's focus on the conditions that afford such a discourse, and the transformations it produces, he says that it 'is helpful at least in beginning to see how we might be interested in the very concept or notion of the algorithm and the way that the discourse framing their material presences may themselves afford transformations, shape fields and reveal something of the conditions through which that discourse is elaborated'.[43] Drawing from Foucault, he acknowledges, 'discursive practices that are intermediary between words and

---

[40]   Foucault, *The Archaeology of Knowledge*, 49.

[41]   Ibid., 88.

[42]   Ibid., 91. By implication, enunciation is by the discourse, not the subject: in doing so it privilege's structure and negates consciousness. Law, as a domain of discursive practice, does care who 'you' are, or what 'you' are aware of. The knowledge from which it is constituted, as exercised in discourse, is power. And this power is structural. Discursive practice so understood enabled Foucault to examine the history of regimes of power, inscribed in agency of their particular practices, this as operationalized by their discourse. Rather than just registering this by revisiting his well-known writing on, for instance, the clinic, discipline, sexuality, discursive practice can be placed in the present to amplify its particular contemporary significance, by situating 'the algorithm' in and as its context.

[43]   David Beer, 'The Social Power of Algorithms', *Information, Communication & Society* 20, no. 1 (2017): 1–13, 9, https://doi.org/10.1080/1369118X.2016.1216147 (accessed 10 March 2023).

things', which he sees as providing 'an approach to algorithms from which we might explore the relations and potential disconnects located in the discursive practices residing and intermediating between the algorithm as a thing and the algorithm as a word'.[44]

Algorithmic technology is now an unavoidable world-transforming agent and part of the advancement of a deterministic technological ecology that heralds the hegemony of an instrumental sensibility wherein function is a liminal horizon of imagination. This condition of limitation is not brought to technology; it is the product of the cultural technosphere. Beer tells us that 'Algorithmic decisions are depicted as neutral decisions, algorithmic decisions are understood to be efficient decisions, algorithmic decisions are presented as objective and trustworthy decisions, and so on'.[45] As this, they represent the objectification of reason, as rational and appear as being independent from the agency that employs them, which can be benign or malevolent, visible or invisible. They undo the historical illusion that the user is in full command of the tools they use, whereas all tools have ontological (designing) consequences for all who use them from the inception of our species to today. For good or ill, tools can change our physical being, produce cognitive change, end our will in ways that future or defuture our worlds, ourselves and our others. But an algorithm, not posed as a tool, but as an instrument of discursive practice, is devoid of the illusion of command; it, to reiterate, 'does not care who "you" are, or what "you" are aware of'.

The notion is that the 'algorithm' is now taking on its own force. As this, it is an evocative shorthand for the power and potential of calculative systems; this, because they 'can think more quickly, more comprehensively and more accurately than humans'.[46] To enable this to happen, the enablers of the technology, and to extend its power, employ a deceit. Using AI, they simulate a human presence to 'humanize' the interface. This is not just an action to make the engagement 'user-friendly', but it is the ontological designing of the acceptance of the onward march of such technology, and to weaken resistance to it. Rather than seeing such action as conspiratorial, it is more an action of the ontological constitution of a particular habitus.

Algorithms are 'deep technology': they are a directive and they reify their inscribed epistemological foundational force within a recursive cybernetic system. As these, algorithms represent the full mechanization of discursive practice. Increasingly, the 'advanced' technological enclaves of especially the Global North, remove any doubt 'that man's language (langues), his unconscious and his imagination are governed by laws of structure'.[47]

In addressing discursive practice, Foucault showed that language, word, sign, and code are all action – 'they do something'. The nature of what discursive practice now does – fifty years after he elaborated his argument – is enacted in

44   Ibid.
45   Ibid., 11
46   Ibid., 11.
47   Foucault, *The Archaeology of Knowledge*, 201.

the grammar of directive big data and algorithmic ordering, which are massively extending their power by ever higher levels of technological incorporation. The application of these economic and cultural informational technologies is on a huge scale, industrially, commercially and within everyday life – from banking to the supermarket, and from medicine to the war machine. They accelerate accelerationism, advance a seeming onward march toward singularity, and function in the service of defuturing, and yet the level of critical concern and inquiry is minimal. Why? Because they are informed by a major lesson learnt about techno-power/knowledge: it places power behind an interface as the desevered (what is close removes all sight of what is near namely: system, network and supporting infrastructure). The profundity of technology now, as the displacement and replacement of metaphysics, as the political, is enormous, but likewise recognition of this transmutation is minimal, not least among the political class.

Contemporary global enviro-climatic circumstances are overriding past understandings of the geometry of governmentality and territoriality.[48] Mass displacement, already prefigured, will vastly increase an abandoned segment of the global population who will be disarticulated from the infrastructure of the modern world. They will destabilize inscribed structures of control (like national borders) and mechanisms of control (the ability to manage migration by regulation and civil and military powers). The reconfiguration of the geopolitics of space as reconfigured is now underway.

The inhabitable and controlled, the inhabitable and contested and the uninhabitable and abandoned – again reiterating – territorially and globally are all elemental to the geometry of the future-present. Space is going to be considerably and unevenly exposed to defuturing by anthropogenically enhanced climate change impacts everywhere and over a protracted expanse of time. And again: the stress placed on environments, economies, food security, civil order and everyday life will be huge.

Contrapractice and a non-Western perspective

Contrapractice so positioned is not that to be created from scratch but is rather that which was, and already is. Two examples make the point.

Yi, the first example, is the ancient Chinese notion that names conduct against/counter to imposed social norms of compliance. *Yi* 'cannot be associated with the sort of order achieved by the imposition of antecedent patterns upon events'.[49] In contrast, it is a form of conduct 'bestowing' fundamental meaning; to 'concrete circumstances'.[50] In doing so, it 'enables people to integrate themselves

---

[48] Gilles Deleuze, 'Postscript on the Societies of Control", *October* 59 (1992): 3–7, *JSTOR*, http://www.jstor.org/stable/778828 (accessed 2 May 2023).

[49] David L. Hall and Roget T Ames, *Thinking Through Confucius* (New York: State University of New York Press, 1987), 105.

[50] Ibid.

into the cosmic order and to participate in an essentially moral universe'.[51] As this it bridges the self and the collective, and opens the way to a right-ness of governance. What is being identified comes down to an indivisible disposition of self and the collective as a realization that defines becoming 'human' as a created, rather than given, condition of being. Seen via contrapractice, *Yi* represents action against de-humanization (a likely consequence of the conditions that abandonment of displaced people will produce).

The second example is cosmotechnics. The epistemological basis of practices of making is not just inculcated in forms of practically applied knowledge to realize individuated objectives. Rather, making is the enactment of the cosmological order. As such, it is not abstracted and reified and expressed as an articulated capability (as with a skill, habitus, craft or facility). Rather, it is who you are and what you do within your culture and historically enabled role. In this respect, the cosmology of the culture does not exist as a commanding narrative, but in the cosmologically imbued practices by which the lifeworld is constituted and replicated practically, socially, spiritually and ritually. It is the fundamental technique of the same becoming futural (unlike 'tradition', which is an elemental supplement of a lifeworld).

CLOSING NOTES

1 On *Praxis*

The meanings of *praxis* are myriad. The aim here is to work through a modest list and arrive at a view of *praxis* appropriate to (bring to) contrapractice. At the most general, *praxis* is understood as a condition of relationality, that is situated, complex and dynamic. It spans a specificity that can be positioned technologically, socially and politically. It is also seen in the context of a relation between being and things. As such, *praxis* is articulated to contemplative thought, calculation, practice, way of making, brought to things and thereafter the consequence of the nexus of materiality and the ethico-political.

For Marx, the term was posited with a particular form directed at a politically informed practice. To undertake and freely participate in action to engage and advance *praxis* is indivisible to changing the self and, in a politically affirmative way, the world as occupied. In contrast, for Heidegger, *praxis* has multiple meanings clustered around 'concernful dealing'.[52] So viewed, it is a condition of engagement of seeing and acting that also implies *poiesis* (contemplative engagement in making) as directed by *phronesis* (practical wisdom and sound judgement). In so doing, *praxis* is taken beyond practice/practical use, political and moral action.[53] So qualified, *praxis* is a defining character of the ontology of

[51]   Roger Ames, *The Art of Rulership* (New York: State of New York Press, 1994).
[52]   Martin Heidegger, *Being and Time*, trans. John Macquarrie and Edward Robinson (Oxford: Blackwell, 1962), 68.
[53]   McNeill, *The Glance of the Eye*, 63–4.

pragmata (things) that are produced by concernful dealing (like, for example, craft skills). Thereafter, such things are engaged in the world concernedly. As a result of this, *praxis* and *poiesis* converge.

The relation between the agency of things, as positioned with the potential to be agents of worldly concern, is realized if engaged by beings exercising and displaying concernful dealings (*poiesis*). *Praxis* so positioned links to *theoria* as it makes the form of worldly engagement perceptibly clear. In turn, this connects back to *phronesis* as understood by Aristotle[54] – it is not science or art, but the ability to reason 'with regards to what things are good or bad for man, for themselves and others'. As such, practical wisdom depends on deliberation, as viewed as the highest intellectual virtue.[55] For Jullien, this thoughtfulness is understood as prudence.[56] For design, to bring things into being concernfully means understanding their ontological agency, and this implies deeming design as *praxis*.

In simple terms, what all this means is that acting with concern and care becomes a condition of being, in a worldly sense, by dealing with things futurally in modest or in expansive futural ways. So understood, it follows that praxis is elemental to being careful, to care for the self and as such it folds into contrapractice in the advancement of Sustainment. By implication, so positioned *praxis* is counter to carelessness, the unsustainable and defuturing and expresses an imperative that commands action.

2 On Praxeology (*Praxis* + *Logos*)

In general terms, praxeology is presented as the study of human behaviour, specifically in the form of practice. It is rooted in Aristotle's moral philosophy of 'the good' and its relation to *theoria* and *praxis* (here as contemplative thought + experiential action) as constitutive of a practice. Bourdieu's theory in sociology has been deemed praxeological.[57] The generative sources of habitus, and what they constituted, became seen as a sphere of complex and directive human activity. So viewed, it specifically influenced the development of action research. Habitus provided the basis to explore the disposition, habits, perceptions, understandings and behaviours that an individual enacts in diverse social settings. Praxeology also has another and earlier and influential history. This was created by the Austrian economist Ludwig von Mises, who applied praxeology to the study of economics, specifically in relation to choices made

---

54   Aristotle, *The Nicomachean Ethics*, trans. David Ross (Oxford: Oxford University Press, 1991), 142–3.
55   Ibid., 142.
56   Jullien, *A Treatise on Efficacy*, 5.
57   Clare Rigg, 'Praxeology', in the *Sage Encyclopaedia of Action Research*, edited by D. Cogh Lan and M. Brydon-Miller (Thousand Oaks, California: Sage, 2014).

in the context of human economic consumptive activity as made in a capitalist free market context.[58]

3 Metis

Metis names strategic manoeuvring as it takes advantage of what is opportunistically found in prevailing circumstances that can't be overcome by brute force.[59] De facto, it informs subversion and grey war. At its extreme, it will not stop at any means to achieve its objective. It was conceived but underdeveloped by the Greeks (as seen in the deceit practiced by Odysseus), who nonetheless deemed it to be an ultimate weapon. It is akin to the strategies of deception and deceit presented in Sun Tzu's *Art of War*, while Michel de Certeau understood it as 'a principle of economy: to obtain the maximum number of effects from the minimum force'.[60]

Politically, an adaptive form of *metis* underpins the development of a strategic instrument of contrapractice. It opens an entry point to change, by redirection and elimination, that destroys, not by brute force but by means that secure an abandonment of the means of defuturing. Specifically, one needs to be able to clearly identify and understand the discursive practices (as with accelerationism) that serve the advance of defuturing. Obviously, this becomes a project in its own right, as does the subsequent creation of redirective practices.

[58] Ludwig von Mises, *Praxeology and History*, https://mises.org/library/human-action-0/html/, 996, 6–38 (accessed 10 February 2023). See also, L. S. Moss, 'Harmony, Conflict, and Culture: An Essay About the Praxeological Ideas of Ludwig von Mises', *Cultural Dynamics* 5, no.3 (1992), https://doi.org/10.1177/092137409200500 (accessed 14 March 2023).

[59] Jullien, *A Treatise on Efficacy*, 8.

[60] Sun Tzu, *The Art of War*, trans. Thomas Cleary (Boston: Shambhala, 1988); Michel de Certeau, *The Practice of Everyday Life*, trans. Steve Rendall (Berkeley: California University Press, 1984), 82.

3 Contrapractice in the End Times

Tony Fry

The destiny of every individual life is crisis – to be, is to be destined to die. But now something has changed. Life itself has been cast into an epochal crisis – a premature terminal condition, named here as a 'compound problem', that has started to arrive. The expected life of the sun is ten billion years. But sometime between now and this moment, planetary life will be extinguished. The consequences of collective actions of the auto-destructiveness of the planet's industrial societies are bringing this fate ever closer, and at speed. It follows that there is an absolute imperative to slow down our species' unthinking and unchecked propensity to destroy the very conditions upon which it, and life in general, depends.

WORLDLY TRANSFORMATION AND ADAPTIVE FUTURES

The impacts of 'our' actions are not uniform. The most vulnerable populations are the planet's poor; they are also per capita among the least destructive. However, they are the most circumstantially exposed to the forces of negation – they face the prospect of displacement in vast numbers. The wealthy and the privileged, again per capita, are most destructive, but believe they can gain immunity from defuturing impacts by retreating into technologically protective environments. The remaining large, diverse and growing global population are starting to realize that they have little choice but to find ways to adapt, in their varied ways of life, to coming conditions. Contrapractice collectively names this adaptive activity. At the most fundamental level, it recognizes that there needs to be a correlation between the performative qualities of the practice and the performative attributes of what it brings into being over time. The aim of contrapractice has to be redundancy. Retrospectively, this will be realized by a history of practices of adaptation and repair. Projectively, the performative qualities of what is created need to be based upon the demands presented by the coming future, rather than just the ones of the immediate imperatives.

To be futural is to counter the defuturing of 'the time of being', and in doing so, *make time* (by negating the forces of negation). Effectively, the dawn of the Heat Age of an unknown duration has begun.[1] Clearly, dealing with it is no simple instrumental act as 'we', differentially, are elemental to 'the problem'. It goes to the very essence of our being as an auto-destructive species. To undertake such a redirective task requires that a new epoch be constituted by and for the displaced and the majority, this by responsive and pragmatic contrapractices ontologically transformative of 'us', and the environmental conditions that 'we' myopically and carelessly created.

The central premise of contrapractice is that: *essentially, nothing changes unless practice itself changes (which implies the ontology of their creators, and what they create, also changes), with the intent of practice directed against that which defutures, and towards what futures (Sustainment).*

Life is now lived in plain sight of an unfolding disaster of unimaginable proportions that is not a hypothetical dystopic projection but rather is a data-underscored and materially driven unfolding reality. What is so remarkable about this overall situation is the extent to which it is being ignored not just by the world's political leadership but also by most of the planet's intellectuals. They mostly stay entrenched in the comfort zone of the division of knowledge of their disciplines and in their career-invested conditions of academic confinement. There are exceptions, but they are a tiny minority of scattered alienated thinkers. The majority function in a condition of, and with, disassociative theory – the appearance of function belies deep dysfunction of thinking that fails to think beyond its horizon of restricted interests.

The scale and danger of the planetary critical situation is still mostly unacknowledged politically, economically and culturally. In large part because the people being most impacted are still the poor, marginal and powerless to effect change, while the rich and powerful are invested in the continuation of the status quo – this with the complicity of the planet's major political 'leaders'. This situation is changing, although the political consequences are still not being appropriately registered – the grip of the status quo, and its reactionary cohort still remains strong, and an acceleration toward a terminal defuturing end-point continues. But the breakdown that is a geopolitical fragmentation looms. One of its major propellent causes, 'the Heat Age', is underway – drought, fire, floods, coming sea level rises and extreme weather are all going to massively increase, and the cost of damage, and the number of people displaced, will be enormous. The likely prospect is that it will create a huge international economic

---

[1]   The most dramatic event of hominoid existence was the Ice Age. It lasted 2.4 million years, decimated their numbers, and forced migration to other parts of the world in search of refuge from the cold and food. Our species emerged in its latter stages 200,000 plus years ago. Human settlement only began at its end, 12,000 years ago. The epochal moment of the present, the dawn of 'the Heat Age', could be of a similar magnitude if a condition of total climate chaos forms as a result of inaction.

crisis. Major cities will be lost, some nations will completely fail, many national borders will break down and conflict will increase. Rather than doomsaying, the prospect rests on logical probability able to be extrapolated from data on causal forces, models and identifiable risks.

Any sense of our species existing in a stable environment is now illusory. The reality of being-in-the-world now is of uneven acceleration toward unpredictable and dangerous conditions as outlined. The displacement of several billion people over the coming century seems unmanageable but probable. Large coastal cities are going to be lost, people will abandon large areas of the planet as they become too hot to be habitable, areas where there was once a plentiful supply of fresh water will have none – this prospect is not probable, but, while the degree remains unclear, it is now certain. As current trends indicate, problems of food security will also be severe.

The end times have been registered as a moment of epochal change, and extant worldly conditions announce its unfolding. The new epoch of danger and uncertainty is underway. Many of the problems posed by the danger, rather than being met with spurious solutions, need acknowledgement as intractable (on the basis of what is currently known and able to be done). Contrapractice is a significant responsive action, one that is realizable and starts from the situated now. Its potential is the creation of conditions of possibility for acting futurally.

On the advancement of practice and contrapractice

While the fundamental premise of contrapractice affirms that nothing changes unless practice changes, it also acknowledges that the creation of affirmative change is no easy matter. There is no ready-to-hand contrapractice template that can be adopted and instrumentally employed to transform some, let alone all extant practices. Rather, contrapractice is an ethos and a project that practitioners themselves bring to their specific practice from a position that recognizes how it is articulated to defuturing. Thereafter, they have to learn how to eliminate (and replace) it, delinking it from its defuturing propensity, redirecting the form of its agency or adapting it so it acts to serve and support that future. To do this is clearly not an easy and purely instrumental task. It requires confronting and engaging one's own habitus, and in doing so, addressing one's embedded knowledge, conduct and values, to form a position where the imperative to become futural overrides short-term interests and conditions of limitation. Taking such action is hard and requires gaining new knowledge, adopting a position of leadership and developing a clear strategy of directed change over time (say one to three years, depending on one's situated complexity). There are, however, some general non-exclusive conditions of possibility (outlined below) open to review in the context of our individual circumstances.

Likewise, there is no shortage of motivating conditions to draw upon: existing practices are clearly often implicated causally in the generation, or amplification, of climate change, its risks and impacts. The list is long: from burning fossil fuels, deforestation and land clearing, to building cities on flood plains, on river deltas, on the edge of forests, at the base of unstable hillsides and in cyclonic belts. Then there is also excessive groundwater extraction and irrigation, the creation of large areas of hard landscape in cities (causing contaminated runoff), toxic leaching from landfill practices, minerals extraction and related land and waterway contamination (also from agriculture and industrial chemicals). There are also the GHG emissions from agriculture and industries, unchecked productivism and hyper-consumption. The point is that defuturing practices remain deeply embedded in the way in which the fabricated world we all occupy is created and used, our ways of life, plus in how conflicts arise and are conducted (including by war). These practices have created the world of our collective dwelling in the world of our dependence but have equally been shown to also be destroying it, and this process of destruction is reaching a point of criticality.

'We' live this dialectic of creation and destruction implicit in consumerism, and its current dislocation from renewal and regeneration. The demand to transform practice extends across all the practices of our individual lives. The imperative is material and pragmatic and grounded in the continuity of being, not just moral. Again, one has to find the source of motivation in the context of one's own life. Here contrapractice breaks the divide between individual voluntarist and collective action: practice is present in common, thus individual action acts with known, but mostly unknown, others in common. As organic, it can pragmatically progress by connection. Like Sustainment, and integral to it, without it, there is nothing.

While contrapractices cannot arrive as an immediate, deliverable and instant overcoming of accelerating defuturing crises, in which technology is situated ambiguously as a propulsive defuturing danger and as an instrument of responsive coping, it can set the stage for a pattern of reactive affirmative change in the situation of the coming adaptive majority of the global population over the next few decades if sufficient interest can be generated. To do this, the frame of adaptation needs a massive level of development beyond its current restrictive and instrumental way of being understood, promoted and employed. For this to be possible, it first requires a series of discursive practices grounded in a change in politics supported by a specific group of applied generative contrapractices.

So qualified, contrapractices will not be marginal action but will need to become central to redirective change. Those practices that perpetuate the defuturing status quo have to be displaced. Making this unavoidable is crucial. Likewise, those existing practices that are futural will need to be newly valorized, exposed and given greater status. While these are predominantly material instrumental actions, they are only part of the means to direct an environment of change. To become fully cognizant of, and emotionally sensitized by, the scale of the dangers of the unfolding deep crisis is elemental to embracing contrapractice, and this implies being ontologically changed by the adopting of a contrapractice.

Experientially realizing that the situation is going to continue to worsen will make emotional and psychological demands on everyone everywhere. Changing conditions are already impossible to ignore. Records for heat and floods are continually being broken worldwide, plants are blooming early before pollinators arrive, animals and birds are dying as a result of climate-induced environmental change.[2] Likewise, people in high-risk regions globally are becoming sick, life expectancy is lowering and infant deaths are increasing, from excessive heat and vector-borne diseases.

Contrapractice does not have a definitive agenda and program. It has a condition of commencement as an adopted action and a developmental potential. Understanding what it is and how it can be advanced can be assisted by the elaboration of a number of discursive practices. To make to point, five are outlined below, after which six community situated material contrapractices will be summarized.

FIVE DISCURSIVE PRACTICES PREFIGURATIVE OF CONTRAPRACTICE

These prefigurative **prompts** to a contrapractice conversation, and its conceptual advance, are directed at progressing its conditions of development.

1   **A new political imagination** has to, and will, arrive to counter the redundancy of the afterlife of the old political paradigm, the politics of despair of the displaced and abandoned, and the authoritarian futurism of corporate techno-elites. A newly imagined politics requires being organic to the adaptive majority as futural and pragmatic. Its fundamental proposition is to address what already exists as a primary resource from which to imagine and create, by adaptation, a viable material future. In this respect, and informed by the coming climate, such action would foreground utility, durability, modesty and repairability as normative adaptive practices. The intent is to keep costs low, maximize the agency of communities' DIY capability, minimize environmental impact and then enable such change at a large scale.

2   **Social reconstruction** would and could be linked to overcoming the social disruption and displacement that is intrinsic to high risk and disaster and the transformation of the built environment – this, so that communities themselves are better able to cope with future climatic conditions and impacts. A major danger of displacement is social devolution. A discursive practice is needed to bring the disaster present as an unavoidable imagery to make apparent the need to repair, and to reconstruct and increase the resilience of the social fabric. Counter to public information and data-driven attempts to motivate public action, a contrapractice would dramatize the coming danger in 'at-risk' communities with, for example, 'a mass community

---

2   Emperor penguins are one example: they lay eggs on sea ice, but the ice is melting before they have acquired feathers, so an entire season of newborns enter the water and drown.

theatre of disaster' – as a strategy of the unavoidable (issue, social and political reaction). At the same time, such action could and would also aim to counter those auto-destructive social and material practices that underpin historically ingrained defuturing capital-intensive modes of urban development, especially in at-risk environments, like flood plains (in 2023, the UN Environmental Program reported that the construction industry, accounting for 37 per cent of total emissions, was the world's largest emitter of GHG[3]).

3 **Relearning, remaking and redressing education in error** – people are not intrinsically agents of the unsustainable. They learn to become so by their formal and informal education and by the habitus they gain via their acquired learnt practices, plus the desires created by the techno-cultural economy in which they become immersed. Redressing this situation requires unmaking and remaking of the ethos of learning and its agency (in contrast to the imposition of a moral agenda of socially correct knowledge). Again, the starting point is to make the failure, the insufficiency, of currently existing education (especially higher education) present. The start point: a discursive practice centred on an imagined completely new education agenda directive of a contrapractice.

4 **A psychology of remade desire** is needed to counter the defuturing desiring machine of the techno-media (that produces the realization of desire by the acquisition of commodities supporting unsustainable ways of life, ambitions and futures). Such remaking centres on the creation of new imaginaries of self-realization and future socially recognized attainment. Here, contrapractice meets TikTok with a desiring machine of liberated imagination (future futuring futurism)

5 **A new social ecology** is established to counter the cultural accelerationist restrictive ecology of technologically mediated social engagement. Creating such an ecology essentially means producing social engagement by collective action, based on a common project and its aim: The demand is finding ways to adapt to changing environmental, material, economic and cultural conditions to provide the context of the dynamic of power of the new social ecology of revitalized sociality – de facto, conceptualizing and organizing futuring as a participatory project: a social prospectus.

FIVE EXAMPLES OF SITUATED PRAGMATIC MATERIAL CONTRAPRACTICES

These examples of general contrapractice activities are able to happen in different contexts. Once the principle of inverting the agency of a dominant practice

---

[3]   UN Environment Program, https://www.unep.org/resources/report/building-materials-and-climate-constructing-new-future (accessed 20 December 2024).

is understood and internalized, the creation of contrapractices would take on an organic form.

1 **Material recovery** from existing abandoned or neglected built structures – this resource would be mined, plus recovering materials from urban and rural waste, all at a scale to reduce extractivism. The scale of such action extends from a few dwellings in a village to an entire large mixed-use city. It would include grading, stockpiling, inventory management and logistics. Such activity would go beyond existing recycling methods and would constitute an industry. The context for this activity is the expected abandonment of many cities at a point when they become uninhabitable due to heat, riverine and sea level rise inundation and destruction. A contrapractice would pre-plan material recovery once abandonment looked to be certain, but before it occurred.

2 **Metrofitting against urban unsustainability** – this action is counter to new urban construction and development. It takes the concept of retrofitting to an urban scale materially, economically and socially. It would structurally enhance and extend the life and enviro-climatic performance of existing built fabric, infill undeveloped existing space, raise roads and infill lower floors of multi-story buildings to flood proof at-risk areas of a city, increase renewable energy uptake and reduce the volume of domestic and industrial energy consumption, create a culture of repair domestically, socially and industrially, be generative of small business and employment directed at metrofitting action. It would also aim to revitalize 'the fabric of community' and the cultural vitality of a city. The ethos would be pragmatic rather than the 'alternative' and 'idealistic'. The overall aim would be to immediately enable a city to cope with a changing climate while also making it better able to sustain itself over time.

3 **Repair and adapt** – A primary everyday responsive practical and economic action to cities exposed to moderate risk, based on a design ethos and practice. The action is akin to a reduced scale of metrofitting, in response to conditions of continuous risk and change, and would focus on expanding the domain of DIY capability and services – this to repair and adapt urban built fabric, as well as interior space, furniture, industrially made goods/domestic appliances. The aim is to extend the life of things and their ability to be modified or improvised if needs/circumstances alter.[4] An economy of bricolage, besides creating a small offset to reduced manufacturing output, would also increase community self-reliance, be a means to reduce the cost of purchasing goods and services, lessen the impact

[4] AbdouMaliq Simone, *Improvised Lives* (Oxford: Polity Press, 2019).

of hyper-consumption and be more affordable for less affluent nations and cities.

4 **Collective allotments of food production** – the need to increase food security is already an imperative, and will increasingly become so as global warming will cause agricultural systems to fail, and heat and drought will make much farmland untenable. Urban agriculture is one response that will become ever-more important. Food seen futurally is not just a positive activity nutritionally and economically, but its urban production can be seen as community development activity (this was evident in Europe during World Two and in Cuba in its economic crisis when the Soviet Union collapsed in 1991). Collective food production can facilitate exchange across cultures, enable social bonds to form and allow knowledge to be exchanged. Placed in the context of the commercial food industry, it is a contrapractice.

5 **Disaster prefigurative action** – in the world of fracture zones, and associated displacement, economic dysfunction, environmental systemic breakdown, social-lifeworld polarization and food scarcity, the conditions of everyday life of vast numbers of communities in many locations are going to become difficult, stressed and dangerous. To reduce the high level of risk of this situation, prefigurative action needs to be taken. Projected situated problems (social, logistical and security) need identification, research and response planning. Conditions of transgression also need to be neutralized. While preventing disasters may now be impossible, mitigating their escalating impact is not. Contrapractice contingent action can be argued as appropriate and needed, in contrast to what is expected: overwhelmed 'after the event' crisis management. Risk assessment, evacuation route planning, the allocation of possible reception areas, avoiding and unstaging conflict, and the logistics of mass involuntary migration are just some of the elements of such action. Failing to plan for assured coming major disasters equates to knowing that one's nation is going to be drawn into a war and failing to plan for its eventuality.

Wargaming is an established practice for understanding what threatens militarily and how to strategically respond to it. Disaster-gaming from a developed scenario would/could not only be a key contrapractice contingency planning action but equally it would be a significant source of images and narratives – to employ in the task of making risk and responsive action clear to communities in danger.

A condition of convergence

As has been made clear, contrapractice is based on prefigurative, redirective and preventive action in contrast to purely being reactive. It has to be anticipatory.

This means signs of change have to be understood, rendered unambiguous and demanded to be met. An actual example makes the point. The relocation of, for example, a small city, can be seen as a contrapractice action counter to its abandonment. Identifying where to relocate it, what moves, how to move, are all part of a known process, and generative of a whole cluster of design, social, economic and cultural contrapractice actions. As a result, it becomes seen and enacted as futural by pre-empting disaster.

Climate change impacts are already making relocation necessary as risks increase. The practice sits between two moments: relocation after a city has suffered a climate event disaster (a common example of reactive action); or relocation as a result of the recognition of growing identified risk (at present, an uncommon action). The latter means there is time to find and select an appropriate and acceptable relocation site, plan to develop a strategic relocation process, and utilize undamaged material resources from the place of abandonment. Such a scenario implicates community members, numerous practitioners and individuals associated with local government, building and construction, public, social and health services, education, the provision of utilities, the operative practices that make up the local economy, and the cultural sector. In each case, relocation invites a review and revision of all these constituent parts, and the potential of adding new ones. Thus, relocation is not merely an instrumental action but one indivisible from the re-conception and recreation of the 'community', its environment, economy and culture.

RESTATING AND RE-AFFIRMING THE CASE FOR CONTRAPRACTICE

Looking at contrapractice as active opposition to situated configurations of global defuturing practices positions it against a great deal of the status quo and all that upholds it. It begs to be employed by a growing community of informed agents who are aggressively advancing futuring practices. Its agency posits futural change that displaces notions and feelings of helplessness and acts to effect affirmative change. As indicated, action taken may be any mix of the social, economic, cultural, material, immaterial, adaptive or redirective engagement. The futural intent is always to make time by confronting, and whenever possible, overcoming the plurality of encountered forms of defuturing.

Practice constitutes things material and immaterial and they acquire force in situated ways that, as François Jullien points out that this 'has nothing to do with personality'.[5] He calls up Daoist thought from the third and fourth centuries BCE, as it recognized a need to 'allow the propensity of things to operate outside you, as their own disposition dictates'.[6] This includes the way they evolve and what they sustain (that is, their futural propensity). Thus, things

---

[5]   Jullien, *The Propensity of Things.*
[6]   Ibid., 39.

'tend of themselves, infallibly, with no need of effort'.[7] Efficacy brought to things can be understood as them having been given a sustainable disposition, while recognizing there is a general propensity to bring other things into being that defuture. Not only is this view of 'the nature' of things foundational and fundamental to ontological design, but it is also central to a materialist ethics that underscores contrapractice and its agency. A design preoccupation with user function and aesthetics does not have the ability to grasp the contra-propensity of the futural designed object.

Things do not bring themselves into being – they require agency. A materialist ethics requires it to be able to create things that redirect the unsustainable and sustain the means of Sustainment. So situated, contrapractice defines a continually evolving re-grounded practice seeking agents directing a strategy. One with defined objectives posited in contexts that overcome and displace established defuturing practices. 'For what counts is no longer so much what we ourselves personally invest in a situation, which imposes itself on the world thanks to our efforts, but rather the objective conditioning that results from the situation: that is what I must exploit and count on'.[8] Thus, the contrapractice exploits the object of its opposition – the future failing practice.

FUTURING CONTRAPRACTICE

There have been three ways indicated in which the agency of contrapractice can be combined to constitute a developable transformative futural force responsive to the imperative of Sustainment. The first goes to delinking an existing practice that is bonded to the production of the unsustainable; the second redirects the agency of the practice away from its existing application toward one that sustains; and the third adapts the form of the propensity of the practice so it ceases to serve the unsustainable and advances Sustainment.

Contrapractice also has to establish a mode of being elemental to four ecologies (technology, psychotechnology, mind and the geo-epistemological) that enable it to organically evolve. Finally, contrapractice has to be embedded within an existing, or new, cosmotechnics that secures those conditions that enable the dependent conditions of life to be secured. Now the three forms of deployment contrapractice, their relation to the four ecologies, and their relation to cosmotechnics will be considered in more detail.

Contrapractice as adaptation, redirection and delinking

To restate: contrapractice, as 'contra to', is against all practices that defuture and thus sustain an unsustainable status quo. It does not allow them to continue

[7]   Ibid.
[8]   Jullien, *A Treatise on Efficacy.*

doing so uncontested. A contrapractice can arrive by invention, but it would more frequently and likely arrive by seeking, discovering and selecting practices to adapt, redirect, or completely remake as they are defined against the opposing practice articulated to specific objects, processes, agents and institutions. The redirective impetus of contrapractice is not contextually delimited to the urban, manufacturing industry and technology; or to education, media and creative industries. In every case, the objective is *the transformation of the practice* directed at the *transformation of what it causally produces* – this in contrast to taking the product (be it system, made object or service as the locus of intervention) to just be 'a thing in itself'. Thus, the agency of practice *as contra* is posited as the primary agency of affirmative consequential change. As responsive and reactive action, contrapractice is always situated, grounded and directed by the pragmatics of an ever-evolving futural ethos. Clearly, there are defuturing practices that seem to be intractable – none more so than war.

As was made clear in an earlier chapter, the danger of war will be ongoing and increase. No effective means exist to prevent and restrain war. The United Nations is not united, the Security Council is structurally dysfunctional, and the institution is impotent (as evident from the Rwanda genocide of 1994 and the destruction of Gaza in 2024). There is no other agency with equal or greater power. There is no peace yet. War is not a definitive and fixed condition: as seen from the fluidity of its form and intensity, which constantly changes informationally, psychologically and technologically. The scale of climate change impacts and the consequential geopolitical and economic instability will result, as said in a vast and unmanageable number of people being displaced. Driven by the will to survive, they will invade cities and cross borders uninvited, looking for sustenance; such action will cause conflict. Likewise, so will competition for diminishing resources (not least fresh water and industry-dependent minerals).

Meanwhile, the forces of political and techno–accelerationism embrace war. They see it, as others have done in the past, as a 'clearing'. The point here is not that a contrapractice can be called on to address and resolve this impasse. But the practice of accelerationist force not only employs war as an extension of political ambition and power but turns it into a normative unbounded condition (unrestrictive war, wherein conflict is elemental to every dimension of political, economic, social and cultural life). The distinction between war and peace has dissolved.[9] This situation demands engaging a massive challenge: the creation of an unrestrictive contrapractice. To recognize war as an imperative of contrapractice is indicative of the scale of what is being proposed. It mirrors the totality of practice itself. But it also follows that the exercise of contrapractice is strategically selective (with, as already indicated, defuturing/unsustainability being the primary general foci of selection). Implicit in what is being argued is that what is being sought is to establish an opening into a generative organic

---

[9]   Michel Foucault, 'Society Must be Defended', Lectures at the College de France, 1975–1976, trans. David Macey (New York: Picador, 1997); and Fry, *Unstaging War, Confronting Conflict and Peace*.

process that will take contrapractice as an idea and inchoate practice into a condition of proliferation and adoption, initially by a 'community of concern'. Prompted by this community, its advance, wider uptake and capabilities would (hopefully will) require a critical mass of thinkers and actors over many decades.

Being-in-the-world: Contrapractice evolution

Contrapractice has to grow out of, and be grounded in, situated environments of organic emergence. Which means it has to be appropriated by practitioners who have identified a practice needing to be displaced, and who have the ability to do so and thereafter replace it with a specific contrapractice they are aware of, or have created. So emplaced, its survival will depend on its efficacy. Its evolution cannot be programmatic and instrumental. Rather, it is modified in its situated context, critically evaluated and engaged – it cannot simply be 'applied'. It follows that it cannot be represented as if it were already fully formed – it would not/does not have one final form, or predetermined condition of realization. In common with practice itself, contrapractice has a process, but the form and content are modified by the nature and the context of the practice it is engaging in order to displace it. It cannot be taken into exclusive ownership (like law, bricklaying, carpentry, accountancy, and a myriad other practices). Nobody owns it, although means of controlling have been, and are, created. It is largely defined by being other than the practice it has opposed and replaced.

With these caveats, the objective here is to create a focus on the evolutionary means that would increase the scale of its critical engagement with a large number of defuturing practices. Specifically, this means contrapractice being adopted, contextually developed, and widely employed within the social ecology of a political community of diverse types of practitioners – a fifth ecology.

The social ecology of political community

As seen in an earlier chapter, Bourdieu's understanding of social practice enfolded particular sets of dynamic relations within a larger frame of power, all positioned by specific configurations of structures, conditions and relations – this animated by the habitus of active social agents. What is being described is effectively a social ecology of communities that are not merely socially functional but also political, which is to say they are active in the relations of power directive of forms of everyday life. Tragically, the political, social, and cultural economy of modernity profoundly damaged the operability of community – this, via specific situated practices that have de-socialized, atomized and commodified so many of the elements of everyday life. The first chapter of Jean-Luc Nancy's 1991 influential book *The Inoperative Community* made this 'dissolution, the dislocation, or the conflagration of community' very clear (in modern developed nations). Its replacement: individualism, commodity-centric culture, and action dominated by self-interest.

Notwithstanding rhetorical appeals to community, with the passage of time, its loss has become even more evident. Yet the universality of the claim to its operability continues to mislead, as do actions based upon its assumed viability. Unquestionably, the dislocation of communities will continue. In spite of Nancy's now dated argument, the potential of community has not been completely erased: there are isolates that retain community, there are informal areas of cities in the global South where community is strong, and there are indigenous cultures, even though damaged by violence directed toward them, that have retained cosmologies that sustain community.[10] For the coming abandoned, dispossessed peoples (dominantly of the global South), the continuity of community, and an ability to share their resources, and to provide mutual care, will be indivisible from their ability to survive.[11] With these qualifications, the ongoing reality of the 'inoperative community' is acknowledged as still a major trend – but one not to accept with resignation as universal. Rather, it demands situated contestation and transformation (two actions needing to be placed in the remit of contrapractice).

As said, the appeal to, evoking of, and calling upon 'community' is commonplace in everyday discourse. Yet in his introduction to *The Inoperative Community*, Christopher Fynsk writes of the name 'community' denoting an absence, announcing what later Nancy will elaborate: a 'community without community is to come, in the sense that it is always coming', as such, this defines the inoperative community as a normative condition.[12] However, mass population displacement is going to cast the issue of inoperability into much starker relief. Earlier, Fynsk had affirmed 'a politics of community is possible', although saying it could not be a program, because community demands it.[13] But, while there can no longer be an unproblematic appeal to community, the demand for and of community requires acknowledgement as an unavoidable imperative of the futural social ecology of collective dependence in the fracture zones of displacement and adaptation. Be it in the conditions of dramatically increased distress, in the coming dangers of the defuturing. A consideration of community needs to be positioned in relation to social ecology and to the significance of 'transindividuality', as an evolving and continually changing relation between individuals and all that constitutes their society.

What social ecology as lived names is the dynamic of our being dependent on others (human and non-human). We all depend on each other directly (family/friends/partners/colleagues), and indirectly, on all those others whose productive activity provides our needs (economic, social, cultural). This is a relation of power, knowledge and variable security and vulnerability. Stating the obvious: born helpless, knowing nothing, to survive, we are all totally dependent upon

[10] Ailton Krenak, *Ideas to Postpone the End of the World*, trans. Anthony Doyle (Toronto: Anansi International, 2020).
[11] Simone, *Improvised Lives*.
[12] Christopher Fynsk, in *The Inoperative Community*, Jean-Luc Nancy, trans. Peter Connor, Liza Garbus (Minneapolis: Minnesota University Press, 1991) xxviii, citing Nancy, 71.
[13] Ibid., xxxvii.

others: our shelter, education, food, goods, services and much more, all come from all the others. Their distributed labour spans a vast complex of created systems, including agricultural, industrial, social, and cultural. *But* the defuturing agency of climate change impacts, related environmental impacts, economic dysfunction and conflict continually place the future of this ecology at risk. It is not completely foreign to us; rather, 'we' have an immediate, proximate, and dynamic relation to its agency. Yet as naturalized operative normality, it goes mostly/totally unthought. Consequently, what is actually being threatened and defutured only has a limited and often abstracted presence – for example, 'we' evoke a crisis of biodiversity as if it were external to 'us', and as if there was ecology and 'us'.

Gilbert Simondon's notion of transindividual makes this evident by linking it to our ontogenic individuation – the process that forms us from all that we have contact with.[14] Whereas, 'our' inner self, our ontology, is created indivisibly from the immediate and foundational (ontic) external world that we engage and that elementally engages us. In this sense, the transindividual is the being unified by the processes of their inner and outer existence as it constitutes an individual 'personalization'. Such a psycho-social process has gained a new dimension with the arrival of digital psycho-technologies. They function, in the frame of transindividuality, as enhanced communication conduits between a subject's inner and outer life. Crucially, such a process is not of singular moments, but a constant one. Thus, transindividuation means a condition of continual making and unmaking of the interface between world, other and self. So understood, the 'connected' being exists in a state of fragile metastability (unstable stability).

Simondon situates the 'technical object in the dialogical process of transindividuation'.[15] This view does not capture the ambiguity of the ontological designing of contemporary technological objects as they, in their difference in use, span operative and enabling capabilities as well as the colonizing and establishing of 'users' within a state of a created dependence. Where possible 'dialogue' exists, it does so having been modified by the mediation of an interface within the 'nature of things' – the technology, media, content, their agency and the omnipresent semiosphere.

Being with/in community

The viability of community is placed in proximity to the efficacy, or not, of a social ecology and transindividuation, so positioned it is exposed to the influences and negation of both. This volatile situation poses fundamental questions to the possibility or not of 'being in common' and the problem of the inoperability community itself. To clarify this issue, a return to Nancy is needed.

[14]   Gilbert Simondon, *Individuation in Light of Notions of Form and Information*, trans. Taylor Adkins (Minneapolis: Minnesota University Press, 2020), 77–281.
[15]   Ibid.

Over three decades ago, he asserted that the Western world 'has given itself over to the nostalgia for a more archaic community that has disappeared, and to deploring a loss of familiarity, fraternity and conviviality – all of which he sees as a pure fiction'.[16] Equally, he asserted that the 'true consciousness of the loss of community is Christian' – that is, community viewed as communion. The 'thought of community, or the desire for it, might well be nothing other than a belated invention that tried to respond to the harsh reality of modern experience'.[17] His views now appear very Eurocentric and dated. His naming of community as an absence felt as loss resonates (for some), but his view that it is we who are lost is problematic.[18] But 'we' are not one, and 'our' diversity ever grows as conditions of fracturing increase geospatially and psycho-socially. While the idea of community is of an 'ontology in which the other and the same are alike'[19] it is equally a 'being in common' that arrives out of a mutual sharing (something valued – a cause, politics, belief and so on) in difference. Problematically psycho-technologies/social media have created a tenuous sharing of ungrounded social connectivity, posited as substantive but is able to vanish in an instant. Nancy's position swung between negating and affirming community.[20] But community does not exist as an abstract universal, but in multiple forms with varied degrees of dysfunction, function, cohesion and resilience. Community does not pre-exist, and then take action. Rather, action makes community.

In total contrast to Nancy's now dated views, Roberto Esposito's concern with community is centred on the notion of 'cum' – being with, together, among each other.[21] But this 'commonality' gathers incommensurable difference: a group of prisoners in an open prison, the inhabitants of a South American favela, a platoon of soldiers, a band of Bedouin gypsies. Surely, circumstantial 'being with, together' is not the same as being together united by a common belief (theological or political)? For Esposito, the common was neither public nor dialectically opposed to the private, the global or the local. 'The common is something largely unknown, and even refractory to our own conceptual categories, which have been held for a long time by the general immunitarian dispositive' – the imperative was to have the capability to 'think around' or rather

16   Nancy, *The Inoperative Community*, 10.
17   Ibid.
18   Ibid., 11.
19   Ibid., 14.
20   A central figure in the thinking community for Nancy is myth. 'Absolute community – myth – is not so much the total fusion of individuals, but the will of community…' and that there is 'no community outside of myth…' plus, the 'interruption of myth is therefore also necessarily, the interruption in community'. He continues, 'there is no new mythology, so there is no community either, nor will there be'. Following this, he states that lamenting the loss of community goes along with lamenting the loss myth, which is a loss that 'defines modern man'. Besides 'modern man' being a problematic designation, s/he is defined by multiple discourses. Moreover, a substantial section of modern humanity retained an attachment to a particular myth (the myth of progress), while its meaning has evaporated, the trace lingers – thus progress is not a completely empty signifier (ibid., 57–8).
21   Esposito, Roberto, *Terms of the Political: Community, Immunity, Biopolitics* (trana. Rhiannon Noel Welch), New York: Fordham University Press, 2012, 2

within the common.[22] Here, the 'in common' is 'an existence which coincides with the exposition of otherness'.[23] In a similar spirit, Frédéric Neyrat comments that in order for there to be commonality, 'there must be something more, something that is different from the proper, the private, or the individual'.[24] But also, the practice and creation of 'something together' can constitute a being 'in common', although this potentiality is debased by corporate capitalism and branding. Community cannot be imposed by a political ideology or by force. Here is a context inviting the thinking of a contrapractice as a point of entry in the remaking community.

At this point, it is important to acknowledge the impossibility of a universal theory of community. Cultural/cosmological difference, not least among indigenous peoples, can have very different understandings of the common and community that is certainly not predicated on Western divisions of knowledge, being and beings, the perception of self and its relation to animals, others, inner life, exteriority, the animate and inanimate. In particular, the significance of kinship structures as regimes of power in many tribal societies begs special recognition as they define with whom authority is posited, social and cultural roles and obligations – this all represents a very different social ecology.

In contrast to community, which refers to something general and open, immunity, or immunization, goes to a particular situation defined by its subtraction from the common condition. This is evident under the juridical profile, according to which 'to have immunity – parliamentary or diplomatic – means not to be subject to a jurisdiction concerning all other citizens… and thus, from the law that is common'.[25]

The exercise of political immunity, and the function of the biological immune system, is to preserve life. In the context of the compound crises which defines the condition of the negation of life on Earth now, and in the recognition that in its condition of auto-destruction (a state of autoimmunity), there is no future for 'us' and so many of our others unless a significant number of the global population gains immunity (from its autoimmune 'self'). Clearly, the extent of fragmentation totally removes the possibility of all idealistic notions of being together.

The situation of the displaced, in their condition of displacement, abandonment, and shared loss, is a moment of rendered dysfunction in the commonality of nothingness and disorder. Subject to power, order, and authority, they are 'imposed upon' as an a-political body exposed to control as dangerous. For them, the coming together to resist helplessness is the beginning – it only has itself for itself.

---

22   Roberto Esposito, *Terms of the Political: Community, Immunity, Biopolitics*, trans. Rhiannon Noel Welch (New York: Fordham University Press, 2012), 7.
23   Ibid., 1.
24   Frédéric Neyrat, 'The Birth of Immumopolitics', *Parrhesia* 10 (2010): 31.
25   Esposito, *Terms of the Political*, 2. Here, one should remember that the concept of immunity was founded in Greek law and disseminated later by Roman law.

The corporate techno-elites, in their retraction into spaces of protection, believe they will have created a condition of immunity. But community is antithetical to their fundamental ontology, which centres on the actual or aspired power of one. Even if a functional collective forms, it will be subordinate to singular(ity) one who constituted the space that accommodates the all. Not only are these conditions not conducive to the establishment of a viable social ecology, but they are also grounded in the perpetuation of conditions of autoimmunity.

For the distributed majority, whose imperative is adapting to change, their prospect would be different. Making together is at the centre of their circumstance. In the variability of their geo-material situatedness, the possibility of community exists as enacted via a contrapractice able to displace a pre-disaster history as an inoperable community. A prospect of diverse and comprehensive projects, situated in different material and social conditions, could create discernible examples of community formation and efficacy in action. Driven by *a social ecology of care* in common (of the locus of dwelling, and of being in common), carefulness would underscore the contrapractices – notwithstanding the physical and emotional hardship of making the means to futurally cope in a harsher biophysical world of likely competing social forces. The quality of the social ecology in this world of utility and of extinguished utopian imagination provides the basis of making a viable, repaired and adapted built environment, of growing capabilities, able to construct futures of an affirmative way of life in difference.

Effectively, what is being signalled here is an ontogenic process established over time by a catalytic socio-political operative leadership, combined with the restorative and protective action of a nascent political community. Here is the Sustainment of the world that was. The unavoidable realism of this reality being: the rehabilitation of as much of the world as possible within the spaces existing between:

- the occupied, potentially reducible spaces, of the displaced and abandoned (as isolates migrate), and
- the artificially sustained protected environments occupied, and commanded by, planetary elites (as they vie between colonizing space or a selective recolonizing selected area of Earth).

Cosmotechnics and survival

The displaced and abandoned are the new to be stateless *indigeno*, the marginalized 'first of the last' fatefully cast into social regression. At present, the majority live in the most exposed nations to climate change and have the least means to cope with the situation. Their fate is to lose their homes, land and meagre income – but they are not helpless. According to circumstances, and by degree, they will strive to survive by that which the collective has as the 'itself for itself' as manifest as the history memory, and skills of improvisation, bricolage, street knowledge, crimes of survival, and their cosmology exercised and enacted by what remains of their cosmotechnics. All this is brought to the environment to which they, by choice or force, migrate.

A decade ago, Yuk Hui made a major contribution in the elaboration, exposure and promotion of the significance of cosmotechnics.[26] But how this can be understood and futured continues to unfold.

A cosmology is not replicated epistemologically but by the world making of its everyday practices (and, less significantly, by its traditions and rituals) of a particular culture. Modernity, via colonial conquest, consciously, and in ignorance, all but obliterated the cosmologies of numerous indigenous peoples (but not all) in the name of bringing civilization and their Christian God. Yet the traces remain, are valued and retain cultural agency.

The critical question now is to think about how such people futurally figure in the coming conditions of total disruption and displacement. Events are going to unevenly accelerate globally toward levels of intensity of crises and breakdown. A great deal of past and present thinking (especially instrumentally, politically, and economically) is going to become redundant/irrelevant, while the demand to think affirmatively and futurally, in the inverted world, is going to be huge. Not least among the challenges of the moment is constituting cosmologies that give meaning and inform transformative action in damaged and fragmented worlds.

In conditions of loss and desperation, and in the complete absence of any form of humanitarian aid, retained, recovered or newly created techniques of survival will be decisive. In this sense, drawing on histories of diversity of cosmotechnics as well as contemporary forms of innovation, created especially in informal settlements, will be crucial for displaced people. They will acquire pragmatic and symbolic significance in conditions where survival depends on what can be done with, and what can be found in, the environment into which fate has thrown displaced people. This is not a new situation, as life in the camps of the already displaced in Asia, the Middle East and Africa confirms.

Cosmotechnology: A question of realization

Contrapractice as futural sees reanimated cosmotechnics as a specific futural practice as (i) an example of a general resistance to hegemonic unchecked defuturing technological advancement, and (ii) as a situated practice developable by people in specific environments of displacement that can help them survive. It does not arrive ready-made. It has to be created out of, and for, the people by people – by them making a world for themselves, from the world they now inhabit, as a structurally recurrent everyday action informed by their transposed way of life. Clearly, cosmotechnics does not have a universal form. A futural contrapractice biased cosmotechnics would be directional and oriented toward the advancement of the Sustainment of displaced people and of the environment

---

[26]   Yuk Hui, *The Question Concerning Technology in China an Essay in Cosmotechnics* (Falmouth: Urnanomic, 2016).

upon which they now depend. It will only be realized for displaced populations who are fortunate to find themselves in conditions of possibility.

Such action cannot be idealized; it presents a harsh and pragmatic existence where sustaining life and creating a viable future would be a continuous struggle, yet one that folds back into the history of the survival of *Homo sapiens*, surviving often against the odds. It is the condition of danger that the displaced are the counter other of 'transhuman' as 'being-towards singularity'. So viewed, cosmotechnical contrapractice can be seen for the displaced and abandoned as the means to counter to regress and social devolution (the possible fate of many), and a path to a realized *praxis* of redirection taking them toward the enfolding ontological qualities of the world of the adaptive majority: utility, durability, repair, modesty, material conservation, stability, skill enhancement and above all care (materialized in the form, use and consequence of/for the conditions of futural dependence).

Cosmotechnical contrapractice, besides contesting the form and direction of technology travelling toward singularity, would be a project of continuous incremental change in response to the consequence of entropic patterns of assured defuturing and systemic breakdowns (economic, environmental, social and geopolitical). The hopeful prospect (if a catastrophic conflict is avoided) is that collapse would arrest the impetus of defuturing, halt genocidal AL, and slow bio-extinction. Within the conditions of epochal change, a process of remaking lifeworlds and futures in difference would start from the foundation of adaptation. This scenario can be viewed as akin to a recovery of the effects of the collapsed empires of the past. However, as transposed onto the scale of the eco-economic impacts of the collapse of the technologically amplified over-populated global empire of industrial capitalism, albeit with hyper-technical enclaves of the privileged and their artificially augmented environments of aspiring (or actual) transhumans.[27] Straying further, and temporarily, into projection, maybe this scattering of 'techno-communities', inspired by Musk's Project Mars and space ambitions, would see Earth as populated by 'regressives' and themselves as the colonizers of other planets and depart.

[27] This position combines technology not only seen as an agent of acceleration but also as being a salvific machine that does not 'save humanity' from environmental collapse but rather becomes the environment of conscious being and its ecology of mind.

4 Reflections and Projections

Tony Fry

Looking back/looking forward conclusion that recognizes that defuturing events are accelerating, but responses to them are not (with the implication that (i) many practices, including in design, are now becoming redundant and (ii) the unfolding situation is making/has already overcome the coping capacity of humanism). Climate change and the inchoate epistemological colonizing AI crises are making this clear.

TO CONCLUDE: AN OPENING STORY

Under current circumstances, to get to a collective viable future requires the creation of the means – conceptual, intellectual, instrumental, existential, together with living with the belief in the possibility of attaining such ends.

In the face of all that threatens, current national and international action is ineffectual. It's too modest in scale, moderate, technocentric, disaggregated and gestural. Globally, there is no common understanding between nations, and few of them act in coordination. The consequences of the actions of the defuturing agents in the coming epochal crisis will converge and transform conditions leading to, and beyond, the described modes of fragmentation and their accompanying ontologies.

Contrapractices, as futural, clearly arrives not just conceptually from imagination but equally responsively as an emergent pragmatic to counter those practices and forms of action that are complicit with defuturing practices embedded in conditions of negation – the relational impacts of climate change, mass extinction, war, the rapid depletion of natural resources and unchecked rapid urbanization all at the fore.

Even if substantive corrective action were taken, there would still be major enviro-climatic impacts, mass population displacement, geopolitical trauma and the risk of major conflict globally, catastrophic economic disruption, plus a huge food security crisis: the dangers are real, already present, interconnected and growing, and there is a wholesale neglect to address them. Those forces committed to maintaining 'business as usual' still dominate, but they are destined to fail.

Christopher Hill (1979), writing of the English Revolution during the mid-seventeenth century, characterized the event and moment in England as when 'The World Turned Upside Down' – this was the turning of a small world.[1] Now, what is metaphorically being turned upside down is the entire world. The scale of epochal change will produce cosmological rupture. A sense of the world, and much of its form, will shatter for the total population of the planet. Mass displaced and abandoned will throw the majority of humanity into a struggle for bare life. Their fate will in large part be decided by the environment they find themselves in being able to sustain them, or not. Techno-salvationists will retreat into their bubbles, but is, in actuality, a synthetic life a desirable and possible mid or long-term enduring future? Would not people living in a techno-fabricated protective environment effectively prefigure a new species, especially if they were also technologically augmented? This prospect is real, and raises profound questions, not least how a relation to them could be negotiated. In recognizing this situation. The relations between the enviro-protected techno-elites, the global majority in difference adapting to change as best they can, and the displaced, if realized, have the makings of a volatile mix.

For the global majority, the process of remaking, adapting and repairing their material conditions of existence will progress unevenly (as impacts will be uneven), involve a lot of relocation, be hard and protracted and, as was indicated in an earlier chapter, would quantitatively and qualitatively be very different from the present.

However, from the perspective of the majority, adaptively responding to the increasing condition of criticality, their pressing issue would be how to make sense, deal with and adapt to the nature and scale of escalating change and resulting radical transformations underway. Confronting this issue prompts an epistemological project of learning how to think, then act otherwise, and futurally, in opposition to inform defuturing global conditions. That this project is not central to the research and pedagogic agenda of universities is indicative of their stasis and embeddedness in business models and instrumentally biased vocational programs that over decades, have reduced the academy to a fate and state of deepening intellectual ruin, first, as detailed by Bill Readings decades ago.[2] While student numbers, and the number of universities, have increased, as has expenditure on capital works, its mission and project, post the after-life of the Enlightenment and beyond social, economic and techno-scientific functionalism, has never arrived. There are individual and marginal program exceptions. But dominantly the intellectual capital produced has serviced the development of the domains of corporate techno-elites, their state economies

---

[1]   Christopher Hill, *The World Turned Upside Down* (London: Penguin Books, 1979).
[2]   Bill Readings, *The University in Ruins* (Cambridge, MA: Harvard University Press, 1996).

and military-industrial complex. Even when critical issues, including climate change and environment crises are engaged the rationale has been underscored by ecologically sustainable development (ESD) rather than the development of ecological Sustainment (DES). Besides ESD sustaining the status quo, it characterizes an epistemological failure to grasp that without making Sustainment foundational, the propensity is for defuturing remaining structural. A core understanding of 'sustainability' and the essence of the 'unsustainable' have never arrived in the plural confusion that defines the ontological condition of the academy. If they had been, the entire curriculum would have been reviewed and transformed, and the project of the university reborn. Whereas the ongoing reality is that universities still induct vast numbers of students into unsustainable knowledge, values and practices and undertake research for, and funded by, unsustainable industries. Dominantly, the normative corporate business model of universities places them firmly in support of the labour market and the unsustainable economic status quo.

Appearances deceive: Sustainability has been taken up by universities predominantly in two ways: instrumentally in terms of operational practices (e.g., energy policy, recycling and waste management, water usage and purchasing policy, etc.); and, in the curriculum of some disciplines (for example, in economics (as triple bottom line accounting, and extended producer responsibility), in sustainable and design in architecture, in renewable technology and sustainable materials in engineering, in environmental studies and ethics and in science in areas like air and water quality and ecological conservation practices). Whatever the developments they have all been, they have not been unified with a rigorous theory of sustainability, or has the unsustainable as the clearly defined foundational condition to which sustainability exists to overcome been rigorously interrogated in every context in which sustainability is engaged – so often it is taken as an established given.

To have taken Sustainment seriously would have meant making its advancement the undergirding principle of the university universally. Thus, it would become the very basis of the mission of the institution in the present age of the acceleration of defuturing. By implication three norms would become directive: the advancement of sustainability (re cast as Sustainment) as an ethical foundation of every domain of practical reason and critical theory and practice; the elimination of all elements of the curricular that demonstrably function in the service of the creation, application and reproduction of unsustainable thought and practice; and the recognition there are areas of the curricular to support that do not directly advance sustainability but nonetheless in advance the critical facility that its development requires. Sustainment also needs to be understood culturally and economically. Inequity, the afterlife of colonialism and its new forms, negates the conditions from which Sustainment can form and emerge. Equity and decoloniality fold into Sustainment as process – as such, they are not reducible to realizable projects. These norms do not eliminate the plural character of the university, but they do displace liberal pluralism. Such a commitment to Sustainment is deemed here to be contingent and essential is the establishment of viable futures in coming, and under, conditions of global socio-geopolitical fragmentation and deepening crisis.

The institutional changes sketched equally require a transformation of sensibility. In particular, the need to move away from the dominant aim of delivering 'solutions' – which does not mean that there are not problems for which there are solutions. But recognizing that there are many problems that cannot be solved as a result of fundamental systemic structural change requires responses that overcome the epistemological condition of limitation that install and support such a misconception. Extant divisions of knowledge and disciplines obstruct understanding relational complexity and associated patterns of causality. A shift in sensibility is vital, and it requires a move to wider and more developed modes of response, and over time – mitigation, redirection, remaking, adaptation and invention, thereby all become possible to reconfigure – underscored by a relational understanding within a relational milieu.

CONFIGURATIONS OF THE BORDERLAND

At this moment of epochal change, we all exist in a borderland. Knowingly or unknowingly, we are all between the end of the world constituted as situated and familiar and the beginning of the world that is going to be. In contrast to graduated and at times of uneven change in the 'developed world', and the protracted trauma of 'the rest', what is to come are times of rupture, break, and dysfunction that will be differentially experienced as indicated as: abandonment displacement, survival by continual and innovatory adaptation and retreat into condition of protection by elites.

Each situation is a borderland between epochs of incalculable duration, as well as itself being generative of a borderland between each of these conditions. In all cases, uncertainty and tension, to a varying degree, will rule.

Clearly, planets do not exist as a condition of stasis. They are dynamic, albeit over a vast expanse of time. Predominantly in the past, the causes of instability have been traumatic geological and biopsychical. But in the present age un-natural induced change (prompted and produced by 'us') and enviro-climatic impacts, produced geopolitical conflicts, omnipresent instability, the abuse of natural resources – these major causal factors of crises with unclear consequences of unknown duration. They are bisected by the equally unknown consequences 'we' (a selective we) have created.[3] There are no lifeworlds that can be insulated from the forces of global instability now in play. Not only is the level of risk to life rising, but the present dangers have no end in sight. A double bind has been created: risk begets risk. As a result, the convergence of problems that constitute what we have named as the 'compound problem' is destined to

---

[3]   The consequences of, for example, the Internet, AI, neuro-invasive technologies and quantum computing have been subject to speculation, but what their causal trajectory will deliver is unknown. This issue is not new, but the magnitude of the reach of these technologies is.

grow. Correspondingly, contrapractices, as a designated response to this situation, have to be created to resist and halt the acceleration of defuturing as
structural. So said, there is a massive disjunction between the way the actuality
of the enormity of the compound problem of defuturing exists, and the way
the disaggregated perceptions, from a limited understanding of the problem,
are currently proposed to be addressed and engaged. Mostly this is by targeted
underdeveloped goals, claimed to deliver solutions from a perspective of temporal
myopia where 'dis-relational action' is proposed in divisions of knowledge over
decades, when the problem is relational, extends over centuries and requires
well-conceived, continuously evolving responsive strategies.

An informed, comprehensive and nuanced understanding of the borderland
begs to be created and embraced. While it names the kind of state of betweenness, it is more than this: it is also a locus of exchange and the engagement of
difference wherein new relations and modes of understanding are, or might be,
formed. These transitional qualities of the borderland converge in the tempo-
rally of a moment of ontological change that would be essential to constitute.
So said, the passage of change within and from the borderland is uncertain and
unpredictable, is likely to produce unexpected inversions of the expected, while
conflict would/will be an enduring disruption and danger.

Positioned between a fate of our own making, and recognizing and acting
upon futural imperative, life is unquestionable in the balance. What is so uncanny
about the precariousness of this collective worldly situation is that it is widely
known but deferred and overlooked. It is as if no matter the scale of the problem,
there is an assumption that at some point, 'a solution' (technological) will be
'found' or created. Even if this were so, it would be for the few, not the many.
Viewed in the medium of time, and from a pragmatic sensibility, *as has been
recognized*, there is an absolute, unequivocal need to restate and address *the
epistemological, communication, enviro-climatic, security and political crisis
of the compound problem* that underscores the emerging epoch. That this is
not being done, that the borderland between epochs is not being recognized,
is very evident. There is a disjuncture between preoccupations of the present
and comprehending the accelerating dynamic of defuturing probabilities. The
disposition to retain a vestige of normality is huge at every level from the local
to the global. A recoil against bad news, a misplaced faith in hope and almost
total dominance of a chronophobic state of mind blocks sight and thought. But
ontologically grasped knowledge (to experience, bare witness, reflect and own)
shatters illusions. Such knowledge is essential to become futural, and thereafter
to confront what threatens and to proactively respond, but it cannot determine
this action.

TELLING STORIES AND EMPOWERING THE
RECOGNITION OF TRUTH IN FICTION

As has been communicated in several ways, the possibility of understanding
the 'complexity of complexity' of the 'compound problem' that is directing the

fate of life on Earth requires a recognizing of the conditions of limitation of knowledge in which we all function. Even so, confronting what threatens us all cannot be fully comprehended, or represented. The relational complexity of this entropic process underway is beyond conceptual recognition and is unavailable as grounded experiential understanding. Likewise, 'we' do not share an equality of understanding – this inequity always has an epistemological dimension. Yet even the most informed and knowledgeable of us are unable to 'call-up' the vast interwoven causal elements of this complexity, and its diverse consequences over time. As soon as a specific entry point to the complexity is adopted, the possibility of grasping the actuality of its complexity disappears. Yet the imperative search for understanding persists, even if the possibility of gaining knowledge and truth eludes. Here, one is reminded of Alfred North Whitehead's notion of 'speculative Reason', which seeks 'always the progress of a better understanding'.[4] And then, 'The whole conception of philosophy is concerned with the discipline of the speculative Reason, to which nothing is alien'.[5] Effectively, the speculative bonds imagination to reason as a means of disclosing the 'to be understood'. In so doing, a narrative of reasoned causality can be constituted, while lacking a truth claim. It still, nonetheless, provides an object of reflective interrogation from which understanding can emanate.[6]

Recoiling from the truth is not merely a dominant feature of the dysfunctional institutional politics – it 'trades' on the illusion of inflated agency. This flaw in its discursive practice makes the difficult task of publicly communicating critical issues even harder, especially in the digital environment of idle chatter, noise and a widespread preoccupation with entertaining trivia. Notwithstanding, contrapractice needs (in positioning itself between myopic popularism and academic abstraction and introspection) to find, shape and mobilize a discourse of influence. Stating and calling for this to be done is totally inadequate, and goes nowhere. There has to be situated action. Passivity, inaction, is complicit with resignation to the terminal.

The shaping of contrapractice exposited in an instructive narrative is obviously not of itself action, but likewise, there will be no efficacious action without the form of the action being prefigured. A well-informed speculative fiction can be a means to give such a narrative a form.

Its intent would not be to be a directive of action, but to be an object of critical reflection that would assist in the creation of a narrative informing how opportunities and options can be conceived in a situated context of action.

The aim here has not been to present contrapractice, claimed and projected as a ready-made practice. But rather to argue for its adoption as a substantial

---

[4]   Alfred North Whitehead, *The Function of Reason* (Boston: Beacon Press, 1929), 38, https://brocku.ca/MeadProject/Whitehead/Whitehead_1929/1929_02.html (accessed 20 November 2024).

[5]   Ibid., para 5.

[6]   Such an approach mirrors the method of the 'observation of observation' of second-order cybernetics employed in design fiction – Tony Fry, *Writing Design Fiction, Relocating City in Crisis* (London: Bloomsbury, 2022).

strategic project that increases the ability to act against practices that, knowingly or unwittingly, serve the unsustainable and in doing so defuture. They need to be resisted, contested and thereafter transformed to be futural and so advance Sustainment. The underlying message of contrapractice is simply 'to understand that nothing changes unless those practices that make and uphold all forms of defuturing existing worlds change'.

The development and advancement of contrapractices is a valid, needed, viable and responsive project to a potential mobilization against the terminal planetary defuturing condition. As such, it warrants an investment of time, effort, commitment and resources – this, in particular, in the coming context of the global population being fragmented into the displaced, an adaptive majority, and a techno-corporate elite by the impact of a 'heat age' and associated problems of the 'compound problem'.

First, it's hard to imagine the implications and feelings of what life would be like to live on a planet that once again has been (and continues to be) massively transformed by a changing climate. The last time was 2.4 million years ago at the start of the Ice Age. Then second, to know that the global population has fractured, and life for likely several billion will be life, as Thomas Hobbes put it in 1651, in 'Nature, red in tooth and claw'. While conversely, another section of the global population retreated into denaturalized technologically sustained protective environments. Meanwhile, the rest do what they can to adapt to changing conditions. Such a future might read like science fiction, but in reality, it is now an approximate characterization of an unstoppable coming future. There is no 'solution', there is just the essential need to respond and adapt to this prospect as it unfolds.

It is against this backdrop that the need and possibility of contrapractice is posed as a means to resist such an emergent defuturing future. It cannot be stopped, it could be mitigated and it will have to be – all in a window of diminishing opportunity that screams to be recognized.

IN CONCLUSION

No matter how the future will come to pass, it will bring unavoidable hardship, pain and suffering for billions of people. The more this prospect is refused, avoided and negated, the worse it will be. That the political leaders of the planet are incapable of facing this situation, let alone dealing with it, firmly positions them within the remit of the forces of defuturing.

In a situation where defuturing is a structural and unsustainability normative worldly condition, contrapractice is fundamental to the very possibility of a future. So situated that it is not an option, but essential. Yet it has no natural status or presence in practice(s): it has to be created and applied with consistency over time to become taken as given and dominant. By implication, this makes it a project for all practitioners. How this can be done has been indicated, but the means outlined are not exclusive or sufficient, but offered as trigger points. Other start points can and need to be situationally created by practitioners attuned to the imperative to which they respond. As has been made clear, there are no templates for contrapractice; rather, it is an acquired and enacted sensibility to be informed by a cadre of practitioners until it becomes a hegemonic practice. By implication, this means it has to be informally learnt in the course of acquiring or re-forming a practice, be formally elemental to institutional education or intrinsic to the exercise of occupational practice per se – all of which is to say contrapractice has to be the essence of the habitus of practitioners. As such, it sits between two timeframes: the speed of the arrival of crises to which it is a response, and the arrival of the recognition of this situation most accelerates its adoption. Metaphorically, there are three moments of this condition of betweenness – the moment of ignition of the concept, the period of it smouldering and then bursting into flames of an unstoppable inferno.

With certainty, what can be said, in these end times, is that the questionable efficacy of political and practical gesturalism and gradualism (that characterized the failure to prevent the arrival of the 'heat age'), now has absolutely no agency. In a world being rendered into desperate fragments, the recognition and response to crises will be futurally decisive.

Moralizing hyperbole offers nothing.

Closing Conversation

Tony Fry and Dulmini Perera

We have shown that the very notion of practice has a complex and contested conceptual history that requires recognition. Moreover, it is clear that the relationship between practices, questions of agency and change forms a complex changing geometry within conditions of acceleration. While design practices are not the only practices that are foregrounded in this book, practices that have some form of design are at its centre and do provide a departure point to explore some of the critical issues, drawbacks and possibilities related to contemporary discussions about practice. This Q&A-driven conversation with Tony Fry discusses some of the issues the book has reflected upon and raises.

A VIEW BEYOND

DP: *Rather than talking about design practice per se throughout the book we have used the word 'practice'. I think we need to differentiate between these words as it matters to the argument on a contrapractice. First the term 'practices' connote all sorts of ways of enacting worlds and relate to the fundamental technological, social, cultural, economic and political relationships that are at play in bringing about 'our' worlds. Thinkers from fields as diverse as philosophy (Ludiwig Wittgenstein), sociology (Pierre Bourdieu, Anthony Giddens, Theodore Schatzki,), cultural theory (Michel Foucault, Terry Eagleton, Eva von Redecker, Carolyn Pedwell), anthropology (Tim Ingold) science and technology studies (Bruno Latour, Isabelle Stengers, Andrew Pickering), Political theory (Karl Marx), critical pedagogy (Palolo Freire), biology of cognition (Umberto Maturana, Francisco Varela), systems and policy research (Donald Schön) have contributed to multiple understanding of the notion of practice.*

While there is no unified idea or method that can be defined as practice theory, these diverse attempts at theorizing practice converge around the idea that 'practices' are becoming a central approach to better understand the human material relationships within a living world in process. Practice essentially is the refinement of action in time with material causal consequences – understanding is intrinsic to it, rather than of – 'you have to know what you are doing' and gaining this is a recursive process. It implies getting better by repetition until a certain level is reached. Particularly with the work of Bourdieu, de Certeau, and Foucault that is foregrounded in a previous chapter, practice becomes part of the everyday habitus. In this sense, all activities, such as cooking, walking, writing or building become sites of practice where a 'habitus' becomes part of enacting worlds and through which power relations are transformed. Their framing of habitus makes it a mediator between conscious processes and the more unconscious processes. Now, if we look at an 'institutionalized design practice' as a specific form of practice, a profession, an institutionalized discipline or a particular form of knowledge, the 'habitus' gets moulded within the institutional apparatus of design in particular ways. Now, one can neither speak about that universally, nor as a generality, but I think there are ways in which one can qualify the nature of an 'institutionalized design practice' within the broader spectrum of practices. What are your thoughts on this?

TF: First, a comment; I try not to engage anything universally. The universal cannot be disaggregated from the history and consequences of the union of colonialism and Euromodernity. On this issue, I totally subscribe to François Jullien's excellent 2014 critique, *On the Universal*. Regarding qualifying the nature of an 'institutionalized design practice', yes, but not positively. I view mainstream design as the practice that Illich called a 'disabling profession'. In terms of 'the nature of an 'institutionalized design practice', I am not interested in qualifying it but overcoming and displacing it. In so many ways for so many years in so many events, books and articles, I have argued for design to be redirected and remade. Contrapractice, as argued in this work, is against design as it is.

DP: *So, I think it is important to ask, 'whose institutionalized design practice?' Certainly, modernity tried to universalize them, and certainly the epistemological colonialism of design practice has been far-reaching. But it could never totally colonize and completely erase the local. As you have argued in your work for 'design by/for/from the global South' in the last two decades, this situation has been recognized and resisted. Moreover, the project of resistance continues in different ways.*

TF: The other issue here is that one of the aims is to counter 'institutionalized design practice' that constitutes a 'restrictive practice' (restriction is the essence of professional practice, as delivered by certification and accreditation, for instance in law, accountancy, architecture). In this context, design is an aspiring profession. But unlike those professions just mentioned, design practice *per se* exists as an intrinsic capability to prefigure/design and so is elemental to our being. As such, design is intrinsic to many occupations a carpenter, chef, bricklayer, plumber, printer, and so on, all make design decisions. But then there are the exclusive design practices of institutionalized, professionalized, accredited and non-accredited forms that constitute design's division of knowledge.

DP: *Then would it suffice if a reader might think of the practices that are discussed in the book by taking into account only everyday practices such as cooking at home or walking?*

TF: Yes and No. Yes, we as beings that prefigure with intent an action prior to undertaking it, this indicates that design (prefiguration) is ontologically elemental to us as a species. It follows that cooking can't be done without intent to cook something, and in a certain way that prefigures the form of the cooked. So, there is a commonality. Walking is more ambiguous. It can be directed by intent or be reactive to an urge or attraction. The primary intent of walking is to arrive at a destination. Although walking with a health intent can be asserted as prefiguring a change in the body. I would add that while the act of design is a product of intent, the practice of designing is not necessarily so – this notwithstanding all the instrumental, and often facile, rhetoric on 'design process and methods', – that a huge amount of designing, as indicated, is also intuitive, embedded in a procedurally ordered habitus and retrospectively rationalized. Correspondingly, a considerable amount of designing is also programmatic – hence design process rendered as commodity, as 'program', designing design. Between these two poles is conscious and critical design practice under erasure. The scale and diversity of design undermines simple classifications. Practices travel with, and are enacted in and by, our plural subject positions. The practices of say, writing, gardening, playing golf, driving, cooking, etc., range from the occasional, to the everyday, to the occupational according to individual difference. We all, I suggest, move through our day and life transitioning from one practice to another, engaging tasks rather than making conscious choices about adopting a particular practice. But then there are circumstances that call practices into being by our everyday life being interrupted. Crises and contingency thus arrive on the scene. Consequently, conditional change brings about new practices.

DP: *What contrapractice makes clear and present is that unless practices change, nothing changes, and that it is predicated upon identifying practices that defuture, resisting, displacing and then replacing them. But perhaps there are theories that already emerge from within design practice that can be helpful to think through such a project. For example, I am thinking of concepts such as 'reflective practice' and 'the reflective practitioner'. Donald Schön's work was pre-figurative of these discussions.[1] Schön's work is interesting because he brings to presence the multiple levels of practice that exist within design, from the practice of, for example, engineering, building and*

---

[1] Donald Schön, *The Reflective Practitioner* (New York: Basic Books, 1983).

planning design, to reflect. His argument was, to a certain extent, helpful to reinstate the value of more vocational or professional-based knowledge models. Schön pointed out how practitioners such as doctors, nurses, lawyers, designers, builders often reflect in the process of working with the situation at hand. This level of reflection as it relates to practices can also be understood with different levels of distance such as reflection in action and reflection on action. This also leads to a better understanding of performativity and operative forms of attention. There is a large body of work that has developed around these ideas to date.

In another practice context, such as architecture, Stan Allen makes a similar argument that design professionals often engage in a specific way of reflection. Allen speaks from what he identifies as a position of 'pragmatic realism' and makes an argument for maintaining a relation to practice that is different from both what he calls dumb theory (critical reflection divorced from a context of practice) and dumb practice (practice without critical reflection). He argues for a 'practice flexible enough' to engage the complexity of what he calls 'the real'. I might not agree with all aspects of their work, but nevertheless, I find their work helpful to think about the questions of practice. But they don't figure in this book prominently. Can we discuss why?

TF: The book is not about design practice as it is, or about reforming it. Secondly, the impact of Schön has not been directly on design practice, but on design methods as mostly a contribution to the instrumentalization of design. Indirectly, as an influence on some design educators, his reductionism got further reduced. Stan Allen's thinking turns design inward. You point out that he wants to discover new uses for theory and bring it closer to the complex problems of 'the real'. But whose theory, what theory? In contrast, a lot of what Schön does is to try to make tacit knowledge/habitus present in its moment of formation. In doing this, he formalizes it and makes it prescriptive (as with an architectural student's matrix). All this is the antithesis of connecting the practice of design to 'the real' world's complexity, as it is indivisible from the complexity of design. In this discussion, a great deal of the situated nature is absent. The relation to practice is far more varied than Schön and Allen present.

Schön says almost nothing about 'intuition' or 'creativity', but a great many designers create with a variable mix of intuitive formalism – a creative impulse within a structure of control inflecting an aesthetic. At the same time, simulation and appropriation undercut and subvert the agency design process. Difference in design practice undermines generalization. Evoking 'the design process' arrives with a claim of reason and method, but it frequently masks action that is lacking in rigour, inflected by taste, style, fashion and other aesthetic considerations.

DP: *So I guess another way to frame this is to say there is something problematic in the politics of their projects, a certain form of universalism and instrumentalization that enters through the back door, perhaps even in unintended ways, as you point out, depending on who has picked up these ideas. In other words, something we have to become more aware of and politically sensitive to, given the current complexity of the relationship between design defuturing processes and practice, and how, for example, all this intersects with questions of 'difference', no matter whether we are talking about class, race or gender, and how they all intersect.*

You have argued in 'Design as Politics', that design is political in so far as it causes positive or negative worldly effects that individually and collectively future or defuture. You also identify this as the ontological performative character of the designed (material immaterial systems) beyond its specific form or function. You argue in the book that the 'designed' always sets forth a set of directional discernible or indiscernible consequences. Most readers are aware of this through the short-handed statement 'design designs'. But you also argue that knowing what and how to design, or the relation of 'the user' to the design, does not mean the worldly futural agency of design is understood. Can you explain this further and how this relates to the critique you made about theories on 'reflective practice?'

TF: Historically, and still, design defutures: the extent of the 'unsustainable' affirms this. It also evidences the overdetermination of design as service provision – which means the designer does not make the most fundamental design decisions, but designs under instruction of a brief – while existentially occupying a position of knowing situated in a condition of unknowing, all as a result of design being a restrictive practice (the product of a disciplinary division of knowledge, a predominantly instrumental education and dominantly subordinate relation to the dictates of market forces).

Placed in the context of Stan Allen's argument for a 'practice flexible enough' to engage the complexity of what he calls 'the real' is irrelevant, and is welded to the status quo. This thinking is part of the problem. Schön gets nowhere near the complexity of the current condition; he does not get close to addressing 'the complexity of complexity' of it. I have tried to deflect away from the misplaced status given to him by the design methods of deadheads who discount the worldly changes in five professions that he engaged in *The Reflective Practitioner* over forty-plus years. Clearly, this sweeping dismissal requires to be justified, albeit briefly. There are three criticisms to be levelled against Schön. The first pedagogic, the second is political and the third epistemological.

The pedagogic criticism in brief is: he underscored and promoted the notion of design 'as a problem-solving activity' – which became a mantra in design education. Yes, design has and does solve some problems, but as its history clearly shows, it also creates them, and some of the problems it creates are massive. But, in addition, what is evident in the present is that so many current worldly problems do not have solutions. Rather, they require adaptive responses. Besides Schön's view being dated and simplistic, it is also mis-directive. For example, sustainable design is presented in design education globally as a means to deliver a solution/solve the problem (as process, object, system). However, the deep structural nature of the unsustainable, which is the fundamental problem, is never adequately recognized and examined. In actuality, the directive force of design is a problem *defining* activity, and places rigorous research centre stage in design practice – Schön's instrumentalism undercuts this, as does design education under his influence.

Design, in common with many practices over the last fifty years or so, set out to gain professional recognition and establish itself as an academic discipline with its induction into the academy in the late '60s/early '70s as a degree course. Schön, as a supporter of the advancement of professions by not just showing 'how professionals think in action' but by instructing such thinking in his exposition of it. The political criticism goes towards this intervention in what is effectively the politics of the advancement of professional practice. In contrast, a critique by Ivan Illich published during the same period of burgeoning recognition of design's status just mentioned, he poses a very different perspective on the professional. Illich contributed the opening essay; it had the same title as the book (a collection): *Disabling Professions*. A few lines into his opening, he proposed to name the moment he was writing, the mid-twentieth century, as 'The Age of *Disabling Professions*, and planetary age in which people had "problems" and experts had "solutions" and scientists measured "imponderables", such as abilities and needs'.[2] Of needs, he remarked, 'It would be pretentious to predict if the age, when needs were shaped by professional design, it will be remembered with a smile or with a curse'.[3] Railing against technocracy, he wrote 'I consider such a descent into techno-fascism as unavoidable unless the major thrust of social criticism begins to change from the support of a new or radical professionalism into the endorsement of a patronizing sceptical attitude towards experts – especially when they presume to diagnose and to prescribe'.[4] The disposition to measure 'imponderables such as abilities' has now been fully realized. The rule of metrics has become an institutional norm, including 'abilities', not least of students and academics in the academy. Likewise, the desire for recognition and status has driven a whole host of territorial divisions of knowledge and subdivisions that directly act against relational understanding and transdisciplinary discourse. What this does is to further constitute a practice as 'restrictive', thereby enabling formal exclusion, the protection of its economic interest (which Illich calls a 'cabal'), and the control of knowledge by the discipline's professional body (the degree to which the system of accreditation of architects by its professional body directs what architects are taught being a good example, as it ties education to the market in the name of professional standards).

Criticism two of Schön's *Reflective Practitioner* (1982),[5] is epistemological. While affirmatively qualifying the 'problem-solving ability' of the five professions he addresses, he elevates the ontological agency and habitus of such professionals. Reflection so contextualized goes to calling up inherently gained knowledge (from the learning and experiential exercise of a practice) to pragmatically identify and resolve a problem within his or her professional

2   Ivan Illich, et al., *Dizabling Professions* (London: Marion Boyars 1977), 11.
3   Ibid., 13.
4   Ibid., 14.
5   Schön, *The Reflective Practitioner*.

remit. Such action is functionally circumscribed – it does not get to identify and engage the problem of the power and knowledge of technocratic professionalism, uncritically serving the political-economic status quo (the issue that Illich foregrounded). So framed, the history of design practice and education is of an obsession with design getting professional recognition and gaining status as a service provision 'profession' – this was indivisible from it gaining recognition as a discipline, and thereafter sub-disciplines like design history and studies (Victor Margolin being one of the major agents of change here). All of these moves lubricated design's passage into the mainstream as a 'restrictive practice' constituting difference, and a wider understanding of design and practice, as on the margins. From this perspective, I see Schön (and his supporters) as part of the problem, as well as them also being implicit facilitators of inducted managerialism. The counter position moves in two directions: an acknowledgement of the huge presence of design/ing outside 'design' and a recognition and understanding of design as one of the agents in the creation of relational/post-disciplinary knowledge.

Theory is evoked numerous times, but its theory is deposited as if the word carried significant meaning in itself; it is used without any *theoretical* substance. The critique of technical rationalism is mild, while positivism is pushed aside and the search for an epistemology declared, but it does not arrive fully enunciated or even suggestively characterized. This is part of the book's appeal – it's an easy read on focussed intelligence of circumscribed practical wisdom.

This condition of limitation goes to Schön's positing of knowledge in/of his real world. It's a vacuous world of anywhere/nowhere western, capitalist, democratic, scientistic and mainstream practices – the dominant comfort zone of design. It is not 'the real world' of conflict, exploitation, crises, injustice, comradeship, pleasure, pain, love, hate, and so on. His real world is banal, his examples of reflections are banal. His presentation of architecture is superficial, as is the associated reflective example of engagement with a student. Design is unproblematically presented via the exhausted cliché of problem solving (that he helped 'fly').

DP: *Yes I think we always pay less attention to the fact that design is also problem creating, and is trapped in the vortex of solutionism that prevents the acknowledgement that in the 'real world' the unsolvable arrives in profusion – this has to be generally addressed by design (amelioration, adaption, mitigation, accommodation, exclusion, etc.). This history has given those designers wanting to be 'radical' a completely inflated sense of the agency of design being at the pointy end of humanism.*

TF: One cannot dismiss the importance of reflective practice, but the scope, means and objective have to go well beyond Schön, in these far more demanding times in the now real, 'real world'. There is a major disjuncture between what worldly circumstances directly should be designed and what continues to be designed. This cannot change unless the practice of design changes, and the transformation of the practice is what changes the design, design education and the designer's habitus. This constitutes the internal agenda of contrapractice. But the external one is even more challenging and ambitious.

DP: *Yes, very ambitious. But this does require more attention to exploring possibilities of radical change within existing conditions. To make a case or take a position on radical change is one thing, but enacting it is of a different order of a challenge. To do this, there seems to be a need to resolve the conflict of interest between upholding the status quo and implementing a decisive measure of radical change, what to sustain and what to let go of completely, and all this within problematic political formations. What are the political challenges associated with the questions of enacting change?*

TF: The short, sharp answer – there is no change without conflict. The status quo cannot be upheld while radical change is created. The forces that negate the future have to be destroyed for there to be a future. The fact that this fact is avoided, or ignored, is what has brought us all to a deepening crisis of which there is no visible end. So framed, to reiterate: contrapractice is about the destruction of defuturing practices, while creating ones that future. The challenge is to take the first steps.

The long answer – sustaining the myopic political order is overriding the sustaining of the means to secure the ongoing Sustainment of the conditions of life. There is an absolute inability to confront the unavoidable fact that the way of life of all, but the world's poor, cannot survive. It is not just the climate that is at a 'tipping point', but rather life as it is currently understood and lived at this moment cannot continue, so will not. The significant unknowing, avoidance and silence of government; the industrial-corporate privileging of the extant global economy, is stupidity beyond measure. The only thing that divides us late-modern beings from recognizing the actual madness of the situation in which we all exist is our chronophobia: our inability to see it in time and to presume the permanence of what we see at the moment. If one could step into the future one would see so much of what is now present swept away. Even if radical action were immediately taken, major cities, whole nations, once viable environments and multitudes of living species will go. These remarks are not dystopic projection, but the reality of available data.

The myopia and short-termism of government and capital effectively sacrifice the future to sustain the present, with the consent of the majority of voters in democratic regimes and with complete disregard for the interests of the total population in those that are not democratic. Yet there is another option, one hard to achieve but essential to voice and work toward. It is an unavoidably difficult redirective change toward material equitable utility as the foundation of a modest way of life, complemented with a massive immaterial investment in socio-cultural post-development. This prospect is not posed in any way as a low-budget utopia. It is not remotely a romantic 'back to nature' vision, devoid of conflict. It would require a huge redirection of technology and adjustment of work and ways of life. The process would be hard, take a century or more and happen in worsening conditions. Life would not be in any way easy. Design activism mirrors in miniature the large disjuncture between crisis and the political. It still serves mostly unknowingly, but marginally critically, the status quo and the sustaining of the unsustainable.

DP: *It is however difficult to imagine the path towards such action given that the 'profession' is bonded to the market economy. Design education feeds this labour pool. It is very difficult to hold on to whatever critical sensibility is acquired during the education process, for as soon as the young designers enter the labour force they conform or are unemployed. Can we say that contrapractice aims to break this mould and can lift practice to a second-order as a supplementary force that can work against institutionalized defuturing politics in demonstrable forms?*

TF: The action is not restricted to design/design education, the practice agenda is much wider. On the issue of a force. It's not about lifting practice up, but, as argued, destruction and replacement. Destruction needs to be understood as not one simple act of violent erasure (although in some cases this might be needed). It can be an act of disassembly, remaking; or redirecting toward other means or ends; it can be a stripping back or an adding on. Again, there is no general answer: the action needs to be specific and situated. Contextually, such change will not happen via voluntarist enlightened action but rather because of the speed of a breakdown arriving from defuturing enviro-climatic and other impacts. Within a wider response to this situation, practices need to acquire the ability to respond to the unfolding imperatives; however, while it remains bonded to market forces, it is unable to do this. Although, as the design labour force shrinks, which it will do as AI becomes a directive force of design, and as economies contract, then contrapractice can potentially attract and create a substantial cadre of designers who can help activate it. But this can only arrive through, and by, an organic 'redesigning design' beyond design professions' design practices.

DP: *So contrapractice can only be achieved through an overt politicization of design, as an intervention within the disjuncture between all that constitutes the condition of global criticality and the inertia of myopic politics in the face of it. Is it correct to say that contrapractice intervenes not only by trying to engage the political institutions directly but also by striving to engage defuturing practices of those who may or may not be aware of the consequences of their action.*

TF: The objective is the overt politicization of practice. Design/designers can assist in this by contributing to the process becoming organic (which means contrapractice being taken up by diverse practitioners and then taking on a life of its own). While there may be material effects, there is also the objective of taking action against the agency of defuturing practice, as they are present and politically unavoidable, as evidence of demonstrable material change. Thus, making such a change needs to become something that political institutions cannot avoid. Such action is not protest, gesture or mere provocation. Rather, it is a process of catalytic action. This process has a starting point and can only advance by a *praxis* formed through 'learning in action', which means going beyond Schön-like reflection to learn the nature of action itself. By implication, this means not just learning *from* action but *about* action in relation to phronesis (practical wisdom) as elemental to *praxis* as an ontological condition of knowing, acting and being.[6]

DP: *Well, in that case it is necessary to talk about the link between 'praxis' and 'particular kind of politics' that starts to appear problematic within the 'accelerationist question'. I am thinking of what Marx wrote in 1845, particularly point XI of Theses On Feuerbach, where he states that 'philosophers have only interpreted the world in various ways; the point is to change it'. The action of changing something demands a theoretical understanding of what needs to be changed and the means to politically act – that is, change requires praxis. Marxist praxis is framed in the earlier section of the book in the following way:*

For Marx, the term was posited with a particular form directed at a politically informed practice. To undertake and freely participate in action to engage and advance praxis is indivisibly to change the self and in some politically affirmative way, the world is occupied. In contrast, for Heidegger, praxis has multiple meanings clustered around 'concernful dealing'.[7] So viewed, it is a condition of engagement of seeing and acting that also implies poiesis (contemplative engagement) as directed by phronesis (wisdom and sound judgement).

While Marx and praxis are introduced, what is left out is how this notion has been picked up in the post-Marxist discourses as a kind of privilege of 'the left', many people understand 'praxis' as a particularly liberatory form that works against particular forms of oppression brought about by capitalism and as having a particular relation to revolution. Those on the left who picked up this Marxist notion of praxis were relatively oblivious to the fact that secular liberalism was also about praxis. It is not only the left that theorizes the world while they purported to be changing it. The right is at it too. Operational forms of neo-liberalism are also a part of praxis, aren't they? It seems to me that there is a need to unpack praxis in this context in a more nuanced way.

TF: There is always a dilemma when evoking Marxism and *praxis*: to pass over suggestively or to start qualifying and potentially bury the argument under a mountain of qualifying detail? To illustrate, Marxism was never singular, but a

---

[6]   *Phronesis* is one form of knowledge, *techne* is another and *episteme* is a third, see William McNeill, 'The Complication of *Praxis*" in *The Design Philosophy Reader*, edited by Anne-Marie Willis (London: Bloomsbury, 2019), 39–44.

[7]   Heidegger, *Being and Time*, 68.

plurality of competing and contesting factions: Trotskyites, Marxism-Leninism, Left communism, Stalinist economism, Libertarian Marxism, Marxist human-ism, Marxist theology, Analytical Marxism, Maoism, et al. Then, with the Fourth International in 1938, a socialist international organization consisting of followers of Leon Trotsky split into contesting groups between and within countries all claiming ownership of the Fourth International doctrine. Thus, there is Marx's understanding of *praxis* (for which I focussed on *concernful dealing*), and then there are Marxism's varied transformed interpretations.

DP: *Equally then there are the various moments of post-Marxism prefigured by Antonio Gramsci, who moved the focus from the economic base, the mode and means of production, to the socio-cultural superstructure. To my mind, he did a lot of work to connect the questions of epistemology(or learning) to the project of change in a way Marx never did. I would say that the notion of 'learning in action' relates mostly to this trajectory.*

TF: Yes, but as you can see, all this was to create divisions among politi-cal activists and philosophers (who strayed beyond Marx). The concept of *praxis* is layered onto this complexity, while also being posited with specific meanings within divergent philosophies and social theories of theory/practice fused in action (concernful dealing). As for the right, their domi-nant ideology and basis for change, is much older and primarily centred on liberalism and was bonded to laissez-faire, to an anything goes 'free-trade' adopted by the colonial trading companies established mostly during the early seventeenth century, and equally on the Enlightenment construction of the individual subject. All of which was to prefigure neo-liberalism and the capitalist market as the primary force of global historical change across political ideologies. Again, there were variations of extreme economic deter-minism to liberal-humanism. *Praxis* cannot be understood and resolved in the abstract. It is conjunctural.

DP: *I find that the different political trajectories and political categories get muddled up when thinking about questions of practice in the context of the 'heat age' where the post/neo-Marxist left accelerationist and right-wing neo-reactionary extremes fold in on each other like a mobius strip. Ideas of techno-affirmative futures that call for technological solutions that could address social issues such as inequality seems very liberating – except some-times they also seem to embrace a Promethean spirit of technology as a force of domination over 'nature' (which then links to techno-solutions as the way to resolve enviro-climatic crises). The right-wing politics that looks to ways of using technology to transcend/erase the limited ways of liberal democracy and thereafter as a means to install a hegemonic regime of corporate control is the other extreme. How and what should we think of the polarity between a techno-left idealism versus a far-right authoritarian realism with political connections and significant economic power?*

TF: Neither techno-left idealism nor far-right authoritarian realism offer a politics appropriate engaging the present nor creating a viable future – they represent the face of political redundancy. They represent political practices that contrapractice has to displace.

DP: *I find it interesting that you often use Foucault to talk about algorithmic technologies and discursive practices and their effects on the production of particular subjectivities, and go on to show how algorithmic technologies in their discursive functions act in a micro-political manner on the very affects and the subject formation of the communities and individuals. In your work, you often explain this by highlighting the ontological designing function of algorithmic technologies and their effects (semiotic). This was, in fact, part of the critique and the updating of Foucault's work that happens through Deleuze and Guattari, where they end up saying that one needs to take 'micro political' resistance seriously. But then, when speaking of de Certeau and his notion of the 'micro-politics of resistance', the argument made in a previous chapter suggests that these subtle minor tactics of resistance of the general public are not modes of resistance but rather modes of coping. This reading of de Certeau seems to indicate that resistance can only be happening at a macro level, something which comes with a clear imperative, which could only be established by a higher level of awareness for a political cause. From a very contemporary perspective, besides being very Eurocentric, de Certeau reads as naïve in the face of the still increased power of the desiring machine of techno-cultural capital. However, a trace of such naivete lives on, but with dark overtones (it can be found, for instance, in Mark Fisher's* Capital Realism*). Twenty years on, the co-authored second volume of 'The Practices of Everyday Life' (de Certeau, 1994) is a compression of the field of inquiry. It looks at micro-histories of adaptive everyday practices in the private domain of the home (like cooking, as well as the experience of life in the public sphere of the neighbourhood). The publisher describes what is presented as the 'subtle tactics of resistance and private practices that make living a subversive art'. This is not resistance. It's what people do and have always done in order to cope, make the best of their circumstances and survive. Would you like to explain the almost contradictory ways the notion of 'micro-politics' is addressed in these two readings? Or is that not the case?*

TF: Both Foucault and de Certeau recoiled from institutional politics, but differently. Foucault occupied a kind of critical libertarian politics. As such, he was critical of the political status quo, and in particular of the power of the state and established institutions. His response was to advance a micro-politics of resistance. At the same time, he also polemically addressed expansive political issues of major social concern, like war and racism, in his 'Society must be saved' lectures of the mid-1970s. But in doing so, he rejected adopting allegiance to any political regime, practices or values. While agreeing with Marx on the significance of power, he theorized power in a more disaggregated way, while Marx viewed structural elements of society as unified blocks (as with class).

Whereas Michel de Certeau's position was, as indicated, more micro-conservative libertarian rather than micro-politics now overridden by macro crises. His relation to everyday practices was more of an existential reaction rather than political and economic. His recoil was more socially biased than Foucault, and his resistance more micro and less political. It was more about the individual coping with life in the political and economic world of the capitalist cycle of production and consumption rather than overthrowing it. His perspective was influenced by both psychoanalysis and spirituality (remembering he was also a Jesuit priest).

DP: *Central to the micro-political in Deleuze and Guattari are notions of addressing the formation of subjectivities at a pre-individual level. This also links to notions of difference understood and framed in affirmative ways that are not based on predefined categories or identities. A difference structured by affirmation does not work with predefined categories, for example between mind and body or nature and culture, nor does it involve a hierarchy between terms. Affirmative difference does not presuppose that the original ontological difference is between that which is and that which is not. Life does not proceed by lack but by mobilization of positive difference along internal lines of divergence where all categories are such by virtue of their relating, not negating. This way of thinking opens up attention to previously sterilize category deviants. Pure difference is both an ontological and an ethical concept. Now as far as I understand, defuturing arrives at affirmation but through a double negation. Can you explain this move a bit?*

TF: Deleuze is searching for a way of thinking about difference that does not view it as meaningless chaos (difference is undetermined – it is everything and nothing). Or as the negation of identities or of things we can represent (if difference is to make any sense, it must be as 'the difference between things'). While Deleuze argues that difference should fundamentally be the object of affirmation and not negation – there are different and multiple forms of defuturing to be negated and not affirmed.

Defuturing as a theory is predicated on a negational logic (but here in the form of a negation of negation) and as such has its alliance with certain fundamental ways of framing the relations between things in the context of historical materialism. What is interesting about affirmative difference is that it utilizes developments in complexity studies, biological systems theory, and other discourses that speak to the complex ways in which living systems evolve through affirmative difference (of minds and ideas, institutions, bodies, communities, organisms). It does so by showing how 'negationally formulated arguments' are in their very nature dualistic, humancentric, and work via 'a social order imposed on nature' – one that negates the natural order of things. Difference posited as value and ungrounded makes no sense (cf Jean-Luc Nancy). It has no independent existence. Difference is difference, 'a rose is a rose' (Gertrude Stein after Hegel). There is no affirmation without an agent. It has also become a cultural trope – it has become a thing to say without meaning, truth, or sincerity (not least in the language of new age parenting of 'wonderful creative children').

DP: *So, what you are saying is that an unqualified affirmation of difference does not help counter the problems of defuturing, it is in fact a part of the problem ?*

I think it is necessary to really articulate what drives the notion of 'the negation of negation'. It is Hegel's dialectic struggle and overcoming of opposites – there is no futuring without defuturing, and futuring cannot arrive without negating the negation that is defuturing. Defuturing is the negation of futuring and thus is a disposition toward negation and the elimination of difference. For example, 'professions' always impose a condition of exclusion, they are a restrictive practice – they are *this* rather than *that; me* but not *you.*

DP: *Let's talk about 'difference' and 'agency' as it relates to the other-than-human context. I think we should make it more clear how contrapractice acknowledges and works with 'difference' as it relates to other agencies that are not human, that still avoids an absolute flattening of human agency in the mix of things (a sort of flat-ontology if you will) as we see in certain contemporary co-design discussions ? For example, I find it very difficult the ways in which some of the current discussions that do take other-than-human agencies seriously place the agency of technology/ technological systems in time and human or the agency of other species within the same flat co-design ontology. I think this, in some sense, completely ignores the structural level of unsustainability (injustice, etc.) that pervades through contemporary ecological crises.*

TF: Contrapractice is an action with specific intent by any cosmologically designated conscious hominoid mode of being. Contrapractice is not an independent agency; it requires a hominoid actor. *Homo sapiens* have to act with and toward their eco-environmental conditions of their existence if they are to survive – this is a fundamental ontological imperative. Contrapractice is a recognition of this imperative and is predicated upon acting against that which negated it. Doing so is not a virtue (i.e., 'respect') but actually an empirical necessity. There are humans and their organic and non-organic others. Some of these others have agency (from the Latin *agentia*: 'active operation, a mode of exerting power or producing effect') others do not.

Thus, to have agency is to have a causal capability beyond a fundamental ontological condition of existence – a horse pulls a cart, eats grass, but a blade of grass is a blade of grass (its nutritional value needs the agency of the horse to be realized). All agency, other than human agency, is 'a difference of'. Non-animate things do not have independent agency (yet) – they require an animatory agent. However, such independence is the ambition of accelerationist autoimmunity (auto-destructive) as the pursuit of singularity as an absolute system without 'us'. Here, with biological collapse (ours and our others), is a speeding toward extinction, and as such is the ultimate object of opposition for contrapractice to

engage. There is no co-design, just an appropriative relation of a thing. Co-design/
actual mutual cooperation (as opposed to its simulated mobilization to thwart
resistance) requires a consensual relation between entities. New materialism
has nothing on offer. All the momentum is towards the inhuman non-human.

DP. *So the essence of ontological design is a posited agency of things. This
is the recognition that ecological change cannot be created by only making
'the masses' conscious. This I suppose marks a shift from overfocus on the
designing of things to look at the effects of design (or the affects) and it has
a resonance with some forms of new materialism.*

TF: Making 'the masses' conscious of ecological change requires a kerb on
consumerism, and the displacement of their market-manufactured desires (everywhere), to start to establish futural Sustainment. This verges on the impossible.
Ontological design, while redirecting the world-formative/performative agency
of designed and made things (toward Sustainment), is hard to emplace *en
masse* (as against the grain of 'market forces'). It is important to work toward,
but not sufficient. Hence, the introduction of contrapractice with its agenda
of eliminating and/or redirecting defuturing practices. This duo increases the
potential of transformative affirmative change – it dramatically expands the
number of 'change agents'. Rather than having a focus on designers its directed
to practitioners at large.

   These ideas were at the heart of the Sydney based EcoDesign Foundation
(EDF). In the early 1990s it was a long way ahead of, for example, Jane Bennett
with her starry-eyed discovery of matter and things: Cameron Tonkinwise and
Anne-Marie Willis wrote an influential book on timber. Willis did a lot of work on
plastics and concrete, and an 'ecology of steel' book was researched and written
by myself and Anne-Marie that was also informed by a decade of architectural
and construction projects aiming to advance sustainable methods and practices.
This history and work put the content of Bennett's chapter on 'A Life of Metal'
in the shade.

THIS CONJUNCTURE

DP: *I think it is important to map out the patterns that connect the main thinkers Bourdieu, Foucault, de Certeau and their take on practice as presented in
the book for the readers, in order to discuss how what is proposed relates to the
present conjuncture's attempts to go beyond some of this work. In different ways,
all these thinkers ground their work in a 'materialist reading' of 'practice'.
Also, though they answer the question at different levels of abstraction and
with different levels of political intensity, all three of them pose their questions
on practice with an interest in 'how practice operates' rather than asking
'what is practice'? Bourdieu comes close to essentializing certain features,
through his theory of habitus, making his work perhaps the least relevant for
those who want to engage the question of transformation and practice and*

most relevant for those who are interested in understanding the transmission process. Foucault's work provides a better understanding of the possibility of transformation, and de Certeau's work falls somewhere in between. Can you elaborate more on how you think the notion of transmission(stasis) vs. transformation(flow) plays out within these three thinkers?

TF: Rather than directly answer this question, I will make a general, and then a specific response.

To 'go beyond' presumes 'our work' is, or has to be, responsive to theirs. Whereas their interests and conjuncture have little in common with ours. What directs the project of this book is to constitute practices against practices that defuture. To do this requires establishing an understanding of practice. What the thinkers addressed is to put in place a history of thinking practice that establishes its significance as 'a matter of concern' that allows our approach and its context to be seen and evaluated comparatively in a field of difference. Yet as recognized, we and they do not occupy the same moment, discourse or objective out of which an understanding and address to practice is constituted. In this sense, there are for us no positions to 'go beyond' but rather they were a foil to think with, and against. In this respect, our work adds to a body of work from circumstances of difference from theirs that really means the milieu of our project is of a different epoch, one less inflected by modernity and a Eurocentric sensibility.

Having said this, Bourdieu, Foucault and de Certeau are not equivalent in general and in relation to practice. Bourdieu really stayed firmly planted within reflexive sociology and, as such, he established and exercised enduring influence in and beyond sociology; de Certeau situated himself dominantly within the cultural theory of the everyday and has become of lesser influence as interest in the area widened, while Foucault and his agenda is of a different order of thinking. His theoretical reach was huge. As a philosopher, historian of ideas and the political, Foucault's influence has extended over so many disciplines, not least because of the ways he addressed the relationships between power and knowledge. Bourdieu and Foucault are regarded as distinctive, if not unique, thinkers, whereas de Certeau is not. Many other engaged thinkers, and the nuanced details, of the everyday, include Henri Lefebvre (on the everyday and everydayness), Maurice Blanchot (on everyday speech) and Alfred Schutz and Thomas Luckman with their two-volume phenomenological study of *The Structure of the Lifeworld*, which dissected the everyday in great detail. Prior to them, and more philosophically, Edmund Husserl and Martin Heidegger engaged the everyday at a fundamental level. So positioned, what de Certeau contributed was to establish 'the everyday' as one of the primary objects of study of contemporary cultural studies.

There are two specific concerns that have influenced what has been argued here: Bourdieu's notion of habitus as a process of transmission from an experiential acquisition, of knowledge, to its embodiment, and then to its situated application, and Foucault's understanding of discursive practice and its agency.

DP: *Clearly the era of Bourdieu, de Certeau and Foucault was very differ-ent from the present moment of crises. Their formative years were between the aftermath of the Second World War and the unfolding of the condition of possibility of reconstruction. Whereas thinking and writing now is with an awareness of 'end times' driven by accelerationist practices. In simple terms, this is the difference between: the hope and expectation of progress as a condition of thought and action, and the present bald fact of the end of progress (with technological innovation being projected as its surrogate). They also represented a moment of post-war ending of European colonial power and the dominance of Eurocentric thinkers. For example, when we conceptualize the 'contra', we have to both celebrate the significant interest placed on questions of decoloniality but also take into account the problematic ways in which 'decoloniality' has been embraced as a trope of intellectual political correctness. As shown, at present it is applied to almost any area of knowledge as if it were a filter that can decontaminate it.*

TF: Yes, the current appeal to decoloniality mostly always fails to grasp the nature of colonization, and its recreated continuation, its power and its inter-nalization. It mirrors what has become a feature of what historian Edward Thompson called 'a poverty of theory', whereby every idea of significance is reduced to a set of pluralistic tropes that stand in for substance and agency – exactly the same fate befell sustainability. As a consequence, a reactionary counter reaction against theory (less academically contained than Thompson's) has been created: 'anti–wokeism'. Eurocentric thought still wields enormous power, this does not mean it should be totally erased (even if this were possi-ble), but rather that its bias be made fully present, critically reflected upon, be selectively appropriated, and contested by/supplemented with other ways of thinking. This demand confronts all of us, for epistemological colonialism touches the colonized and colonizers alike. Most fundamentally, 'decoloniality' starts with engaging one's self.

Situated critical analysis is elemental to contrapractice. However, and essen-tially, it has to be constituted in a situated conjuncture. It cannot be reduced to 'a method'. Methodologies mostly are/have become handmaidens of technological rationalism/instrumental reason – they are part of the problem as they invite mechanistic and universal application. It follows that what can be taken from our three highlighted thinkers is not methods, but the imperative of immersion in transformative thought. In this sense, what one is doing when committing to advance contrapractice is fundamentally to ontologically transform one's own practice, and thereafter the practices of others. Certainly, this is what Bourdieu did, this is what Foucault did.

DP: *Clearly, contrapractice cannot be reduced to 'a method'. But you do speak of a certain necessity of setting Sustainment as an imperative and working towards finding a commonality in difference to work towards. You also point out that it may not come through incremental choices but almost requires a certain form of imposed order. But the issue with Sustainment is always finding out what needs to be sustained and how to work with that, but also maintain relative openness to variety. But then defuturing does not tell us how to grapple with the very problem of setting up the imperative in the first place, and perhaps this is something that contrapractice could be more specific about. To me, this is still a question related to the operationality of practice and of methods (albeit framed in a broader way than how you qualify the term earlier). How should one think of imperatives in a broken, scattered and polarized world?*

TF: Sustainment is not 'an imperative', it is *the* imperative. Without Sustainment, there is nothing but entropic finality. So positioned, Sustainment names the underpinning project that consolidates all actions that are futural. In this sense, it is not a single unified, somehow centrally managed, exercise but a diverse and growing accumulative gathering of action, with transformative agency, authored by the imperative becoming directive of the concept realizable in difference. As a project, it is of a scale greater than the Enlightenment as it accompanied European expansionism. Unlike the Enlightenment, the concept is not based on a universal epistemological imposition but a negation of that which is unsustainable and its replacement with that which sustains the condition of futurality. As effect and consequence, neither of these sought effects are reducible to just phenomenal forms, although both have specific agents directed at elimination of what defutures and the creation or adoption of what sustains (e.g., a claimed sustainably designed house can only be designated to deliver Sustainment if all that constituted it) from the point of the extraction/manufacture of all of its employed materials, and the way of life of its occupants – are sustainable. Sustainment is not relative, and neither the unsustainable nor Sustainment are defined by designation but by predetermined or retrospectively verified effect. Likewise, neither can be delimited: both exist as a potentiality.

Sustainment is futuring as process. Notwithstanding the proximate relation to the notion of 'sustainability', as indicated, Sustainment is not reducible to an attained end, or instrumental actions. Contrapractice thus needs to be understood as the transformative agent acting against unsustainable practices – material and immaterial, mental and physical – and for the establishment of practices that are agents of Sustainment.

DP: *Insofar as practices are informed via instruction, training and education (and are learnt recursively) Sustainment and contrapractices need to be firmly embedded in the very core of education at every level from the nursery to the university, and across all vocational education and training. Starting from the status quo, it is a project of unlearning, relearning and new learning. The contemporary problem of how 'sustainability features in education' is worthy of consideration. For example, sustainability or ecological education as present in different universities predominantly takes the following two forms: (i) as curricular content scattered across a wide variety of disciplines (like engineering, architecture, design, environmental stud-*

ies, law, business and the sciences) at varied levels of significance. As such, it does not disturb the structure of the divisions of knowledge; and (ii) as unevenly applied policy and practice, such as waste management, transport, purchasing goods and services, mode of energy uptake and its management. How could it be otherwise?

TF: Sustainment could and should be the foundational directive intent of education. It is not simply the 'what is to be learnt' but the ground of learning upon which all education stands. As such, it places education at the forefront of the continuity of the vitality of being itself. It is not an 'add on' project, subject, course, program or discipline, but the reason for learning once the scale of what needs to be learnt is grasped as being totally relationally interconnected in the service of Sustainment. Currently the plurality of disciplines, divisions of knowledge, specialisms, practices and their subordinate structures are de-relational and serve competing interests – epistemological, pedagogic, economic, social, political, scientific, technical, environmental, contemporary, historical, cultural – in doing so they create an incoherent condition of induction into knowledge and practice that future and defuture, are un-sustain-able, and sustain-able (a situation made all the worse by business models, funding structures and modes of administration). Effectively, education has become out of joint with creating, enabling and maintaining the fundamental condition necessary for the continuity of being: Sustainment. Obviously, it's not possible to sweep everything away and start again, but it is possible to retrofit the educational edifice and its practices. Sustainment has to arrive as 'the project', as the screen that filters what needs to be removed, repaired or remade from what needs to be advanced and developed, newly created and woven into the entirety and the connecting conduit through which the evolving presence and force of Sustainment flows and grows. Some will view this as ideological imposition and incredulous. The available evidence indicates it is not. STEM education (Science, Technology, Engineering, and Mathematics) has arrived and is being introduced from K to PhD. It's presented as responding to an instrumental imperative. In actuality it is responding to, and ideologically supporting, the unsustainable economic status quo. Education centred on Sustainment as outlined is its absolute other; in this respect, it is political, and essential to the continuity of being: there is nothing more or less ideological than it and being. That is why, in contrast, in order to make the university futural, Sustainment should undergird and relationally direct its curriculum to become its 'logic of practice'.

DP: *I think some of the issues that stand in the way of setting Sustainment as imperative can be found within the history of ecology that points towards the ways in which ecological consciousness has developed through the years since the 1960s, perhaps. For example, although the level of concern about ecological questions has increased, there is no coherent characterization of ecological consciousness and green politics. In fact what it has in some ways a contradictory and contested history from the 1930s to the present evident in the writings of, for example: Walther Schenscher (ecofascism), James Loveloch*

(Gaia), Arne Naess (deep ecology), Warwick Fox (transpersonal ecology), Vandana Shiva (Eco feminism), Green Anarchism (Murray Bookchin), David Suzuki (bio-essentiaism), Enrique Leff (economic rationalism), John Bellamy Foster, Andreas Malm(Eco-socialism), Ecological epistemology (Gregory Bateson), Felix Guattari (ecological complexity), Eric Hörl (general ecology). But what all these approaches seem to share is a critique of the ways in which the search for an ecological consciousness intersects with a certain form of 'false consciousness' that assumes that, in some ways, they are dealing with the problem, when in reality they are still having trouble locating the ecological problem. This is also reflected within some of the issues around green politics. What are your thoughts on this?

TF: First, the whole discourse of 'ecological consciousness' has dissolved into the polarization and pluralization of the concept of ecology itself. There is still a dominant biocentric view of ecology in circulation, and its pluralist positions, as you listed. But then there is also the going beyond the biological (as the book has discussed) of Gregory Bateson, with his straying away from the biology and into an ecology of mind in the 1970s, and then Felix Guattari's three ecologies (mental, social and environmental) of the 1980s. Followed later by Erich Hörl's General Ecology of a 'thousand ecologies' from the natural, to the technological and artificial as engaged via mind, information, media to the political, power and perception and more. Effectively the ecological/consciousness distinction has collapsed, in its place and open question: a consciousness of what? As for false consciousness, it was a concept introduced into Marxism in the 1920s by Georg Lukács, influenced by Kant's distinction between the real (the noumenal) and appearances (the phenomenal), and later displaced by making the connection between ideology and consciousness, implied by Antonio Gramsci and overtly stated by Louis Althusser (this was a major issue of theoretical Marxism in the 1970s[8]).

As for the incoherent directionality of 'green politics' (biocentrism and social reform), and the 'green new deal' (the technocentric quasi-socialist version of green politics), plus transitionalists (politically idealistic, gradualist, biocentric, systems reformist, and functionalist) who all hover on the political margins and often are complicit with the mainstream and dysfunctional social demo-cratic politics and its inability to confront the scale of the defuturing problem. Additionally, it constitutes its agenda via 'the ecological' division of knowledge that negates the political reality of an enviro-climatic actuality of an extraordi-nary and complex relationality. In common with the mainstream, single-issue ecopolitics refuses to confront the present nature and scale of the crises, which the clichéd and now vacuous call to 'save the planet' epitomizes.

DP: *Accelerationism further complexifies the project of green politics/practice. Putting accelerationism into this frame of reference requires recognizing accelerationism as historically structurally elemental to modernity. The*

---

[8]   Centre for Contemporary Cultural Studies, *On Ideology* (London: Hutchinson, 1977).

problem of defuturing, and the eco-environmental crises that fold into this as part of a still-growing compound problem, as you refer to it in your previous work. Discussions around the 'great acceleration' have acknowledged this and asserted that it is an urgent issue to respond to. The far-right and left accelerationists seem to share the view that an ecological disaster cannot be avoided. The right then wants to 'let it rip' so as to move into a dominant technocentric corporate future – with all that is outside its operational structure abandoned, while the left, who are equally technocentric, present an idealized residually humanist Eurocentric Promethean powered utopian future.

TF: Yes, the right takes a Chinese-like authoritarian capitalism on steroids as its model, while the left accelerationism is stranded in a techno-romantic fairyland. All that far-right accelerationists offer is the speeding of defuturing to a post-defutured techno-authoritarian dystopia for who-so-ever survives in a condition of biophysical and socio-political collapse. From this 'clearing away' the building of their 'new world' begins. The staggering-on status quo, and its margins, has no ability to slow this dynamic of defuturing because of its political impotence. All the critiques of humanism (via postmodernity, new materialism etc.) are correct in their analysis but even more bereft at providing a means to act. There are few options, and they are dictated by circumstances and are without a political actor to animate them. A declaration of a global 'state of emergency' could be called if there were an entity to call it and administer it well, and even then, compliance would not be total (in some respects, the history of Covid confirms this). One can say that chaos, breakdown and total disaster is the likely future, while most are recoiling from this prospect in the hope that another possibility will be created and salvation will arrive.

ON POSITIONALITY

DP: *I would like to discuss the work of Bourdieu, Foucault and de Certeau further. They can all be critiqued for speaking of practice in a Eurocentric way. In others words, it is important that the 'practice question' and the question of 'resistance' are also read through a 'subaltern/southern' frame. Perhaps some of our readers might want to take this up as a project. I would say that such a task is necessary, but I think to do that we need to see how their work opens up the possibilities of such a project also. All of them were located within the French intellectual culture in a specific way. In other words, I think their work does carry an 'oppositional consciousness'[9] of a particular kind. Perhaps, you can explain how you see this 'oppositional consciousness' in relation to the milieus they come from and their particular relationships to politics?*

---

[9]   Chela Sandoval, *Methodology of the Oppressed* (Minneapolis: University of Minnesota Press, 2000).

TF: In going back to Bourdieu, Foucault, and de Certeau, I said earlier that 'they are not equivalent' and in relation to Eurocentrism I would point out Foucault's powerful recoil against racism and Bourdieu complex relation to anthropology – both seen in relation to 'oppositional consciousness' refracted through the history and presence of racism in France. In relation to politics, I think I have already partly answered the question, but there is more to say. Implicit in what I have already said, 'dealing with' Eurocentrism is not a selective process. The ontology it is predicated upon, and the shaping of a consciousness that is expressed in its disposition, is present in its said and unsaid. It is also relative, and so is enunciated by degree and at a particular level, according to the extent of an individual's exposure to a critique of it, and their prior awareness (or not). Once one is cognizant and sensitive to Eurocentrism, which again is by degree, it becomes just another element of the critical lens through which one views, reads or hears any mode of worldly representation. The fundamental problem is its naturalization: its views are dominantly read as universal.

Returning to the issue of 'oppositional consciousness'. It is complex in that it does not exist as a disaggregated checklist. It becomes synthetic and as such frames a disposition that then may get addressed more specifically within a particular context – like for example, a Eurocentric-grounded discussion on migration and politics. Thus, an awareness of it exists prefiguratively (as knowledge), but becomes conscious via contextual prompts. Politically, such an awareness is part of a learnt politics, one that establishes a political position that is then mobilized in various ways (like reading, writing, speech and discussion). But fundamentally in the end, the issues come down to 'oppositional consciousness' which means nothing unless it is translated into political action.

DP: *These three thinkers, again by degree, all had some degree of awareness of an 'oppositional consciousness', but they also seem to display a form of akrasia. Would you say that in part this was generational in relation to France and colonialism, and also because the discourse of decoloniality, a product of post-colonial intellectual culture, was not historically formative in their intellectual development?*

TF: A contemporary thinker of Bourdieu et al., Jean-Paul Sartre, makes this clear. He does this in his famous Preface to Fanon's *Wretched of the Earth* in 1961, where, on the very first page, he cuttingly confronted the epistemological colonialism of the 'European élite' in 'manufacturing a native élite'. Just prior to this publication Sartre had published Volume One of his *Critique of Dialectical Reason* (in 1960, with the second volume published in 1985 and which was unfinished). This project, started at the commencement of the colonial war in Algeria, was to situate universal class struggle in a revisionist dialectical theory of history grounded in what he hoped to be a revitalized Marxism. Although volume one had eighteen pages addressing colonialism – this in the over thirteen hundred pages of the two volumes – it did so in the context of its place in history as a relation between the colonized and the colonizers. My point is: notwithstanding the Fanon Preface, Sartre's sensibility remained Eurocentric because of his inculcation/individuation (Simondon being another of his contemporaries), and his habitus – all of which reiterated Eurocentrism (as an ontology). I would add that *'oppositional* consciousness' puts (academic) careers on the line. Its lack of action has been very evident in recent decades in the inability of academics to act in defence of the humanities and their revitalization. Likewise, to the colonizing project of STEM.

DP: *Why I ask this question is because I think we need to bring the notions of practice and the form of 'oppositional consciousness' that is part of their arguments in conversation with those who have mapped this question by actually taking 'subalternity' (the South) into account. In doing so, I think we might find an alliance between the critique of their positions made in this book and others who speak of practice questions in the South. This alliance between positions of oppositionality is also important in thinking of a particular kind of an intellectual who is politically active, does work towards a 'certain imperative' using their roles to steer everyday action to a realm of resistance and contrapractice. I think both Spivak and Gramsci talk about this in different ways.*

For example, I think it is interesting to look at Foucault and Deleuze's 'intellectuals and power' conversation and Spivak's response to it in the essay 'Can the subaltern speak?' When Foucault and Deleuze start to talk about a new relationship between theory and practice, what they denounce is the need for a certain idea of representation, and at the extremes, they make a case for all forms of micro-political resistance at all levels of practices, very similar to de Certeau's tactics. As Deleuze says:

> *A theorizing intellectual, for us, is no longer a subject, a representing or representative consciousness. Those who act and struggle are no longer represented, either by a group or a union that appropriates the right to stand as their conscience. Who speaks and acts? It is always a multiplicity, even within the person who speaks and acts. All of us are 'groupuscules'.*

But as Spivak critiques this and brings in the questions of subalternity and representation she speaks to the needs for a certain kind of representational practice, or perhaps a certain kind of trained individual who has a better idea of what you in your previous work call 'imperatives'. But who can speak about imperatives? Who can act on imperatives? Are there aspects of this question that need more grounding before being answered?

TF: First, I would add that one cannot separate the conceptual from the actual when addressing what Spivak has to say in the voice of the subaltern. Born in 1942, she grew up and was educated in Calcutta. In 1961, she moved to the USA and joined the graduate program in English at Cornell University. A year later, she transferred to the new Comparative Literature program, with a dissertation under the supervision of Paul de Man (to become one of Derrida's most significant interlocutors). It was from this background that she translated Jacques

Derrida's *Of Grammatology* – Derrida being a French Algerian Sephardic Jew, born in Algiers in 1930, who moved to study in Paris at the age of nineteen. It was Spivak's translation of Derrida that projected her into international academic visibility.

Her 'Can the Subaltern Speak', regarded as an influential, if not seminal, essay, concludes with the stark declaration: 'The subaltern cannot speak'. It is framed a few lines earlier with these words of Jacques Derrida calling for a rewriting of '... that interior voice of the other within us'.[10] Here, one remembers that both of them left their native land in the South aged nineteen. I choose to read 'us' as 'he and she'; there are clearly others.

Now it is important to recognize that a common (global) understanding of the South cannot be assumed. The very notion of the South is now under attack from the South as being reflective of a condescending designation. At the most basic, it cannot be seen just as a geographic and stable designation. People of the South exist in socio-economic margins of the North as migrants, the displaced and abandoned; for example, La Courneuve, a poverty-stricken municipality of Paris. Likewise in the North (Trump's USA) people of the South (migrants of varied status) are being 'rounded up' (a cattle industry metaphor) and returned to *the* South. The ethnic mix, culture and history of these two populations are very different, but they share a common condition of silence.

On the question of practice, the meta-practice of the South is that of survival.

DP: *Agreed. I was born into the middle class in Sri Lanka, lived through a civil war as a child and educated as an architect within the Sri Lankan system. I am familiar with the meta practices of survival. Whether it's at the level of the household I grew up in, or the level of the broader society or the practice contexts of architecture, many other modes of engagement became subservient to basic questions for survival. The hopeful side of these practices is evident in the tactics of improvisation, bricolage, sharing, social cohesion and the common. On the downside, it produces a culture of violence, and crimes of survival. One of the dimensions of life in the South is the manifold and constant representational presence of the North as a disabling desire. Hence for example from a very early age one would aspire to move to the North in search for better conditions not only for economic sustenance but in order to find the freedom to think to be futural. One could say that Life is lived in an all-encompassing 'in-your-face' confrontation with 'the lack' – often not just of economic means of subsistence, but of a future. This is a condition that worsens with every subsequent crisis whether it's of a political or economic kind. In fact, it almost seems that the South is continuously structurally defined through a crisis that manages to reinforce its deficient geometry.*

TF: Here, we should perhaps invert the question 'Can the subaltern speak?' and ask 'Can the subaltern be heard?' Bringing these questions to the present,

---

[10]   Gayatri Chakravorty Spivak, 'Can the Subaltern Cannot Speak', in *Marxism and the Inter-pretation of Culture*, edited by Gary Nelson and Lawrence Grossberg (London: Macmillan, 1988), 308.

it is absolutely clear that in an age where climate change impacts are going to increase, together with abandonment, displacement and conflict, silence threatens. The global spatiality of the South is growing, and will do so at a faster rate. The situation is now going beyond and recasting the colonial/decoloniality binary, together with the coming displaced as a mass silent global minority. Likewise, the significance of re-colonization, and new mode of psychic- re-colonization, are going unspoken. It is not that issues of the South and its past are no longer valid, but rather they are being added to, and partly displaced, by those of the present. In a geopolitical world of fragmentation, which is being mirrored geo-culturally, the metaphor, the tragic narrative of Chinua Achebe's classic novel *Things Fall Apart* increasingly and painfully resonates.

DP: *One can presume Deleuze's theorizing of the intellectual 'for us', was actually to have been for the audience of L'Arc, or maybe to more broadly the French reader. Not unreasonably, one can take his position here to be Eurocentric, and situated in European culture. While over fifty years ago, what has changed?*

TF: Now, certainly in the North, it's clear that there are almost no public intellectuals (currently, at the time of writing, the ninety-five-year-old Noam Chomsky has been called the last public intellectual). Another cultural difference is that universities are no longer 'hotbeds' of intellectual life. Certainly, in most 'advanced economies', academics have become service providers within a business model and within a career structure determined by metrics (the hegemony of metrics being a definition of instrumentalism) – evidenced by performance indicators and the like. Education product delivery, monitored by 'teaching and learning' administrators and directed 'learning outcomes' is delivered to a mass-market of 'customers' (students), this to meet primacy of market needs and a required delivery of graduate employability, all accompanied by the de-socialization of academic life (not least by technological mediation). The result has been the arrival of structured conformity, reduced academic freedom, with consequent large numbers of disgruntled, disheartened, alienated academics. The occupation has been reduced to just another job option, with career ambitions displacing political and intellectual culture. As a result, there is now a huge schism between the daunting conceptual and intellectual demands of the age, and the market myopia of educating for 'business as usual', along with the dominant instrumentalism of the institution.

Will the normative condition now in place remain? Will generational change happen as crises deepen? Are there exceptions? Of course, but there are few. Certainly with geopolitical fragmentation, intellectual culture will itself fragment.

The very notion and significance of the 'organic intellectual' addressed by Gramsci (but not recognized by Deleuze) in his opening discussion of 'The Intellectuals' in his *Prison Notebooks* begs acknowledgement.[11] One cannot

---

[11]   Antonio Gramsci, *Selection from The Prison Notebooks*, trans. Quintin Hoare and Geoffrey Nowell Smith (London: Lawrence and Wishart, 1973), 5–23.

speak of an organic intellectual in generality, for they emerge out of specific conjunctural conditions and have agency in that context. So said, the potentially emergent conditions of contrapractices need to be seen as a potential fertile environment for their formation.

DP: *All this points to two forms of change. One type of change takes the form of a significant break, and another points to gradual and incremental change. In some ways, those who accompany the less privileged part of this complex geometry, such as those in the South, often only can think of the gradual process of change and how that figures in practices. I think Eva von Readeker's recent work on Praxis and Revolution frames the possibility of gradual/ incremental change through notions of anchoring practices.*[12]

I think in the context of this discussion, anchoring can also be related to positionality in a different way. With the notion of 'anchoring', there's literally the idea of ground in two ways. There's the idea of being grounded, which is both being realistic and being in place, being situated. Then there is the notion of ground as an epistemological foundation, or taking a position and holding one's ground.

TF: For me, grounding is more a dynamic way of understanding a response to practice than trying to anchor something. Because for me anchoring is holding something in place. I feel the task at hand is breaking, creating, holding new ground.

DP: *Yes, but anchoring can also mean relationships across practices. How different practices relate, that is more than holding something in place. It is about how certain practices can work together in order to help develop a contrapractice, perhaps. I guess if you want to change something, a habit or whatever, you always have this kind of a constellation of practices that you have to work with. So, for an example, very simply speaking, the reason why we're talking about contrapractice and not talking about contra design. But then the question is, how are these practices related to each other? How are they anchored?*

In von Readeker's work, she defines anchoring relationships in three ways. One version is when a praxis becomes a schema for other practices in the narrower sense. so that it defines them. So there is a kind of praxis that then forms a schema for multiple practices. So there is this idea that there could be a more fundamental proxy schema. And then there are like more narrow practices that somehow get anchored. Then the other version is when norms, internal to a particular practice, are extended beyond that practice and become evaluative criteria for broader areas of the social world.

TF: I see relationships across practice as strategic, fluid, collaborative and potentially dynamic. Anchoring connotes fixity and inflexibility. Anchorage

[12]   Von Redecker Eva, *Praxis and Revolution* (New York: Columbia University Press, 2021).

in conditions of crisis may deliver security, but equally maybe be a state of extreme vulnerability. As for what *von Readeker* proposes as you outline it, I find it abstract and (ironically) unlocated. It needs substance to be evaluated. On her anchoring relationships in three ways, first *as when a praxis* becomes a schema for other practices – when I used Heidegger's notion of *praxis* in chapter two as 'concernful dealings' it precisely names a scheme for other practices. As for the other two ways of anchoring they do not provide any sense of what is to be anchored where or why.

DP: *And then, of course, the third one, which I find interesting actually is how the constitutive rules of a particular practice serve as an indispensable prerequisite for entering other practices. So, for example if we are thinking of training the attention to be able to understand the problematic political economy that surrounds the act of designing an object, other practices such as writing or listening can function as anchor practices that aid in the same process of training attention. How does this relate to what you just said about ground?*

TF: First, I repeat that what is proposed does 'not provide any sense of what is to be anchored where or why'. Second, practices are inherently relational: at the moment I am reading and writing; a carpenter making a table of timber is measuring, cutting, assembling, and so on. Within a practice, there are moments of movement and transitory anchoring. What I am recoiling from is the programmatic presentation of anchoring when many relations in practice are contingent, and so circumstantially reactive and fluid.

As for ground, it is foundational and situated and is not simply spatial. As such it is the locus from where things emanate (epistemologically, socioculturally, and in a situated sense: the place from where a practice originates – but recognizing that acceleration exists on the structural conditions of the ground of unsustainable defuturing, so is fated to become groundless).

DP: *We have tried to highlight that abandonment is taking many forms. And within the multiplicity of those forms it is becoming difficult to address questions of practice, agency and positionality by using specific categories (geographical, gender, class, age) that are often used to invoke 'the othered'. It is perhaps important to understand how they all intersect and ask difficult questions, as the familiar categories of the past and present have become fluid and expanded. For example, in what class is the transhuman situated? Are they abandoned as a class beyond and under usual class classifications? Effectively, there are only situated positionalities. Thus, global/universal categories have no descriptive value. In sum, new domains and forms of injustice are overshadowing those of the past that remain unresolved. New modes of oppression and colonization are forming and arriving. The past geography of inequity is breaking down as populations are fractured and move. Consequently, the North and the South can and do exist in the same place. This situation will become even more complex when more people are displaced, or abandoned and as populations are relocated.*

But recently, you also suggested that the nature of these changing geometries and the fractures they produce make the practice aspiration towards the 'pluriversal' problematic due to the nature of incommensurability of the many worlds that are forming within the fractures. For example, you have been talking about the three worlds formed through the techno-accelerationist agenda (of Thiel, Musk et al. – deemed by some to be full of possibility), the worlds of the abandoned (which is emptied by impossibility), and the worlds constituted by the rest (remaining population whose future is preoccupied with a struggle to adapt to continuous conditions of change in the world of fracture zones). In what ways do these three together undercut the proliferation of a 'pluriverse of equivalent worlds of difference'?

TF: The time of the equivalent worlds of difference of the 'pluriverse' – 'a world where many worlds fit'[13] – is passing. It presumed a plural co-existence of 'humans' living in worlds accommodated within a whole in which they all 'fitted', but this is not a sharing of the whole in difference. But the emergent condition is of the 'incompossible', of 'ill-fitting' fragmenting worlds.[14] There is the world of social regression (the abandoned being 'thrown back' toward 'bare life'. of as the retention of much of a familiar world as possible. Then there is the world of the majority population adapting to retain the qualitative condition of life in their dynamically changing worldly conditions as best they can. Finally, in difference, there is the world of mutation of beings (*Homo technicus*) 'evolving' in a 'post-natural' artificial condition of being) retreating into a world of artificially sustained protected environments (spheres and bunkers). Here the commonality of being (of beings and of dwelling, be it in inequity) has ended. Besides the geological mass of planet Earth, there is no one world into which the world in fragments fits. Planets are given, worlds are made: epistemologically, culturally and materially as places of being and dwelling in the widest sense.

The constructed illusion of Anthropos as the sum of *Homo sapiens* no longer holds. The repressed plural identities of the being of different cosmologies have been overtaken in a 'fragmenting world' by the commencement of the fragmentation of 'our' species. The actuality of categorical difference of the other within the same ends, this as the other who is totally other (a bio-technic hybrid) starts to arrive. The pluriverse (as the one in which all fit) cannot accommodate non-concomitant worlds of incompatible world-making beings.

---

[13]   Arturo Escobar, *Designs for the Pluriverse* (Durham, NC: Duke University Press, 2017), xvi.

[14]   Incompossible-used in this context meaning: not mutually possible.

Appendices

Tony Fry

Appendix 1: On an elaboration on Bourdieu's understanding of habitus

1   For Bourdieu, practice is constituted by social action, and is a conduit
    of it. But for practice understood as materially grounded, it also
    emanates from productivism (a classical understanding of matter as
    formed by structural properties – the foundation of atomic theory –
    the ability to make/produce a 'some-thing' via a practice).

2   Bourdieu's anti-science view of practice rested with an implicit action
    grounded in the privileging of the 'intuitive' embedded in habitus. Of
    the practitioner, let's say an artist, he says '… there is every reason
    to think that as soon as he reflects on his practice, adopting a quasi-
    theoretical posture, the agent loses any chance of expressing the truth
    of his practice, and especially the truth of the practical relation to the
    practice'.[1] What Bourdieu is claiming, and in various ways elsewhere
    saying, is that the structures, socially formed and materially
    concretized as a locus of practice, constrain practice in the very
    attempt to make it present. It follows that reflective practice (not least
    by the artist), is antagonistic to gaining knowledge of practice. More
    simply, one could say, artists are mostly antagonistic toward reflecting
    on their practice, and this raises the question of the relation between
    intuition and habitus.

3   Central to Bourdieu's address to practice is that it 'has a logic which
    is not the logic of the logician', again he rests upon a totalizing,
    essentially abstract and grounded in an Eurocentric epistemological
    perspective, whereas all practices have a consequential coherence
    does not mean they in themselves are all logical.[2] The logic of a

---

[1]   Pierre Bourdieu, *The Logic of Practice*, trans. Richard Nice (Stanford: Stanford University
      Press, 1992), 91.
[2]   Ibid., 86.

practice needs to be seen in its consequence. The logic of the relation
of practice *to need* and the *need of* practice arrives a few pages later
in his *The Logic of Practice* when he observes that practical sense
goes before and selects objects and actions on the basis that there
is something to be done.[3] This voluntarist view is clearly not wrong,
but it is insufficient as a 'practical sense' gets reified and systemized
by discursive practices within a performative ontological setting and
process. So said, logically, practice requires a need, but not all needs
are logical. Neither is the application of a logical practice necessary.
logical. Enormous numbers of logically constituted practices have
contributed to bringing numerous forms and conditions of defuturing
into being. The epistemologically posited value of logic cannot
be disarticulated from the object or practice of its application.
Therefore, a distinction needs to be made between the internal logic
of practice and the external worldly application of it. Effectively, the
logic of practice has to be bonded to, and be evident in, a logic of its
application.

4   The critique of habitus by Anthony King, and others, characterizes
it a reductive interaction between individuals as an objectified
transmission, which is undercut by it being cast as an 'intersubjective
interactions between individuals'.[4]

5   Bourdieu's agenda lacks recognition of the link between ontological
agency and 'the world of things', – this in the current, especially fluid,
relation between communication practices, technological change and
culture. Obviously, as he died over twenty years ago, he could not
have been aware of the scale of change in cultures of communication
(but his reader should be, not least in how they now inflect how
habitas is formed and viewed). However, the ontological agency of
things was well recognized in the intellectual culture in France of his
time. For instance, Sartre, writing in 1960, addresses the discovery of
the 'dialectical investigation is that man is "mediated" by things to the
same extent that things are "mediated" by man'.[5] Practice is intrinsic
to this recursive dynamic – this observation directly resonated with
the materiality of things that defuture.

6   Operationally, 'habitus is posed as an 'integral part of an apparatus
of production as unthinkable'.[6] It is therefore elemental to all
practices and material conditions of production are either intuitive
or autonomous. Clearly, this would include the way acceleration

[3]   Ibid., 89.
[4]   Anthony, King, 'Thinking with Bourdieu against Bourdieu: A "Practical" Critique of the
      Habitus', *Sociological Theory* 18, no. 3 (2000): 417–33., *JSTOR*, http://www.jstor.org/
      stable/223327 (accessed 2 May 2023).
[5]   Jean-Paul Sartre, *Being and Nothingness*, trans. Hazel, E. Barnes (New York: Simon and
      Schuster, 1984), 79.
[6]   Bourdieu, *The Logic of Practice*, 116.

has been, and increasingly continues to be, seen as elemental to the practices integral to advanced capitalist means of production. But Bourdieu says 'to assign a quality to an abstract totalization of all practices of, but beyond the mechanical, means no "good" practices are acknowledged'.[7] What is displayed here is a refusal to recognize practice, as situated, is often overdetermined by technical systems.

For him, system is understood as a complex social network, wherein individuals interact on their habitus. He also rails against science as it 'tends to destroy practice by imposing on it the intemporal time of science'. Leaving a question of the voracity of this statement he moves between an instrumental view of practices to a singular one that can assume it to be social. Thus, what is actually being said is that science destroys social practices. Problematically, Bourdieu also posits meaning in the temporal structure of practice: 'its rhythm, its tempo, and above all its directionality'.[8]

In actuality, Bourdieu's moment, analysis and disposition fall between an industrial culture material era of practice and the 'post-industrial' cultural economy (an immaterializing era of practice), which is now poised on the edge of conditions of an epoch of global fragmentation where practice will be thrown into plural situated and disparate temporalities. Even so, the exercise of practice always has an ontologically constituted state of being biased toward futuring or defuturing.

---

[7]   Ibid., 80.
[8]   Ibid., 81.

Appendix 2: Michel de Certeau and *Practices of Everyday Life*

Practices of everyday life[1] for de Certeau were urban and European. Volume one spanned everyday culture, art, the spatial, language and modes of belief. It was also placed in, and responded to, a field of critical concerns on issues of the everyday – here de Certeau engaged Bourdieu and Foucault. Volume two was a collection of micro-studies focusing on the home and home life. In contrast to Bourdieu's reflexive sociology, de Certeau offered a form of quasi-celebratory cultural studies of everyday life; this, embracing a view of consumer constraints and very situated adaptive resistance to 'the market', including the power of the cultural industries. Resistant action was of an individuated customizing of use-acquired commodities for the self. It did not include what are now called hacking systems, direct action, organized politics in opposition to market forces, or means directed at collective economic transformations of consumer culture. As such, the approach reflected familiar cultural politics of Europe in the late 1970s and early 1980s.

The consuming subject was cast as active, not passive, but within the confines of their immediate lifeworld. This very much reflected how cultural studies was to embrace a critical, but increasingly celebratory, relation to popular culture as a domain of resistance. From a contemporary perspective, de Certeau reads as naïve in the face of the still-increasing power of the desiring machine of techno-cultural capital. Although a trace of such naivete remains, it now does so with dark overtones (as can be found, for instance, in Mark Fisher's *Capital Realism*).[2]

The actual dividing line between 'user' adaptation/product modification and producer product innovation is very thin. Seen from the viewpoint of current hyper-consumerism, the power of the appropriation of micro-resistance is

[1]   Michel de Certeau, *Practices of Everyday Life* – Volume one first published in France in 1980, English translation 1984, volume two respectively 1994/1998.
[2]   Mark, Fisher *Capital Realism* (London: Zero Books, 2022).

unbounded – rap music, the tattoo industry, TikTok, fashion hacking: whatever is cool is the rule. Dominantly, resistance is reduced to an aesthetics (and thereafter commodified). Such action may have had some purchase in the past, but this moment has gone.[3]

Placed in the orbit of defuturing, de Certeau's embrace of consumption as a site of liberatory action of the everyday is a soft politics, spanning progressive and reactionary culture, and is devoid of any substantial agency. It can even be seen as complicit with the forces of unsustainability, and self-delusion. This is not an argument against people hacking the market, and customizing their lifeworld, but it is one against a claim that such action is any kind of resistance to the power of market forces, and resistance to the colonizing capability of psycho-technologies.

The co-authored second volume of *The Practices of Everyday Life* arrived almost twenty years after the first.[4] It has an even more compressed field of inquiry, looking at micro-histories of adaptive everyday practices in the private domain of the home (like cooking), as well as the experience of life in the public sphere of the neighbourhood. The publisher describes what is presented as the 'subtle tactics of resistance and private practices that make living a subversive art'. This is not resistance. It's what people do and have always done in order to cope, make the best of their circumstances and survive. It is life in informal communities, during times of economic hardship, and in a more general way, the action of people making what is usually a minor effort to be a 'responsible consumer'. To some degree it is recognition that the home is a primary site of material destruction to which a vast output of 'product' from numerous industries are directed – this in an economy predicated upon continuous consumption of consumable and the replacement of durable goods that, together with the packaging from these goods, the detritus of domestic destruction heads to landfill via regular collections by waste services. Bourdieu's praxeological theory maintains that social life is always in relationship to multiple phenomena; that agents and agency are more than simply structurally determined cultural behaviours, able to be understood through the study of micro-practices in a specific context and in relation to the macro world of structural influences. Does de Certeau do this? Yes, to a limited extent, but his project offers almost nothing in the face of unfolding enviro-climatic and geopolitical crises.

---

[3]   Tony Fry and Madina Tlostanova, *A New Political Imagination, Making the Case* (London: Routledge, 2021).

[4]   Michel de Certeau, Luce Giaed and Pierre Mayol, *The Practice of Everyday Life, Vol 1 Living and Cooking*, trans. Timothy J. Tomasik (Minneapolis: University of Minnesota Press, 1998). Note: the 1980 publication of *The Practice of Everyday Life* was not designated as volume 1.

Appendix 3: Peter Sloterdijk's theory of practice

One of the common catch cries of 'progressive' liberal democrats is for individuals who want change to become aware, use their vote and act politically as change agents as active recyclers, the owners and drivers of an electric car, eaters of organic produce, composters of green waste, people who have insulated their home and installed PV, and so on. Philosopher Peter Sloterdijk has atomized another politics of practice to promote a subjectivist counter position in contrast to action that transforms the structural social order of classes or collectives and the ontological agency of their agency, independent from their level of consciousness. Whereas de Certeau's appeal is to change your individual practice to effect change, Sloterdijk is saying adopt a practice to change yourself, so in your newly gained awareness 'you' will change your life – this on the basis that if enough people do this, everything changes.

So positioned, Peter Sloterdijk's conception of the practice is applied to the discipline of self-production – a position heavily influenced by 'the masters' of the training of body and mind from the cultural traditions of East Asia. This is especially evident in his *You Must Change Your Life*, and is extended in *The Art of Philosophy: Wisdom as a Practice*.[1] In the Introduction to the former work, he summarizes his understanding of practice as the oldest form of self-referential training with the most momentous consequences.[2] Its results do not influence external circumstances or objects, as in the labour or production process. Rather, they develop the practicing person 'himself' and get 'him into shape' as the subject-that-can. The result of practicing is shown in the current 'condition' (that is, in the practicing person's state of capability). Depending on the context,

---

[1]   Peter Sloterdijk, *You Must Change Your Life*, trans. Wieland Hoban (Oxford: Polity, 2009) and Peter Sloterdijk, *The Art of Philosophy: Wisdom as a Practice*, trans. Karen Margolis (New York, Columbia University Press, 2012).

[2]   Sloterdijk, *Must Change Your Life*, 1–10.

this is defined as constitution, virtue, virtuosity, competence, excellence or fitness. The subject, seen as the protagonist of his training sequence, secures potentiates and skills by putting 'himself' through his typical exercise regime.

What is presented can be seen as a 'pitch' to a very particular self – an enlightened self who has risen above the distained masses (not least in East Asia) to realize the idealized self who is 'a general ascetologist, a studier of self-disciplines, and an athlete in pursuit of *mechané* (cunning) of anthropotechnics (the language and practicing of self-forming), and of the *bios theoritikos* (the contemplative life)' all summed up as a 'philosophical multisport'.[3] So considered practice folds into his ideology of discrimination (in all senses of the word), but this does not imply that this is always the case.

Contrary to creating an elite of individual multi-sporting philosophers, and the transformative reach of anthropo-technically transformed subjects are accommodated under the roof of a constructed 'greenhouse' for 'the selected' – this to undergo another kind of practice. One wherein such a self becomes essential to bringing into being a collective within the remit of a counter-practice. One that recognizes its absolute inter-dependence within a social ecology – this in the knowledge that 'it' cannot come to be, and continue to be, without a 'you'. Biophysically 'self' is inextricably linked to its animality, and that of its Others.

Criticism of Sloterdijk arrives from plural viewpoints.[4] Just on the issue of the self, as Adam Robbert points out, changing the self means knowing the self, and this implies self-knowledge,[5] but this knowledge does not necessarily deliver a practice of self or worldly transformation. Sloterdijk views life futurally in structures of social containment (signalled by the metaphorical use of the 'greenhouse') and as elaborated in detail in his Spheres trilogy, 1998, 1999 and 2004.[6] As has been discussed at length in the book, the future is now being recast as, and by, a deepening enviro-climatic and geopolitical crises and the instability they portend. Against this backdrop, Sloterdijk's vision now resonates with the accelerationist corporate techno-elite delinking from the biophysical world and a withdrawal into constructed protective artificial environments. It also resonated with the cultural selectivism and eugenic trace that is an undercurrent of accelerationism, and that figures in Sloterdijk's history.

Peter Sloterdijk gave a speech in Basel on 15 June 1997 entitled 'Rules for the Human Zoo'.[7] It was repeated in Oberbayern on 17 July 1999. The issues

---

3   Ibid., 47.
4   Oliver Davis, 'Anthropotechnical Practising in the Foamworld', *Angelaki* 26, no. 1 (2021): 109–23, https://doi.org/10.1080/0969725X.2021.1863600 (accessed 15 February 2023); Adam Robbert, 'Cosmos and History', *The Journal of Natural and Social Philosophy* 13, no. 1 (2017): 1–14, https://cosmosandhistory.org/index.php/journal/issue/view/31 (accessed 16 February 2023).
5   Robbert, 'Cosmos and History', 3.
6   Sloterdijk, *Spheres* trilogy: *Bubbles* (1998); *Globes* (1999) and *Foam* (2004), see details as listed in references.
7   Eric Brown, 'The Dilemmas of German Bioethics', *The New Atlantis* (Spring 2004): 36–53, https://thenewatlantis.com/wp-content/uploads/legacy-pdfs/TNA05-Brown.pdf (accessed 11 November 2024).

he raised became widely published. He argued that media saturation, popu-lar culture and consumerism were undoing the humanist project of creating moral, political, and civilized subjects: for him, 'man has not been tamed' and was regressing. But advances in reproductive biology and genetic science can reverse this situation by altering the human genome, so conscious control over our species breeding, along with managing human reproduction, will enable 'us' to become fully domesticated human beings. Unsurprisingly, the ideas he voiced evoked memories of eugenic, selective breeding, Nazi fascist genetics and concentration camps. Unsurprisingly, what he said generated a massive public and academic controversy, the resonances of which linger. Then, more recently, Sloterdijk has been arguing that a new type of being will be coming into existence. 'It' will be a biological being fused with its technological pros-thetic extension. Here then is transhuman being – Homo-technicus – at one extreme, a techno-augmented human, at the other an operative system, linked to an information ecology supported and managed by AI – able to simulate a civilized being (but equally able to be coded otherwise).

Appendix 4: Technology revealed and cybernetics stripped bare

French physicist and mathematician André-Marie Ampére first coined the word 'cybernetique' in his 1834 essay 'Essai sur la philosophie des sciences'.[1] He used the word to describe the science of civil government. The idea died, but unaware of its first birth, it was reborn with Norbert Weiner's *Cybernetics. Or Control and Communication in the Animal and the Machine*, first published in 1948.[2] Drawing on the ancient Greek word 'kynernan', which means 'steer', Wiener named the systems concept he was developing as cybernetics. Etymologically, this links to its function in relation to 'control', 'regulate', and 'govern'.[3]

Cybernetics has become integral to modern technological and biological systems theory with profound consequences. Martin Heidegger recognized and rehearsed its significance early in its development in numerous texts, and on many occasions. For him it demonstrated that metaphysics itself became technology and a terminal moment of philosophy.[4] In his infamous 1967 *Der Spiergel* interview, published after his death, Heidegger stated that 'philosophy

---

[1] See entry on André-Marie: Ampérehttp://www.ampere.cnrs.fr/textes/essaiphilosophie/pdf/essaiphilosophiesciences_1.pdf (accessed 7 November 2024).

[2] Norbert Weiner's, *Cybernetics. Or Control and Communication in the Animal and the Machine*, published in *Cybernetics. Or Control and Communication in the Animal and the Machine* (Cambridge, MA: MIT Press, 1961).

[3] What Wiener did was to create a model and method of cybernetics able to be brought to anything presented and 'positioned' as a system of control. For example, industrial production, traffic management, prison administration, urban planning, air-traffic control and so on. Early applications also focussed on self-organizing systems, information systems, and production control.

[4] Martin Heidegger, *The End of Philosophy*, trans. Joan Stambaugh (1954, Chicago: The University of Chicago Press, 2003), 93.

dissolves into the individual science: psychology, logic and political science'.[5] Then, when asked 'what or who takes the place of philosophy?' he immediately answered: cybernetics.[6]

During the opening of Heraclitus Seminar (1966/1977) – based on a discussion between Heidegger, Eugen Fink and other participants – there is a crucial exchange on Heraclitus fragment 64: 'And thunderbolts steer (my emphasis) the totality of things'.[7] As a metaphor, thunderbolt is discussed as an 'outbreak of light' and a 'bringing forth' that in darkness enables 'movement'.[8] Here then is cybernetics is the essence bringing to light and movement (disclosure and action). This also leads to consideration of steering as coercion (a claim made by Fink, that Heidegger questioned and that Fink restated). After which Heidegger poses a rhetorical question, and in doing so makes a leap in thought and time, saying: 'Isn't present-day cybernetics itself also steering'.[9] One could now also say that the forces of steering have now been amplified – not least by algorithms (as they employ cybernetic memory).

Yuk Hui states: 'Cybernetics as a universal reflective thinking has displaced the role formally played by philosophy as reflective thinking'. But one would add, only in a restrictive sense: cybernetics does not, for example, reflect on ethical, epistemological or existential issues. Although, extended by/as AI, simulated reflection is created. Likewise, second-order cybernetics makes the nature of reflective thinking more complex. Hui also states that cybernetics marks the end of 'the metaphysical dualism in ontology and epistemology'.[10] But here one needs to draw a distinction between the conceptual and operative functions. Hui goes on to pose a crucial question: 'Will cybernetics be the solution to the ecological problems that we face today'? This he links to a question of the long-standing overcoming 'shadow' (de facto consequence) of (Euro)modernity.[11] Taking the implications of the questions in turn.

The answer to Hui's question is a definitive no. There are some (often instrumental) problems that cybernetics, in its pervasiveness, can and may solve, but it will not solve the 'compound problem' that most threatens. As argued in this work, the situation is such that some problems, like the loss of species in the general context of lost biodiversity, don't have solutions. Where

---

[5]   This view reflects an evolving position. For example, in 1952 in the Holzwege collection (Young and Haynes (trans and ed), 2002), he had argued that philosophy in the age of completed metaphysics had become anthropology.

[6]   Martin Heidegger, Der Spiegel 'Only God can Save US Now' Interview (1966), https://archive.org/details/MartinHeidegger-DerSpiegelInterviewenglishTranslationonlyAGodCan (accessed 22 October 2021).

[7]   Marting Heidegger and Eugen. *Heraclitus Seminars*, trans. Charles H. Seibert (Evanston: Northwestern University Press, 1979), 9–10. Thunderbolts is also translated from the Greek as lightning.

[8]   Ibid., 10.

[9]   Ibid., 12.

[10] Yuk Hui, 'Machine and Ecology', *Angelaki* 25, no. 4 (2020), 56, https://doi.org/10.1080/0969725X.2020.17908320205 (accessed 8 January 2022).

[11] Ibid., 58.

irreversible change has occurred, the only option is adaptation. The obverse question clearly is, has cybernetics contributed to the problem? Certainly, as it has become structurally elemental to technology, it is implicated in many unsustainable industries; the answer is yes. More specifically, as elemental to the 'enframing' (Gestell[12]), the power of technology and of the instrumentalization of especially working life and of education, is an even a more emphatic yes. Of itself, cybernetics does not have an intrinsic moral value, but its uses, like technology, can be used for good or ill.

A question to return to Hui, would be: 'Is there a potential contribution that second order cybernetics can make to cosmotechnics (a significant issue of concern to him) as a steering toward Sustainment?' Certainly, this is a question that contrapractice has to consider. Then there is also a question for more general contemplation: can a situated new cosmotechnics be turned into an 'event' that steers the cybernetic essence of contemporary technology away from its passage toward autonomy (singularity)? The next question thus arises: Can cybernetics be redirectively steered toward its becoming a contrapractice? The tension between general systems theory and second order cybernetics is perhaps a fissure that could be widened to become an opening for this question.

[12]   Martin Heidegger, *The Question Concerning Technology and Other Essays*, trans. William Lovett (New York: Harper and Row), 47.

Appendix 5: Degrowth/Regrowth

Degrowth/Regrowth poses issues emanating from the current Global North and the elites of the South. It presents wealth and income reduction, and reduced consumption, standard of living, industrial production, and, by implication, waste and pollution (including GHG emissions) as the path to solving unsustainability and global warming. The problem is how to make this action happen at a sufficient scale to make real differences, and with understanding and lasting actual consequences – making the argument in itself has no agency – events are 'in the saddle'.

Likewise, the history of action when imposed austerity is not good. It produces hardship, civil unrest and is politically extremely unpopular. Degrowth so positioned would be even worse. It could not arrive via democracy and would have to be imposed. It has partly arrived in wartime via a coalition government, but positive impacts are negated by a massive increase of production post the war effort (often funded by debt on the basis of it being repaid once the post-war growth economy returns). Economically, two major arguments are posed against degrowth: it dramatically reduces income from the tax base, thus impoverishing the government, and it dissuades investment. The counter position is that such measures can be countered by longer-lasting, higher-priced products, combined with behavioural change, immaterialization and an increase in the service economy. The counter view is that this would not halt the arrival of a major recession, hardship and increased inequity, especially for nations in the Global South.

Degrowth as a mechanism of deceleration has the ability to create stasis. Rather than just slowing down, it causes economies to come to a stop. Here, Rosa uses the example of a traffic jam reaching a point of blockage as a metaphor for this stasis.[1] The whole economic discussion of acceleration/growth vs deceleration/degrowth is conducted within extant economic structures (cf. Rosa).

---

[1]   Rosa, *Social Acceleration: A New Theory of Modernity*, 84.

'The economy' is given an absolutely substantive value. But it emerged out of conditions of iterative change (reductively described as stages of development). The lacuna of the present nature of economics indicates that, in the defuturing conditions of the compound problem, this economy (like extant politics) is no longer fit for purpose. Climate change will remain unchecked and is going to create degrowth! The proposition carried here is that 'a solution' will not arrive, and be delivered by economic policy, or by 'adjustment' of the economic status quo. Rather, it will be those practices responsive to the unavoidable crisis destined by climate change that will drive adaptive change able to regrow a recursive economy, within the pertaining condition of limitations, predicated upon securing futurality (Sustainment).

Glossary

This glossary exists to clarify terms that may be unfamiliar to some readers. Not all have a consensual meaning. All have a complexity beyond the summaries given.

ANTHROPOCENE The Anthropocene has been named as the emergent epoch and denotes the moment when the Earth's climatic, geological and ecosystems became critically impacted by human activity. The actual moment when this commenced is contested, but is often cited as with the arrival of the industrial revolution in the late eighteenth century. The Anthropocene was preceded by the Holocene, which commenced at the end of the last ice age almost 12,000 years ago, marking the history of our species' development that was initiated with settlement, agriculture and advances in basic technologies.

CHRONOPHOBIA It was Friedrich Nietzsche who bonded *chrono* (time) to *phobia* (fear) so as to define the fear of time as a human quality. It is evident in two ways: fear of the future and a linked inability to think futurally; and living with an illusion of permanence. What connects these two expressions of fear is the mortality of our being and the way that 'being toward death' throws us into a continual present. In conditions of increasing unsustainability, chronophobia represents a substantial obstacle to acting with urgency and forethought toward actions that secure a more viable future.

COMPLEXITY OF COMPLEXITY It names the complexity concealed beyond any existing understandings/theories of complexity. It presumes an excess of the unknowable, an indivisible presence of the functional and dysfunctional, and a mutational relation between systems in their situatedness. It has no definable cosmological limit in space or time. Thus, while 'it' can and needs to be acknowledged, it remains beyond any access, is ungraspable and so beyond the comprehension of us all. Yet collectively our generative action continually adds to it and its relational dynamic.

COMPOUND PROBLEM (THE) The relational interconnection and interaction between, and convergence of what are currently individuated problems that combine to constitute the sum and complexity of a defuturing global crisis. It is what the Anthropocene (and other meta-discourses) aims, but fails, to be able to name. The disaggregation of a problem from its relational environment by the exercise of a division of knowledge can, and does, get justified as pragmatically needed and appropriate, but it always has a causal consequence of variable significance that begs investigation/consideration prior to action (such action goes to the frequency of 'solutions' producing problems).

COSMOTECHNICS Names the traditional relation between a cosmology and the means by which it creates, and reproduces, its world of habitation through its enacted everyday technological practices. Cosmotechnics as such are not abstracted as knowledge, but are simply the way things are done in relation to the making and operation of the material and immaterial forms of the culture. Cosmotechnical practices are transferred intergenerationally by assigned roles, functions, rituals and their significance and values. While often associated with indigenous cultures, they are not exclusive to them. However, they were and are marginalized, displaced and in many instances replaced by the scientific, spiritual and metaphysical cosmologies of colonizing modernity.

DECOLONIALITY Decoloniality is a theory-informed critical practice that emerged out of the people of colonized nations coming to the recognition that their colonization was not just political and economic but was also cultural, psychological and epistemological. Thus, the processes of decolonization and the arrival of a post-colonial structural order did not mean liberation from the effects of being colonized. For this to happen, there had to be a critique, a resistance to, and an overcoming of the ongoing epistemological power, inculcated values and psycho-social identities constituted by a colonial imposition of knowledge, conduct, values grounded Eurocentric worldview and mode of being as it was enacted over generations, while at the same time often violently repressing the people's indigenous culture. By implication, this meant that while the colonial power may have withdrawn, its ontological presence remained and continued in its colonized subjects until a process of decoloniality. Delinking from the apparatus of colonization is a hard and painful process that requires a radical revision of the history of the once colonized people, drawing attention not just to the physical destruction of their lifeworld but confronting the destruction of a great deal of their traditional culture and knowledge. Decoloniality is futural – it requires the creation of *border thinking* and *a border land* that recovers traditions and knowledge from the past, appropriates what is deemed to be of value from the present, and creates what is needed to establish a bridge to both to form a viable future. This view of decoloniality does not conflate with a popular appropriation and use of the term that totalizes the decolonization of virtually all and everything by everyone.

DEFUTURING Defuturing names any actions by individuals, material or immaterial objects, industries, commercial organizations, systems (social, political, economic and military) that negate our future as a species and indivisibly, the biosphere upon which we and all other species inter-relationally depend. Underscoring the concept of defuturing is the recognition that life on this planet, including our own, is finite. The more the actions of our species deplete natural resources, reduce biodiversity and pollute the atmosphere, oceans and rivers – and in so doing damage aquatic and terrestrial ecologies – the more the duration of life is reduced. Inculcated unsustainable values, desires and modes of behaviour are all elemental to the process of negation.

DESEVERANCE Coming especially from the issue of the mediated proximity between a representation and the object in the world represented whereby the object appears to be near but is not, and cannot not, be brought close. Thus, bringing to presence as appearance also denotes an act the deservers between object and its image

DISCOURSE The common meaning of the word 'discourse' is as an ordered mode of communication through linguistic exchange. However, what it meant was extended by Michel Foucault to include the use of language, and linguistic practices, to produce knowledge and meaning within particular social and historical contexts. It did this often within specific rule-governed social or historical contexts that determined what could be said, how and by whom. Discourse so positioned is therefore linked to power relations, their structures and practices. As such, it is implicated in the construction and deployment of knowledge, as well as influencing the creation of subjectivities.

DISCURSIVE PRACTICE Such a practice designates the way and form that specific discourses are produced and distributed within a society and its institutions. For example, the law, education and the military have all created their own distinctive types of discursive practices. The employment of discursive practices is accompanied by those that are non-discursive. In the case of the law, it delivers forms of punishment; education directs forms of behaviour; and the military mobilizes directed force.

EUROCENTRISM Eurocentrism names the universalization of the epistemological ground of the Western mind that commenced with European colonial global expansion, as it established its rule, imposed governing institutions and thereafter their material social, economic and political forms. In doing so, the very designation, ontologically, of Anthropos (the human) was introduced and used to erase the specific indigenous mode of understanding of its 'self'. The history of the destruction of these people's original sense of their being is one where genocide, cruelty and racism were common. The interpellative force of colonization was unbounded, and thus did not end with decolonization as the withdrawal of the colonial power. The material and psycho-social reality it created, often over centuries, lingered. The discourse of decoloniality as *praxis* has recognized that, over generations, colonization as a subaltern subject was constituted. Not only was this subject marginalized socially, politically and culturally excluded from positions within the nation's dominant structures of power, *but* equally, much of their knowledge, imagination and self-image was, and often continued to be, shaped by the ongoing agency of cultural and epistemological modes of colonialism. To recognize this is to get a full measure of the scale of the challenge of the process of decoloniality. This, not least because the agency of such colonization continues as Eurocentric knowledge remains normative universally, and sustained by the form and a great deal of its curricular content. Specifically, the 'modern academy' still functions as a global paradigmatic model of higher education (which in turn overdetermines the nature and direction of the curricula in prior levels of education). The instrumental and cultural capital it imparts to students, not least from the Global South, remains an international currency.

EVENT Like discourse, 'event' has a common meaning – action/activity within a particular time frame – but it also has a more complex philosophical way of being understood. What it recognizes is that things inanimate or inanimate are an occurrence in the medium of time. As such, some have the potential of being generative of events in their own right. A political leader gives a speech to the nation on TV, and as a result of this event three months later an election takes place; a life is constituted the sum of the events that gave it its form and historicity; a city is not just a place but an environment animated by a massive and continuous flow of events over time that give it its character, and determine it fate. For philosophy, 'event', its most fundamental, is simply 'being'.

EXOSOMATIC Exosomatic refers to something existing or actively taking place outside the body. Examples in the context of the human activities body include: the storage of memory, real-time displayed data on biofunctions or the testing of a blood sample.

FUTURING Futuring is a critical practice without a consensual meaning. It is used, for example, by 'futurologists' to name what are often speculative technocentric futures; likewise, it is used to name foresight thinking. It is also used in design and architecture to visualize the form of structures and environments. More substantially, futuring is a way of thinking about futures (as well as futural action) that recognizes and engages defuturing forces that negate the future for life as it is now understood. At the same time, 'futuring' also recognizes that the future is not a void but an obstacle course filled with 'things' thrown into it from the past that constantly arrive in the present (climate change impacts being a good example, as its future impact results from the addition of past greenhouse gas emissions to those from the ever-unfolding present). Beyond these critical perspectives, futuring is also about creating the ontological quality of material things performatively that negate defuturing and have a futuring effect.

GATHERING Gathering, as understood here, is brought within the orbit of critical practices. Importantly, it brings together two understandings of 'gather' – to bring together and to comprehend. Such a unification of action and thought is expressed and grounded in the Indo-European root of 'leg' as it means 'to collect', this, seen in the Greek 'legein' and the Latin 'legere'. Collecting the scattered thus becomes ordered, unified (re)counted, spoken and thereafter reflected upon, hence the link to the law of a reasoned process (logos). So understood, gathering therefore prefigures relational thought and 'operationalizes' it in forms (including designed forms) that make it present and active. Gathering so understood also links to bringing our being into being, this, as the event of becoming. We become as we gather/appropriate language, knowledge, skills and all else that constitutes our embodiment and habitus over the appropriative even of our individuated being.

HUMAN (THE) Cultures once created their own cosmology, within which a specific understanding of their own being was constituted. This being's understanding of itself was obviously not based on the same characteristics posited with an anthropoid identity. Thus, the culturally constructed human was not universal, although colonialism sought to make it so (in the name of advancing 'civilisation'). Difference, mostly centred on the perception of, and in relation to, animality. The colonial imposition of Anthropos travelled with modernity and, thereafter, the Enlightenment knowledge upon Others. That many other cultures did not make a distinction between animality and their own being was given no status, value or right to exist. Many indigenous cultures still live with the aftermath of the violence of this history, while retaining a sense of difference. In the current epoch, rather than the difference continuing to disappear, it is actually arriving and increasing – but not because new cosmologies are arriving. Rather, because our species is fragmenting. At one extreme are the growing numbers of abandoned people of refuge, who are nomadic or living in 'the camps' (at danger of social regress). At the other end are a segment of technocentric 'hyper-digitized natives' in economically advanced nations who seek and embrace becoming transhuman via technological forms of physical and chemically induced means of augmentation. The coexistence of the dehumanized and modes of posthuman being portend a fracturing of 'our' species and its natural evolution.

LOGOS Many disciplines lay claim to the meaning of *logos*. However, the approach to this key ancient Greek term to be engaged comes from the pre-Socratic philosopher Heraclitus. He took it to be the form of an ordered account, the structure of knowing, that functioned with directive force. His understanding of *logos* evolved and became understood as underscoring logic that linked to the rise of reason/reasoned argument. What a historical reflection on *logos* exposes is that 'reason', and the thinking that was predicated upon it became, as a result of the Enlightenment, a normative form of thought and intrinsic to late modernity, advances in the sciences, modern society and an extension of the universalization of Eurocentrism. Reason needs to be understood as being more than just a mode of cognition because it became, through the Western Enlightenment, a carrier of values and of a system of belief based upon it being deemed superior to all other ways of thinking. As such needs become bonded to instrumentalism and functional ends, while problematically lacking the ability to recognize the ethical consequences of what it enables to bring into being.

METROFITTING Retrofitting refers to the refurbishment of existing buildings to improve their environmental performance, such as introducing materials or systems to reduce their energy consumption. Metrofitting takes this action up to an urban scale, but it is much more than this: it is not merely an instrumental technical exercise. Metrofitting centres on remaking and repairing the constituent elements of a city. This means addressing a city as material fabric, as relationally connected operational and social systems, as a cultural environment, and as a designed (informally and formally) designing event that enfolds its social, economic, political and cultural everyday life. Metrofitting fundamentally acknowledges the imperative of 'correctively dealing with, and sustaining, what already exists', this, rather than the production of the new (the dominant approach of architectural and urban design). It is also based upon 'designing in time'—which means once commenced, it is a project without an end, ever responsive to present and future threats and identified enviro-climatic impacts.

MODERNITY Early modernity emerged from the early Renaissance as an overcoming of the 'dark ages'. It arrived with the nascent idea of making the world modern, not least by bringing 'civilisation', via colonial conquest, to the Godless. Its 'dark side' thus travelled with its ascent. By the time of late modernity, marked by the coming of the Industrial Revolution in the final decades of the eighteenth century, the modern has been linked to technological and scientific development, agents of progress supported by the Enlightenment and the socio-political order articulated. The material advances it heralded were employed to extend the reach and extractive power of dominant European colonial nations, while equally speeding the development of their capitalist economies. In doing so, a negative dialectic was firmly entrenched: the enormous creative output of modernity was equally matched by a huge amount of destruction evident in destroyed environments, the lives of colonized people and in metropolitan nations, ways of life, traditional practices, values and cultures and craft industries. Modernity produces a temporal transformation: it also transformed existential time by increasing the speed of everything: change; work; extractive industries, manufacture, the movement of materials, goods and people; building construction, city life, the war machine and more.

NEW POLITICAL IMAGINATION The scale, nature, complexity and defuturing agency of the compound problem of the planetary crisis is demonstrably beyond the capabilities of all existing regimes. Their vested interests in the economic and political status quo, dependencies and inertia not only obstruct the possibility of taking the kinds of action establishing futural conditions of sustainment demands, but they make it impossible for them to imagine how the political systems could be other than they are. Notwithstanding the extent of ideological differences, there is no political regime able to go beyond the current conditions of limitation. The need for a new political imagination that can visualize and mobilize a new political order is not an idealist dream but a stark and unavoidable reality. Without a politics that is capable of establishing the foundation of a social order and mode of governance that is viable and futural, there is no operative social order, or way of avoiding a collapse into the chaos of a speeding passage toward entropy. The possibility of the realization of a newly imagined political system is non-existent. The imperative of overcoming a seemingly impossible situation seems absolute – but a geospatial catalytic situated force of resistance has to be made possible out of an adaptive culture whose very existence would have defied the seemingly impossible.

ONTOGENESIS Ontogenesis is a process of staged development from inception to full maturity. The concept draws on its original biological meaning of the processes of transformation – this, from a simple organism to its state of completed development.

ONTOLOGICAL DESIGN Ontological design is both a way of understanding and of practicing design. Starting from an understanding of the ontological as concerned with the nature of being and becoming, ontological design emphasizes and focusses upon how designed things are understood as performative in that how they are designed is directive of their designing. For example, a pen as well as the writer designs the writing style, likewise the form, weight and sharpness of an axe, as well as the skill of its user, designs the efficiency of its use. Moreover, in that design development is incremental, the already designed performs as the basis of the newly designed (be it a minor modification or a major transformation). From this understanding, the primary concern of designing then shifts to what the designed object (material or immaterial) performatively brings into being, and with what consequence environmentally and for a user. By design or neglect, things have a good or bad environmental impact during their use or at the end of their life. They equally can have ontological impacts on users: ergonomically (by making a task easier or harder), psychologically (by making a task rewarding or frustrating), physiologically (by making a task the body healthier or doing harm). At the most basic, consequences can be viewed as sustaining or un-sustaining, futuring or defuturing – this, from the almost imperceptible to the obvious and dramatic.

POSTDEVELOPMENT Within Development Studies, it has become increasingly recognized that a great deal of activities conducted in the name of development have been impositional, destructive and defuturing. The main issue is that development was, and still is not, either generated by the people to be developed, nor is it neutral. Rather, 'development' is the contemporary face of a long history leading from *modernity* to modernization and to the designation of *un*developed people as *under*developed – this, according to Eurocentric norms of what it means to be developed. Responding to this situation, postdevelopment sets out to assist in establishing the conditions from which another path to a viable future is created, this not least by indigenous people of the Global South. It follows that postdevelopment directly connects to *decoloniality* and *border thinking*.

POSTHUMAN The term does not have one meaning, and the meanings are fluid: they change with discourses and circumstances. One meaning comes out of critical humanism that sees the posthuman as 'the more human' human (kinder, more considerate of others, less aggressive, etc.). Another is grounded in a technophilic view of the future of 'our' species becoming increasingly technologically enhanced and morphing into a transhuman condition convergent with technological singularity, able to survive a biological apocalyptic crisis. Such views stand on a universal totalized biologically reductive understanding of what 'we' are and will become. From the first use of stone tools by *Homo sapiens* hominoid ancestors, technology has always been an ontologically transformative change agent of our being. As technology has become ever more diverse and unequally available, so has our difference. Not only will this trend continue, but it may well fragment 'our' evolution. Thus, 'our' future will become less disposed toward the universal and more plural.

PRAXIS/PRAXEOLOGY As stated at the end of Chapter 2: The meanings of **praxis** are myriad. The aim here is to work through a modest list and arrive at a view of *praxis* appropriate to (bring to) contrapractice. At the most general, *praxis* is understood as a condition of relationality, that is situated, complex and dynamic. It spans a specificity that can be positioned technologically, socially and politically. It is also seen in the context of a relation between being and things. As such, *praxis* is articulated to contemplative thought, calculation, practice, way of making, brought to things and thereafter the consequence of the nexus of materiality and the ethico-political. In general terms, praxeology is presented as the study of human behaviour, specifically in the form of practice

PREFIGURATION/PREFIGURATIVE Prefiguration names the essence of design as integral to the cognitive condition of our species being, irrespective of geo-cultures or other differences. The ability to prefigure realized as an envisioned effect, affect or object is actually a characteristic that partly defines, in difference, the modes of 'our; being'. Prefiguration is design as an intuitive thought process that goes ahead of design as a conscious act. It puts 'the what is to be designed' before the act(ion) of design – thus indicating prefiguration to be elemental to imagination when the intent to create a 'something' occurs.

PSYCHOPOWER In the inequity of the current post-industrial age of the digital empire and of the hyper-consumption of consumer classes of privilege, market forces mobilize psychopower. What it names is the enhanced agency of the means of the creation of desire for immaterial, imbued qualities of material commodities. Born with marketing, the development of this agent of the libidinal economy became continually refined and extended by the rise of the power of signs in tele-visual media (a product of the psychotechnologies of cinema, television, video and digital media). The increased presence of these media in so many people's lifeworlds, as afforded by personal devices, has dramatically increased proximity to the semiosphere of the libidinal economy and its articulation to the fiscal economy. The reach of psychopower knows no limit beyond the wealthy and well off; it includes the old, the sick, the poor and children. Moreover, it functions to colonize imagination and negate memory.

REDIRECTIVE PRACTICE Redirective practice is a post-disciplinary divisions of design knowledge. Politically, it seeks to remake the ground and content of one's own knowledge. Even more fundamentally, it implies an ontological transformation of what it means to be a designer in order to constitute a commonality of intent across different practices that aim to contribute to the development of Sustainment by addressing what already exists (from built environments, to industries, products, services, media and practices). In so doing, it understands that the divisions of knowledge that underpin most practices are a product of a political economy that exercises power and control by de-relationalizing, and then managing, its elements;

RELATIONALITY Relationality is an operational dynamic within all ecologies, a functional feature of, and between (linked), systems and descriptive of the articulation of the elements of an epistemology. It is also counter to the practices, modes of thinking, divisions of knowledge, disciplines and specialisms that organically delinks, disaggregate and abstract an entity from its situated environment. While initially enabling means of command and control, the eventual consequence of de-relational action over time is breakdown and dysfunction.

REMAKING/UNMAKING Dealing with a world being made unsustainable requires dealing with what is, be it: modes of thought, theories of knowledge, professional and creative practices, institutions, industries, government, systems, products or services. Such a listing will include much that needs to be eliminated, and it can come in two forms: destruction or unmaking. Unmaking does not only mean the disassembly of an object or structure to recover material to reuse. It also means unmaking values, habits, beliefs, affiliations and knowledge that obstruct acting against the unsustainable and acting for sustainment. Likewise, remaking is not just about repair, retrofitting or adaptive reuse. It is also about remaking cultures of learning, social ecologies, relations to sustaining traditions of the past, and more. Both practices beg recognition and development.

SUSTAINMENT Sustainment names the futural performative quality of being. Sustainment is not 'sustainability' (with its propensity to sustain the unsustainable). Rather, Sustainment (or 'the Sustainment') is a condition and a vital intellectual and pragmatic project of discovery marking a vital turn to another kind of earthly habitation and understanding. One that recognizes a process of continual decay and regenerative recreation that is the essence of being itself. This absolute imperative overrides all actions that in damaging environments, biological, social, psycho-cognitive (mind), while also increasing global inequality and conflict, are all effectively defuturing terminal forces. Sustainment, so understood, is the most important, the most urgent and the most overlooked and the most neglected project that collectively befalls us all, and for as long as can be imagined. So understood, Sustainment can unite difference in difference: it does not reduce to the same.

TECHNOCENTRISM Technocentrism is a sensibility, spanning the functional to the idealistic and romantic perceptions of technology, adopted by individuals and organizations that cedes power to technology and its instrumental agency. It sees it as the means of meeting and overcoming major global challenges, like delivering solutions to social, climatic, environmental, food security, urban, health, logistics problems and crises. In doing so, technology is deemed as liberatory and the instrument to secure a viable future. But what it fails to be able, do is to comprehend and address issues like: structural inequity, racism, injustice, unethical conduct,corruption, violence. Even worse, it can and does get employed to serve and meet these undesirable means and ends. The critique of technology that technocentrism invites does imply that technology is not valued, but rather than it should not be viewed and posited with total deterministic power.

TECHNOGENESIS Technogenesis is based on the application of the staged process of ontogenesis (see above) to the co-evolution of the human and technology, as a result of their ontological interaction from the moment of the first use of tools to the present immersion of humans in the technosphere.

UNLEARNING The importance of unlearning requires learning. What subsequent understanding recognizes is that unsustainable knowledge, values, desires and practices are learn informally (by inculcation, media, mimesis and example) and formally (by educational programs and instruction). Sustainment is not the foundation of learning for parents and educators at every level. A fundamental reform of education has not even been recognized, let alone implemented. When sustainability arrives in the education system, it does so on the margins, and so often bound to the economic and political status quo. As such, it ends up sustaining the unsustainable. One of the main reasons for this is that the actual embedded complexity of the unsustainable goes unrecognized and unlearnt. What actually arrives is superficial and implied by obvious malpractice, like the pollution of land, air and water. These conditions are symptoms, not causes – and these sequentially examined slate back to 'us' and our lack of knowledge, values, desires and defuturing conduct. This situation does not demand moral condemnation but an unlearning of the learnt and a new learning at a mass structural level (which implies the comprehensive remaking of educators, curricula and education).

UNRESTRICTED WARFARE The concept 'unrestricted warfare' was created by two Chinese Airforce officers in the 1990s as a way to attack and defeat the USA. While never formally adopted by the nation's government, its ideas have been influential (including in Russia). It aims to expand conflict to include and engage trade areas as broad as finance/economics, technology, terror, ecological destruction, piracy and smuggling, cultural aggression, use of drugs, aggressive use of the media, law, psychological war and cyber war. Unrestricted warfare is devoid of any ethical principles or adherence to the laws of war. Operationally, it prefigures or accompanies conventional and asymmetric modes of war fighting. What it does is dissolve any distinction between war and peace. Although omnipresent, it is now mostly existing at a low level of intensity as a feature of the geopolitical environment. However, it is capable of becoming more aggressive if tensions rise between adversaries.

UNSETTLEMENT In an age of climate change impacts and significant conflicts in the world, and with the prospect of these problems worsening, the number of people becoming displaced and unsettled is expected to dramatically increase. Numbers are likely to exceed the ability of humanitarian resources to cope with the situation – chaos would then be a real prospect. The physical conditions of unsettlement equally produce a psychological one. The feeling of living in an unsettled and increasingly dangerous world, with a bleak future, ever grows everywhere.

UNSUSTAINABILITY A structural condition of unsustainability emplaced by modernity
  – as produced by unrestrained extractivism, environmental destruction, failures
  of the modern economies, its modes of production and forms of consumption
  – has created high levels of atmospheric, terrestrial and ocean pollution and
  intractable waste. They have all combined with a still-growing global population
  to accelerate the generative forces of unsustainability, as has an increasing risk
  of global conflicts. Specific knowledge and a general sense of the situation and
  prospect relationally link to, and feed, a widespread sense of unsettlement.

References

Ames, Roger, *The Art of Rulership*, New York: State of New York Press, 1994.

Arendt, Hannah, *The Human Condition*, Chicago: The University of Chicago Press, 1958.

Aristotle, *The Nicomachean Ethics*, trans. David Ross. Oxford: Oxford University Press, 1991.

Armed Conflict Location and Event Data, https://acleddata.com/conflict-index/index-july-2024/ (accessed 10 January 2025).

Bacon, Francis, in his *Novum Organum*, 1620, https://oll-resources.s3.us-east-2.amazonaws.com/oll3/store/titles/1432/0415_Bk_Sm.pdf (accessed 20 June 2021).

Bateson, Gregory, *Steps to an Ecology of Mind*, New York: Paladin, 1973.

Beer, David, 'The Social Power of Algorithms, Information', *Communication & Society* 20, no. 1 (2017): 1–13, https://doi.org/10.1080/1369118X.2016.1216147 (accessed 10 March 2023).

Blair, Alex, 'UN warns "climate breakdown has begun" after hottest northern hemisphere summer on record', news.com.au, 7 September 2023, https://www.news.com.au/technology/environment/climate-change/un-warns-climate-breakdown-has-begun-after-hottest-northern-hemisphere-summer-on-record/news-story/bb8437677864d5c9b950b5dc5a521f4f (accessed 11 November 2023).

Bourdieu, Pierre, *Outline of A Theory of Practice*, trans. Richard Nice, Cambridge: Cambridge University Press, 1977.

Bourdieu, Pierre, *The Logic of Practice*, trans. Richard Nice, Stanford: Stanford University Press. 1992.

Braidotti, Rosi, 'The Virtual as Affirmation Praxis: A Neo-Materialist Approach', *Humanities* 11, no. 62, http://doi.org/10.3390/h11030062 (accessed 2 March 2023).

Braverman, Harry, *Labor and Monopoly Capital*, New York: Monthly Review Press, 1974.

Brown, Eric, 'The Dilemmas of German Bioethics'. *The New Atlantis*. Spring (2004): 36–53, https://thenewatlantis.com/wp-content/uploads/legacy-pdfs/TNA05-Brown.pdf (accessed 11 November 2024).

Carlson, L. Thomas, 'Perpetual Peace: What Kant Should Have Said', *Social Theory and Practice* 14, no. 2 (1988): 173–214.

Carson, Racntosbel, *Silent Spring*, 1962, Boston: Houghton Mifflin, 2003.

Centre for Contemporary Cultural Studies, *On Ideology*, London: Hutchinson, 1977.

Chenna, ZamZam, 'Lethal Autonomous Weapon Systems', *Geopolitical Monitor*, March 26, 2004: 1–4, https://www.geopoliticalmonitor.com/lethal-autonomous-weapon-systems-a-gamechanger-demanding-regulation/ (accessed 2 April 2024).

China Digital Space, June 26, 2022, https://chinadigitaltimes.net/archive.

Clifford, James, *The Predicament of Culture*, Cambridge, MA: Harvard University Press, 1988.

Cockcroft, J. D., A. G. Frank and D. Johnson, *Dependence and Development*, New York: Doubleday, 1972.

Crutzen, P. J., and E. Stoermer, 'The Anthropocene', *IGBP* Newsletter, 41 (2000): 17–18.

Dargan, James, 'Quantum Computing Companies: A Full 2024 List', *Quantum Insider*, 29 December 2023, https://thequantuminsider.com/2023/12/29/quantum-computing-companies/ (accessed 8 June 2024).

Davis, Oliver, 'Anthropotechnical Practising in the Foamworld', *Angelaki* 26, no.1 (2021): 109–23, https://doi.org/10.1080/0969725X.2021.1863600 (accessed 15 February 2023).

De Castro, Eduardo Viveiros, *The Relative Native, Essays on Indigenous Conceptual Worlds*, Chicago: Hau Books, 2015.

de Certeau, Michel, *The Practice of Everyday Life*, trans. Steve Rendall, Berkeley: University of California Press, 1980.

de Certeau, Michel, Luce Giard and Pierre Mayol, *The Practice of Everyday Life, Vol 1 Living and Cooking*, trans. Timothy J. Tomasik, Minneapolis: University of Minnesota Press, 1998.

Deleuze, Gilles, 'Postscript on the Societies of Control', *October* 59 (1992): 3–7, *JSTOR*, http://www.jstor.org/stable/778828 (accessed 2 May 23).

Derrida, Jacques, *Dissemination*, trans. Barbara Johnson, Chicago: The University of Chicago Press, 1981.

Derrida, Jacques, *The Truth in Painting*, trans. Geoff Bennington and Ian McLeod, Chicago: The University of Chicago Press, 1987.

Diamond, Jared, 'A Brand-New Version of Our Origin Story', *New York Times*, 20 April 2018, https://www.nytimes.com/2018/04/20/books/review/david-reich-who-we-are-how-we-got-here.html (accessed 10 September 2023).

Doray, Bernard, *From Taylorism to Fordism*, trans. David Macey, London: Free Association Books, 1988.

Eriksen, Thomas Hylland, *Overheating: An Anthropology of Accelerated Change*, London: Pluto Press, 2016.

Escobar, Arturo, *Designs for the Pluriverse*, Durham, NC: Duke University Press, 2017.

Esposito, Roberto, *Terms of the Political: Community, Immunity, Biopolitics*, trans. Rhiannon Noel Welch, New York: Fordham University Press, 2012, 7.

Esposito, Roberto, 'Community, Immunity, Biopolitics', trans. Zakiya Hanafi, *Angelaki* 18, no. 3 (2013): 83–93, https://doi.org/10.1080/0969725X.2013.834666 (accessed 10 August 2021).

Fisher, Mark, *Capital Realism*, London: Zero Books, 2022.

Foucault, Michel, 1966. *The Order of Things*, New York: Vintage, 1973.

Foucault, Michel, *Discipline and Punish*, trans. Alan Sheridan, Harmondsworth: Penguin Books, 1979.

Foucault, Michel, *The Archaeology of Knowledge*, trans. A.M. Sheridan Smith, London: Tavistock Publications, 1985.

Foucault, Michel, '*Society Must be Defended*', *Lecture at the College de France, 1975-1976*, trans. David Macey, New York: Picador, 1997.

Frier, Maxwell and Sarah Adler, 'Twitter, Musk and Why Online Speech Gets Moderated', *Bloomberg*, 3 October 2022, https://www.washingtonpost.com/business/twitter-musk-and-why-online-speech-gets-moderated/2022/10/03/0cb0ae68-434f-11ed-be17-89cbe6b8c0a5_story.html (accessed 9 February 2023).

Freire, Paulo, *Pedagogy of the Oppressed*, London: Penguin Classics, 2018.

Fry, Tony, 'Switchings' in *RUATV, Heidegger and the Televisual*, edited by Tony Fry, 24–44, Sydney: Power Publications, 1993.

Fry, Tony, *Becoming Human by Design*, Oxford: Berg, 2012.

Fry, Tony, *Unstaging War, Confronting Conflict and Peace*, London: Palgrave Macmillan, 2019.

Fry, Tony, *Defuturing: A New Design Philosophy*, London: Bloomsbury, 2021.

Fry, Tony and Madina Tlostanova, *A New Political Imagination, Making the Case*, London: Routledge, 2021.

Fry, Tony, *Writing Design Fiction, Relocating City in Crisis*, London: Bloomsbury, 2022.

Fry, Tony, *Political Breakout*, Wilmington, DE: Vernon Press, 2025.

Fynsk, Christopher, 'Foreword', in *The Inoperative Community*, edited by Jean-Luc Nancy, trans. Peter Connor and Lisa Garbus, Minneapolis: University of Minnesota Press, 1991.

Gardiner Michael, 'Critique of Accelerationism', *Theory, Culture and Society* 34, no. 1 (2016), https://doi.org/10.1177/0263276416656760 (accessed 18 February 2023).

Gibson, William, *Neuromancer*, New York: Ace Books, 1984.

Gilbert, Daniel and Faiz Siddiqui, 'Elon Musk's Neuralink Says it Has FDA Approval for Human Trials: What to Know', *Washington Post*, 26 May 2023, https://www.washingtonpost.com/business/2023/05/25/elon-musk-neuralink-fda-approval/

Giri, A., S. Heckathorn, S. Mishra and C. Krause, 'Heat Stress Decreases Levels of Nutrient-Uptake', *Plants* 6, no.1 (2017), https://doi.org/10.3390/plants6010006 (accessed 27 October 2022).

Gowen, Annie, Niko Kommenda and Saiyna Bashir, 'Pakistan Bears the Brunt of Global Extreme Heat Illness and Mortality' *Washington Post*, 5 May 2023, https://www.washingtonpost.com/climate-environment/interactive/2023/pakistan-extreme-heat-health-impactsdeath?utm_campaign=wp_the7&utm_medium= (accessed 5 September 2023).

Gramsci, Antonio, *Selection from The Prison Notebooks*, trans. Quintin Hoare and Geoffrey Nowell Smith, London: Lawrence and Wishart, 1973.

Guattari, Felix, *The Three Ecologies*, 1989, trans. and edited by Ian Pindar and Paul Sutton, London: Athlone, 2000.

Hall, David, L. and Roger T. Ames, *Thinking Through Confucius*, New York: State University of New York Press, 1987.

Haraway, Donna, *Staying with the Trouble: Making Kin in the Chthulucene*, Durham: Duke University Press, 2016.

Haraway, Donna and Anna Tsing, 'Reflections on the Plantationocene: A Conversation with Donna Haraway and Anna Tsing', moderated by Gregg Mitmann, 2019, chrome-extension://efaidnbmnnnibpcajpcglclefindmkaj/https://edgeeffects.net/wp-content/uploads/2019/06/PlantationoceneReflections_Haraway_Tsing.pdf (accessed 9 February 2023).

Hari, Johann, *Stolen Focus*, New York: Crown Publishing, 2022.

Harman, Graham, *Tool-Being, Heidegger and the Metaphysics of Objects*, Chicago: Open Court, 2002.

Harvey, Chelsea, 'Warfare's Climate Emissions Are Huge but Uncounted' E&E News, *Scientific American*, June 1, 2024,https://www.scientificamerican.com/article/warfares-climate-emissions-are-huge-but-uncounted/ (accessed 10 March 2023).

Heidegger, Martin, *Being and Time*, trans. John Macquarrie and Edward Robinson, Oxford: Blackwell, 1962.

Heidegger, Martin, *The Question Concerning Technology and Other Essays*, trans. William Lovett, New York: Harper and Row, 1977.

Heidegger, Martin, *On The Way to Language*, trans. Peter D. Hertz, San Francisco: HarperCollins, 1982.

Heidegger, Martin, 'The End of Philosophy and the Task of Thinking', in Martin Heidegger, *Basic Writings*, edited by David Farrell Krell, San Francisco: HarperCollins, 1993.

Heidegger, Martin, *The Fundamental Concepts of Metaphysics*, trans. William McNeill and Nicolas Walker, Bloomington, Indiana University Press, 1995.

Heidegger, Martin, *The End of Philosophy*, trans. Joan Stambaugh, Chicago: The University of Chicago Press, 2003.

Heidegger, Martin and Eugen Fink, *Heraclitus Seminars*, trans. Charles H. Seibert, Evanston: Northwestern University Press, 1979.

Herring, David and Rebecca Lindsay, 'Hasn't Earth Warmed and Cooled Naturally Throughout History?' 2020, https://www.climate.gov/news-features/climate-qa/hasnt-earth-warmed-and-cooled-naturally-throughout-history(accessed 9 October 2022).

Hill, Christopher, *The World Turned Upside Down*, London: Penguin Books, 1979.

Hornborg, Alf, 'The Political Ecology of the Technocene: Uncovering Ecologically Unequal Exchange in the World-System', in *The Anthropocene and the Global Environmental Crisis: Rethinking Modernity in a New Epoch*, edited by C. Hamilton, C. Bonneuil and F. Gemenne, 57–69, Routledge, 2015.

Hui, Yuk, 'Algorithmic Catastrophe—the Revenge of Contingency', *Parrhesia* 23 (2015): 122–43.

Hui, Yuk, *The Question Concerning Technology in China: An Essay in Cosmotechnics*, Falmouth: Urbanomic, 2016.

Hui, Yuk, 'On the Unhappy Consciousness of Neoreactionaries', efflux, 81 (2017), https://www.e-flux.com/journal/81/125815/on-the-unhappy-consciousness-of-neoreactionaries/10 (accessed 6 January 2023).

Hui, Yuk, 'Writing and Cosmotechnics', *Derrida Today* 13, no. 1 (2020): 17–32.

Hui, Yuk, 'Machine and Ecology', *Angelaki* 25, no. 4 (2020): 54–66, https://doi.org/10.1080/0969725X.2020.1790835 (accessed 8 January 2022).

Illich, Ivan, K. Zola Irving, John McKnight, Jonathan Caplan and Harley Shaiken, *Disabling Professions*, London: Marion Boyars, 1977.

Institute for the Study of War, daily report 20 March2024, https://understandingwar. org/backgrounder/russian-offensive-campaign-assessment-march-20-2024 (accessed 21 March 2024).

IPCC, Synthesis Report of the Sixth Assessment Report, 2023, https://www.ipcc.ch/ ar6-syr/(accessed 8 February 2023).

Jamieson, Michelle, 'The Politics of Immunity: Reading Cohen through Canguilhem and New Materialism', *Body and Society* 22, no. 4 (2016): 106–29.

Jullien, François, *The Propensity of Things, Towards a History of Efficacy in China*, trans. Janet Lloyd, New York: Zone Books, 1995.

Jullien, François, *A Treatise on Efficacy*, trans. Janet Lloyd, Honolulu: University of Hawai'i Press, 2004.

Jullien, François, *On the Universal*, trans. Michael Richardson and Krzysztof Fijalkowski, Oxford: Polity, 2014.

Kant, Immanuel, 1795. *Perpetual Peace: A Philosophical Essay*, trans. M. Campbell Smith, London: George Allen & Unwin, 1917, available at https://www.gutenberg. org/ebooks/50922.

King, Anthony, 'Thinking with Bourdieu against Bourdieu: A "Practical" Critique of the Habitus', *Sociological Theory* 18, no. 3 (2000): 417–33, *JSTOR*, http://www. jstor.org/stable/223327 (accessed 2 May 2023).

Kirby, W. Maurice, *Operational Research in War and Peace*, London: Imperial College Press, 2003.

Ko, Hyun, 'Origins of Human Intelligence: The Chain of Tool-making and Brain Evolution', *Anthropological Notebooks* 22, no. 1 (2016): 55–22, http://www. drustvoantropologov.si/AN/PDF/2016_1/Anthropological_Notebooks_ XXII_1_Ko.pdf02.03.23.,http://www.drustvoantropologov.si/AN/PDF/2016_1/ Anthropological_Notebooks_XXII_1_Ko.pdf (accessed 12 March 2021).

Kolbert, K., *The Sixth Extinction: An Unnatural History*, New York: Henry Holt and Company, 2014.

Krenak, Ailton, *Ideas to Postpone the End of the World*, trans. Anthony Doyle, Toronto: Anansi International, 2020.

Land, Nick, *Fanged Noumena, Collected Writings 1987–2007*, edited by Robin Mackay and Ray Brassier, Falmouth: Urbanomic, 2011.

Land, Nick, 'Narcissism and Dispersion in Heidegger's–Trakl Interpretation' (in *On the Way to Language*, 1959 (1982), 140–157) in *Fanged Noumena, Collected Writings 1987–2007*, edited by Robin Mackay and Ray Brassier, Falmouth: Urbanomic, 2011, 81–122.

Land, Nick, *Xenosystems Fragments*, https://www.apostategallery.com/exhibitions/ xenosystems-fragments/ (accessed 1 March 2023).

Latour, Bruno, 'How Better to Register the Agency of Things', The Tanner Lecture on Human Values delivered at Yale University, 26 March 2014.

Liang, Qiao and Wang Xiangsui, *Unrestricted Warfare*, [FBIS Translated Text], Beijing: PLA Literature and Arts Publishing House, 1999.

Limone, P. and G.A. Toto, 'Psychological and Emotional Effects of Digital Technology on Digitods (14–18 Years): A Systematic Review', *Health Psychology* 13 (2022), https://doi.org/10.3389/fpsyg.2022.938965P (accessed 10 July 2021).

Litt, Thomas, Jürgen Richter and Frank Schäbitz, *The Journey of Modern Humans from Africa to Europe*, Stuttgart: Schweizerbart Science Publishers, 2021.

Lorber-Kasunic, Jacqueline, 'Practice Theory, Practices', in *Bloomsbury Encyclopedia of Design*, edited by Clive Edwards, London: Bloomsbury, 2016.

Mackay, Robin, 'Nick Land: An Experiment in Inhumanism', 2012, (unpaginated), http://readthis.wtf/writing/nick-land-an-experiment-in-inhumanism/ (accessed 17 August 2021).

Mackay, Robin and A. Avanessian, *Accelerate: The Accelerationist Reader*, Falmouth: Urbanomic, 2014,

Marx, Karl, 1843. 'Introduction', *A Contribution to the Critique of Hegel's Philosophy of Right*, trans. A. Jolin and J. O'Malley, Cambridge: Cambridge University Press, 1970.

Massey, Doreen, *Spatial Division of Labour*, London: Macmillan, 1984.

McIntyre, Alister, *After Virtue*, South Bend: University of Notre Dame Press, 1981.

McNeill, William, *The Glance of the Eye*, New York: State University of New York Press. 1999.

McNeill, William, 'The Complication of *Praxis*" in *The Design Philosophy Reader*, edited by Anne-Marie Willis, London, Bloomsbury, 2019.

McNeill, William, *The Fate of Phenomenology*, London: Rowman and Littlefield, 2020.

Mignolo, Walter, *The Darker Side of Western Modernity*, Durham, NC: Duke University Press, 2011.

Mignolo, Walter D. and E. Catherine Walsh, *On Decoloniality, Concepts, Analytics, Praxis*, Durham, NC: Duke University Press, 2018.

Mises, Ludwig von, *Praxeology and History*, 1996, https://mises.org/library/human-action-0/html/pp/638(accessed 10 February 2023).

Moss, L. S., 'Harmony, Conflict, and Culture: An Essay About the Praxeological Ideas of Ludwig von Mises', *Cultural Dynamics* 5, no. 3 (1992), https://doi.org/10.1177/092137409200500 (accessed 14 March 2023).

Muller, A., C. Shipton and C. Clarkson, 'Stone toolmaking difficulty and the evolution of hominin technological skills', *Nature, Sci Rep* 12 no. 5883 (2022), https://doi.org/10.1038/s41598-022-09914-2(accessed 9 January 2023).

Murphy, G. Jeffrey, 'Kant on Theory and Practice', *Theory and Practice* 37 (1995): 47–78, https://www.jstor.org/stable/24219524(accessed 12 March 2023).

Nancy, Jean-Luc, *The Inoperative Community*, trans. Peter Connor and Lisa Garbus, Minneapolis: University of Minnesota Press, 1991.

NASA Science - Climate cycles, 2024, https://science.nasa.gov/science-research/earth-science/milankovitch-orbital-cycles-and-their-role-in-earths-climate/ (accessed 19 September 2024).

Nasrollahzadeh, Mmoudah and S. Mohammad Sajadi, 'Risks of Nanotechnology to Human Life', *Interface Science and Technology* 28 (2019): 323–33, https://www.sciencedirect.com/science/article/abs/pii/B9780128135860000079 (accessed 20 January 2023).

Neyrat, Frédéric, 'The Birth of Immumopolitics', *Parrhesia* 10 (2010), 31.

Noble, F. David, *Forces of Production*, Oxford: Oxford University Press, 1986.

Noys, Benjamin, *The Persistence of the Negative*, Edinburgh: Edinburgh University Press, 2010.

Our World Data 2023, https://ourworldindata.org/internet (accessed 22 February 2023).

Parenti, Christian, Eileen C. Crist, Justin McBrien, Donna J. Haraway, Elmar Altvater, Daniel Hartley, and Jason W. Moore, *Anthropocene or Capitalocene?: Nature, History, and the Crisis of Capitalism*, Oakland, CA: PM Press, 2016.

Parikka, Jussi, *The Anthrobscene*, Minneapolis: University of Minnesota Press, 2015.

Partlow, Joshua, 'Alaska Glacier Melting', *Washington Post*, 4 September 2023. https://www.washingtonpost.com/climate-environment/2023/09/04/juneau-flood-alaska-glacier-mendenhall/ (accessed 12 November 2023).

Prokop, Andre, 'Curtis Yarvin Wants American Democracy Toppled. He Has Some Prominent Republican Fans', *Vox*, 24 October 2022, https://www.vox.com/policy-and-politics/23373795/curtis-yarvin-neoreaction-redpill-moldbug (accessed 10 January 2023).

Readfearn, Graham, 'Antarctica Warming', *Guardian*, 8 September 2023, https://www.theguardian.com/world/2023/sep/08/antarctica-warming-much-faster-than-models-predicted-in-deeply-concerning-sign-for-sea-levels (accessed 11 November 23).

Readings, Bill, *The University in Ruins*, Cambridge, MA: Harvard University Press, 1996.

Reich, David, *Who We Are And How We Got Here – Ancient DNA and the New Science of the Human Past*, New York: Pantheon Books, 2018.

Rigg, Clare, 'Praxeology', in *The Sage Encyclopaedia of Action Research*, edited by D. Coghlan and M. Brydon-Miller, Thousand Oaks, California: Sage, 2014.

Robbert, Adam, 'Cosmos and History', *The Journal of Natural and Social Philosophy* 13, no.1 (2017): 1–14.

Rosa, Hartmut, *Social Acceleration: A New Theory of Modernity*, trans. Jonathan Trejo-Mathys, New York: Columbia University Press, 2015.

Rosa, Hartmut, *Resonance: A Sociology of Our Relationship to the World*, trans. James C. Wagner, Oxford: Polity Press, 2016.

Sainato, Michael, 'Stephen Hawking, Elon Musk, and Bill Gates Warn About Artificial Intelligence', *Observer*, 19 August 2015, https://observer.com/2015/08/stephen-hawking-elon-musk-and-bill-gates-warn-about-artificial-intelligence/ (accessed 10 February 2023).

Sandoval, Chela, *Methodology of the Oppressed*, Minneapolis: University of Minnesota Press, 2000.

Santos, Bonaventura de Sousa, *Epistemologies of the South*, Boulder, CO: Paradigm Publishers, 2014.

Sartre, Jean-Paul, *Being and Nothingness*, trans. Hazel E. Barnes, New York: Simon and Schuster, 1984.

Savransky, Martin, *Around the Day in Eighty Worlds*, Durham, NC: Duke University Press, 2021.

Scarry, Elaine, *The Body in Pain*, Oxford: Oxford University Press, 1985.

Schmitt, Carl, *The Nomos of the Earth*, trans. G. L. Ulmer, New York: Telos Press, 2003,

Schön, Donald, *The Reflective Practitioner*, New York: Basic Books, 1983.

Simondon, Gilbert, 'The Genesis of the Individual', in *Incorporations*, edited by Jonathan Crary and Sanford Kwinter, New York: Zone Books, 1992, 297–319.

Simondon, Gilbert, *On the Mode of Existence of Technical Objects*, trans. Cecile Malaspina and John Rogove, Minneapolis: University of Minnesota Press, 2017.

Simondon, Gilbert, *Individuation in Light of Notions of Form and Information*, trans. Taylor Adkins, Minneapolis: University of Minnesota Press, 2020.

Simone, AbdouMaliq, *Improvised Lives*, Oxford: Polity Press, 2019.

Sloterdijk, Peter, *The Art of Philosophy: Wisdom as a Practice*, trans. Karen Margolis, New York, Columbia University Press, 2009.

Sloterdijk, Peter, *Bubbles, Spheres Volume 1*, trans. Wieland Hoban, Cambridge, MA: MIT Press, 2011; German edition, 1998.

Sloterdijk, Peter, *You Must Change Your Life*, trans. Wieland Hoban, Oxford: Polity. 2013.

Sloterdijk, Peter, *Globes, Spheres Volume II*, trans. Wieland Hoban, Cambridge, MA: MIT Press, 2014; German edition, 1999.

Sloterdijk, Peter, *Foam, Volume III*, trans. Wieland Hoban, Cambridge, MA: MIT Press, 2016; German edition, 2004.

Spivak, Gayatri Chakravorty, 'Can the Subaltern Speak?' in *Marxism and the Interpretation of Culture*, edited by Gary Nelson and Lawrence Grossberg, 271–316, London: Macmillan, 1988

Steele, Wendy, John W. Handmer and Ian McShane, *Hot Cities: A Transdisciplinary Agenda*, Cheltenham: Edward Elgar Publishing, 2023.

Steffen, Will, J. Paul Crutzen and R. John McNeill, 'The Anthropocene: Are Humans Now Overwhelming the Great Forces of Nature?' *Ambio* 36, no. 8 (2007): 614–621.

Stiegler, Bernard, *Technics and Time, 1, The Fault of Epimetheus*, trans. Richard Beardsworth with George Collins, Stanford: Stanford University Press, 1998.

Stiegler, Bernard, *Taking Care of Youth and the Generations*, trans. S. Barker, Stanford: Stanford University Press, 2010.

Stiegler, Bernard, *States of Shock*, trans. Daniel Ross, Oxford: Polity, 2015.

Stiegler, Bernard, *The Neganthropocene*, trans. Daniel Ross, London: New Humanities Press, 2018.

Stiegler, Bernard and Irit Rogoff, 'Transindividuation', *e-fflux Journal* 14, (2010), https://www.e-flux.com/journal/14/61314/transindividuation/ (accessed 18 January 2021).

Stringer, Chris, *The Origin of Our Species*, London: Allen Lane, 2011.

Stringer, Chris, 'What Makes a Modern Human', *Nature* 485, no. 7396 (2012): 33–5.

Sun Tzu, *The Art of* War, trans. Thomas Cleary, Boston: Shambhala, 1988.

Swayne, Matt, 'Quantum Computer AI: Explained', *Quantum Insider*, 8 August 2022, https://thequantuminsider.com/2022/08/23/quantum-computer-ai-powering-computers-with-quantum-brains/#:~:text=Quantum computers possess tremendous (accessed 22 February 2023).

Tan, Rebecca and Ragine Cabato, 'Behind the AI Boom, an Army of Overseas Workers in "Digital Sweatshops"', *Washington Post*, 28 August 2023. https://www.washingtonpost.com/world/2023/08/28/scale-ai-remotasks-philippines-artificial-intelligence/ (accessed 12 September 2024).

Taylor, Josh and Alex Hern, '"Godfather of AI" Geoffrey Hinton Quits Google and Warns Over Dangers of Misinformation', *Guardian*, 2 May2023. https://www.theguardian.com/technology/2023/may/02/geoffrey-hinton-godfather-of-ai-quits-google-warns-dangers-of-machine-learning (accessed 10 September 2023).

Thompson, Edward, *The Poverty of Theory and Other Essays*, London: Merlin Press, 1978.

Tollefson, Jeff, 'Climate Change is Hitting the Planet Faster Than Scientists Originally Thought', *Nature*, 22 February 2022, https://www.nature.com/articles/d41586-022-00585-7 (accessed 20 December 2022).

Trottein, Serge, 'Of an Enlightenment-Conservative Tone, Recently Adopted in Philosophy', *Angelaki* 26, no. 1 (2021): 38–50.

UN Environment Program, *Building Materials Report*, https://www.unep.org/resources/report/building-materials-and-climate-constructing-new-future (accessed 20 December 2024).

US Council on Foreign Relations Conflict Tracker, currently https://www.cfr.org/global-conflict-tracker(accessed 10 January 25).

Vaccari, André, 'Neosubstantivism and Cosmotechnics, Gilbert Simondon Versus the Transhumanist Synthesis', *Angelaki* 28, no. 4 (2020): 39–53, https://rid.unrn.edu.ar/bitstream/20.500.12049/8365/3/10.1080%400969725X.2020.1790834.pdf(accessed 8 January 23).

Vaccari, André, 'Cosmotechnical Thought Between Substantivism and the Empirical Turn', *Foundations of Science* 27, no. 394 (2022): 1279–84, https://philpapers.org/rec/VACCTB (accessed 3 January 2023).

Virilio, Paul, *Speed and Politics*, trans. Mark Polizzotti, New York: Semiotext(e), 1977.

Virilio, Paul, *The Original Accident*, trans. Julie Rose, Oxford: Polity Press, 2007.

Von Redecker, Eva, *Praxis and Revolution*, New York: Columbia University Press, 2021.

Walker, Pat (ed.), *Between Labour and Capital*, Brighton: Harvester Press, 1979.

Washington Post, Report on Urban Africa, 20 November2021. https://www.washingtonpost.com/world/interactive/2021/africa-cities/?utm_campaign=wp_main&utm_medium=social&utm_source=facebook&fbclid=IwY2xjawHz_M1leHRuA2FlbQIxMQABHXIa6vijARTUmB9XsFAWly4BVbPOs6pVrVREza6CT30nWhtkUvlhhAJ0w_aem_TVVAiptVGZ7EELtbiEMbVQ (accessed 9 April 2022).

Whitehead, Alfred North, *The Function of Reason*, Boston: Beacon Press, 1929, 38, https://brocku.ca/MeadProject/Whitehead/Whitehead_1929/1929_02.html (accessed 20 November 2024).

Wiener, Norbert, *Cybernetics. Or Control and Communication in the Animal and the Machine*, Cambridge, MA: MIT Press, 1961.

Williams, Alex and Nick Srnicek, *#A Manifesto for an Accelerationist Politics*, 2013. https://criticallegalthinking.com/2013/05/14/accelerate-manifesto-for-an-accelerationist-politics/ (accessed 5 January 2020).

Willis, Anne-Marie (ed.), *The Design Philosophy Reader*, London, Bloomsbury, 2019.

Wilson, Joss, 'Cosmetic Surgery is on the Rise with Technology and Hollywood is at the Center of It', *Forbes*, 18 January 2023, https://www.forbes.com/sites/joshwilson/2023/01/18/cosmetic-surgery-is-on-the-rise-with-technology-and-hollywood-is-at-the-centre-of-it/?sh=7da9fcd51d91 (accessed 2 March 2023).

World Bank Knowledge Portal - Climate Change 2024, https://climateknowledgeportal.worldbank.org/country/guyana/heat-risk (accessed 14 October 2024).

World Health Organization, *Teens, Screens and Mental Health*, 25 September 2024, https://www.who.int/europe/news-room/25-09-2024-teens--screens-and-mental-health (accessed 2 January 2024).

Index